Digital Compositing
with Nuke

Digital Compositing with Nuke

Lee Lanier

Focal Press
Taylor & Francis Group

NEW YORK AND LONDON

First published 2013
by Focal Press
70 Blanchard Road, Suite 402, Burlington, MA 01803

Simultaneously published in the UK
by Focal Press
2 Park Square, Milton Park, Abingdon, Oxon OX14 4RN

Focal Press is an imprint of the Taylor & Francis Group, an informa business

Notices
Knowledge and best practice in this field are constantly changing. As new research and experience broaden our understanding, changes in research methods, professional practices, or medical treatment may become necessary.

Practitioners and researchers must always rely on their own experience and knowledge in evaluating and using any information, methods, compounds, or experiments described herein. In using such information or methods they should be mindful of their own safety and the safety of others, including parties for whom they have a professional responsibility.

Product or corporate names may be trademarks or registered trademarks, and are used only for identification and explanation without intent to infringe.

Library of Congress Cataloging in Publication Data
CIP data has been applied for

ISBN: 978-0-240-82035-4 (pbk)

Contents

Contents

Contents

Contents

Introduction

Of all the areas within the visual effects and animation industries, the one that I never grow tired of is digital compositing. Every shot that I composite becomes an intriguing challenge whereby aesthetic improvements are always within reach. Instead of fading away with the rapid development of technology, digital compositing has become more powerful over the last few years. The Foundry's Nuke software is the epitome of these developments, with 32-bit floating-point color space, optical flow algorithms, and stereoscopic processing as just a few of the standard features.

You, the Reader

Digital Compositing with Nuke is aimed at digital artists who have a desire to learn Nuke from scratch or have a need to transition to Nuke from another digital compositing package. If you are unfamiliar with Nuke's tools and general workflow, this book is for you. If you have a desire to composite with Nuke in a professional capacity within a visual effects, feature animation, or broadcast design environment, you'll find all the critical information and theory necessary to achieve your goal.

A Brief History of Nuke

Digital domain, the visual effects studio founded by James Cameron and Stan Winston, developed Nuke as a command-line image-processing program in the 1990s. Early versions of the software were used to create digital effects on *True Lies* (1994) and *Titanic* (1997). Nuke 4 was the first commercially available version of the program and was licensed through D2 Software. At present, The Foundry owns the intellectual property rights to Nuke. The Foundry was founded in 1996 and produced the Tinder plug-in set for Flame. The Foundry has gone on to become a leading developer of visual effects and image-processing technologies for film and video postproduction.

Topics Covered

Digital Compositing with Nuke takes you from an introduction of the program interface to important compositing tasks that include keyframe animation, rotoscoping, matte pulling, motion tracking, and filter application. In addition, the complexities of bit-depth management and stereoscopic camera work are covered in Chapters 3 and 9. Expressions and Python scripting are introduced in Chapter 10. If you have prior compositing experience with Adobe After Effects or Apple Shake, you'll find a handy node/effect/operation conversion guide in Appendix A. If you're forced to work with interlaced video or suffer from 3:2 pulldown or rolling shutter artifacts, suggested solutions are included in Appendix B.

Installing Nuke

This book was written with Nuke versions 6.1v2 and 6.3v6. Any significant differences between v6.1, v6.2, and v6.3 of the software are noted in the text.

Nuke Versus Nuke PLE Versus NukeX

Nuke is the standard commercial release of the program. A 15-day trial version is available at *www.thefoundry.co.uk/products/nuke/*.

Nuke PLE (Personal Learning Edition) is available for free and may be downloaded from *www.thefoundry.co.uk/products/nuke/ple/*. While the PLE is a fully functional version of the program, it places a watermark in the Viewer and on any render. In addition, a handful of nodes are disabled, including Primatte and WriteGeo. The PLE script files are encoded, which means that commercial versions of Nuke cannot read them.

NukeX builds upon Nuke by including an integrated 3D camera tracker, image-based modeling tools, deep compositing tools, particle generation nodes, and the FurnaceCore plug-in set. These features are covered briefly within the book. A 15-day trial version of NukeX is available at *www.thefoundry.co.uk/products/nuke/*.

You can "rent" Nuke, NukeX, and various plug-ins on a quarterly basis. Any questions concerning the rental or purchase of Nuke can be directed to *sales@www.thefoundry.co.uk*.

A Word About Plug-Ins

This book touches on the most useful and powerful plug-ins and plug-in sets provided by The Foundry. These include FurnaceCore, Keylight, Ocula, Rolling-Shutter, and CameraTracker. While NukeX is bundled with FurnaceCore and CameraTracker, all the plug-ins are available as a free 15-day trial. Visit *www.thefoundry.co.uk/products/all/* for more information.

System Requirements

Nuke will run poorly unless your computer's hardware and operating system software meets minimum criteria. The criteria are carefully spelled out at *www.thefoundry.co.uk/products/nuke/system-requirements/*.

Supplemental DVD

The supplemental DVD is an important asset and includes over two gigabytes of Nuke script files, digital video footage, CG image sequences, texture bitmaps, digital stills, and FBX geometry files. The files are placed in the following directory structure:

Chapters/Chapter*n*/Scripts/	Nuke scripts (`.nk`), LUT files (`.vf`), and FBX files
Chapters/Chapter*n*/Plates/ *PlateName*/	Digital video footage, converted to image sequences (Targa `.tga` files)
Chapters/Chapter*n*/Renders/ *RenderName*/	CG image sequences (Targa `.tga` or OpenEXR `.exr` files)
Chapters/Chapter*n*/Bitmaps/	Texture bitmaps and digital stills (Targa, TIFF, and MayaIFF files)
Tutorials/Tutorial*n*/Scripts/	Tutorial-specific Nuke scripts, LUT files, and FBX files
Tutorials/Tutorial*n*/Plates/ *PlateName*/	Tutorial-specific digital video footage, converted to image sequences
Tutorials/Tutorial*n*/Renders/ *RenderName*/	Tutorial-specific CG image sequences
Tutorials/Tutorial*n*/Bitmaps/	Tutorial-specific texture bitmaps and digital stills

Using the DVD with Windows, Mac, and Linux Systems

If you are running Nuke on a Windows system, I recommend copying the contents of the DVD onto your own C: drive before opening any script files. If you are running Nuke on a Mac or Linux system, I recommend copying the contents onto your root drive.

If you are running Nuke on a Mac or Linux system, any Read nodes contained within the sample Nuke scripts will be unable to locate their associated image sequences, bitmaps, and geometry files. You can solve this problem in one of two ways:

- Open the Nuke script. Locate the node(s) that are missing files. Open the matching properties panels and relocate the files by clicking the File parameter browse button.
- Open the script's `.nk` file in a text editor. Search for and replace any hard-coded Windows paths. For example, replace `C : /` with `/` or another appropriate location. Note that Nuke automatically replaces the Windows `\` backslash with a Mac/Linux `/` forward slash.

Note that the book's screen captures are taken from Nuke 6.1v2 and 6.3v6 running on a 64-bit Windows 7 system.

Naming Conventions

Digital Compositing with Nuke uses common conventions when describing mouse operation. A few examples follow:

click	Left mouse button click
LMB-drag	Drag while pressing left mouse button
RMB-click	Right mouse button click
Shift+Opt/Alt-click	Left mouse click while holding Shift and Opt/Alt keys

When discussing various functions and interface features of Nuke, I've used terminology established by the program's help files. When discussing compositing theory, I've used terminology commonly employed in the visual effects industry.

The Ctrl key on a Windows or Linux system and the Cmd key on a Mac PC serve the same function; hence, a call to press either key is written as Cmd/Ctrl. The Alt key on a Windows or Linux system and the Option key on a Mac PC serve the same function; hence, a call to press either key is written as Opt/Alt.

Updates

For updates on topics in *Digital Compositing with Nuke* and more information, please see the book's website, www.digitalcompositingwithnuke.com.

Tutorial Footage

Much of the tutorial footage included with this book was culled from "Forgive Me," a dance video produced and choreographed by Jenny Savage and directed by myself. Please see the `license.txt` file on the DVD for copyright and licensing information, as well as permitted use.

FIGURE I.1 The cast of "Forgive Me." Top row, from left to right: Ryan McVeigh, Kimberly Barbeau, LaTrice Harper, and Michael Tomlin III. Bottom row, from left to right: Fabienne Maurer and Jenny Savage. Photo by Vien Chau.

Contacting the Author

Feedback is always welcome. You can contact me at *comp@beezlebugbit.com* or find me on popular social media networks. To see my work, visit www.beezlebugbit.com.

Special Thanks

I'd like to thank Tim Kelly, Christoffer Hulusjo, and Steve Wright for serving as technical editors on this book. I also want to thank all the loyal readers who've purchased copies of my books over the years.

CHAPTER 1

Nuke Interface

Nuke was designed to create digital visual effects on feature films. As such, it carries a robust set of tools that make high-end postproduction available to professional digital artists, independent filmmakers, students, and hobbyists alike. The core of Nuke's functionality is a system of connected nodes. Although node manipulation may seem odd to an artist who has mastered layer-based programs, the efficiency and power of nodes comes to light after a basic knowledge is achieved.

This chapter includes the following critical information:

- Overview of interface panes and panels
- Comparison of layer-based and node-based compositing
- Node manipulation, including creation, connection, adjustment, and arrangement
- File importation and output rendering
- Timeline and flipbook playback

Interface Components

By default, Nuke's main window is divided into three panes: the Viewer pane, the Node Graph/Curve Editor pane, and the Properties Bin/Script Editor pane

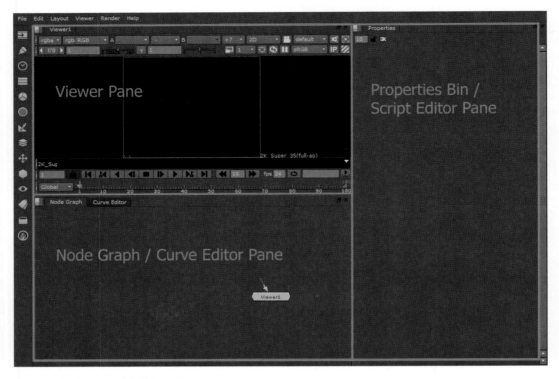

FIGURE 1.1 The three panes of the Nuke window.

(Figure 1.1). Any given pane may have more than one tabbed panel. For example, you can switch from the Node Graph panel and Curve Editor panel by clicking the Curve Editor tab. Each pane includes a content menu, as represented by a gray-checkered Content Menu box at the top left of the pane. If you click on the Content Menu box, a pop-up menu opens and displays a set of options you can use to customize the pane.

The menu bar is located on top left of the Nuke window. The bar hosts commonly used dropdown menus, including File, Edit, and Viewer (Figure 1.2).

FIGURE 1.2 The menu bar, as seen in NukeX 6.3.

The toolbar is located on the left side of the Nuke window and contains between 13 and 17 icons, depending on the version of Nuke you are using. The icons represent different categories of nodes such as Image, Draw, and

Time (Figure 1.3). You can use the toolbar to add nodes to the Node Graph. To do so, click on an icon and choose a node from the resulting dropdown menu. It's also possible to add nodes through an RMB shortcut menu in the Node Graph; this is described in the "Using the Node Graph" section later in this chapter.

Layers Versus Nodes

Adobe After Effects, which is the most widely used compositing package in the world, is layer-based (Figure 1.4). Adobe Photoshop shares a similar layer structure (Figure 1.5).

Nuke, on the other hand, is node-based. A *node* is a discrete unit used to build linked data structures. On a more basic level, you can think of a node as a box that contains specific information that can be shared with neighboring

FIGURE 1.4 Adobe After Effects CS5 Timeline with four layers. The lower the layer number, the higher the layer is in the layer stack.

FIGURE 1.5 Adobe Photoshop CS5 Layers window with four layers. The checkered areas within the layer thumbnails represent transparency.

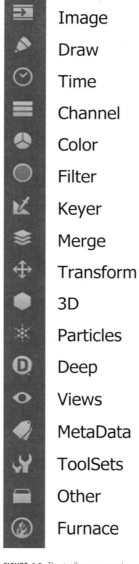

Image
Draw
Time
Channel
Color
Filter
Keyer
Merge
Transform
3D
Particles
Deep
Views
MetaData
ToolSets
Other
Furnace

FIGURE 1.3 The toolbar, as seen in NukeX 6.3.

3

node boxes. In Nuke, a node is represented by a rectangle icon in the Node Graph (see Figure 1.6 in the next section). The information the node carries is displayed as parameters through its properties panel.

With layer-based compositing, each utilized image sequence, still image, and movie file is placed on a layer. Each layer has its own set transformations and carries an optional set of filters. Layers are stacked and processed in order from bottom to top. This is roughly analogous to a stack of cut-out magazine photos. Higher layers win out over lower layers unless nonstandard blending modes are selected or the higher layers possess transparency. Photoshop PSD files store layer transparency information. Other image formats, such as Targa or TIFF, store transparency through a fourth channel known as alpha.

With node-based compositing, each utilized image sequence, still image, and movie file is represented by a unique node. In Nuke, the Read node fulfills this duty. The output of each Read node is connected to the inputs of other nodes, including various filter nodes and merge nodes. The final result is output to a Viewer node (for display in the program) or a Write node (to write an image sequence to disk).

A Nuke node supports a limited number of inputs. However, you can connect the output of a Nuke node to an unlimited number of nodes. When multiple nodes are connected through their inputs and outputs, the structure is known as a node network, tree graph, process tree, or node graph. In Nuke, the work area that you use to create and edit such node networks is called the *Node Graph*; the Node Graph can carry multiple networks. More specifically, the node networks are a directed acyclic graph (DAG) where information only flows in one direction for each connection.

There are several advantages to using a node-based compositor:

- You can easily create complex node networks. In contrast, you can only stack layers. With a layer-based system, it's difficult to connect the output of a single layer to the input of multiple layers; workarounds require the nesting of composites or prerendering certain layers to disk.
- When carefully set up, a node network is easy to interpret. Complex layer-based composites can be difficult to navigate due to the sheer number of layers that are required.
- High-end compositing systems used in the feature animation and visual effects industries are node-based. The systems include Flame, Inferno, Shake, Fusion, and Toxik.

Node Anatomy

Any given node in Nuke has a set of input and output pipes. A *pipe* is a connection between nodes that allows the flow of information between nodes. A pipe can only send information in one direction. Before a node is connected to another node, the pipes are broken or are indicated by arrow stubs (Figure 1.6).

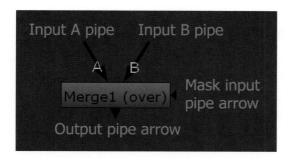

FIGURE 1.6 A Nuke node with input and output pipes. Note that many nodes only possess a single input pipe.

More specifically, a pipe carries one or more channels. A *channel* is a discrete component of a digital image that represents specific information as scalar values (whereby a pixel of a single channel can only carry in single magnitude or intensity); the information may be the distribution of a primary color, such as red, or the distance an object is from the camera, as with a Z-depth channel. Channels commonly used in Nuke include red, green, and blue (RGB) color channels; alpha channels; Z-depth channels; and U and V direction channels. Thus, a node affects the quality of the channels that pass through the node. That is, the numeric values of the channels are affected by the node. Channels are discussed in more detail in Chapters 3 and 4.

If a node is connected to one or more nodes, Nuke indicates the channels that are flowing through a node by adding small colored lines to the bottom left of the node icon (see Figure 1.18 later in this chapter). If the channel is affected by the node, the line is long. If the channel is unaffected, the line is short. The color coding follows:

Channel	Color
Red	Red
Green	Green
Blue	Blue
Alpha	White
Z-depth	Purple
U	Pink
V	Cyan

5

In addition, Nuke indicates the channels a node is affecting by printing a word at the bottom center of the node icon. For example, (red) is printed for the red channel and (all) indicates that all input channels are affected. For information on channel control, see Chapter 4.

Importing Files

To import an image sequence, still image, or movie file, you must create a Read node. To do so, follow these steps:

1. Click the Image icon on the toolbar. Choose Read from the dropdown menu. The File Browser window opens (Figure 1.7).

FIGURE 1.7 The File Browser window with the built-in viewer displayed.

2. Navigate to the file you want to open. (For tips on navigation, see the next section.) Once the files are listed in the Pathname field, click the Open button.
3. The File Browser window closes and a Read node is placed in the Node Graph. Nuke numbers new nodes consecutively. To view the imported file, you must connect a Viewer node to the Read node. The Node Graph is provided with a Viewer1 node by default. To make the connection, LMB-drag the dotted 1 pipe extending from the Viewer1 node and drop it on top of the Read1 node (Figure 1.8). The output of the Read1 node is thereby connected to the input of the Viewer1 node through a pipe. Alternatively, you can select the Read node and press the 1 key to automatically connect to Viewer1.

FIGURE 1.8 The Viewer1 node is connected to the output of the Read1 node.

Note that Nuke automatically recognizes numbered image sequences and lists them as under a single name with the format *name.placeholder .extension startFrame endFrame*. For example, a sequence might appear as `name.%02d.tga 1 60` or `name.##.tga 1 60`. With these examples, the %02d and ## represent the total numeric placeholders, where the original files are named `name.01.tga` to `name.60.tga`.

Using the File Browser

The File Browser window offers several ways to navigate the directory structure. The Favorites section features icons for commonly used locations such as the Nuke working directory, system root directory, or various hard drives. To jump to a Favorites location, click the location name so it turns orange. You can add your own Favorites location by navigating to a directory and clicking the + button at the bottom of the Favorites section. To remove a Favorites location, highlight the location in the Favorites section and click the − button. In addition, the window provides Create New Directory, Up One Directory, Previous Directory, and Next Directory buttons at the top left (Figure 1.9). To preview a selected file or image sequence in the File Browser,

Next Directory
Previous Directory
Up One Directory
Create New Directory
Embedded Viewer

FIGURE 1.9 The File Browser navigation and viewer buttons.

click the black arrow at the top right. A viewer with playback controls is embedded in the window (see Figure 1.8).

Supported Image Formats

Nuke supports a wide array of image formats. A few of the more commonly used ones are described here.

AVI (`.avi`**).** The AVI (Audio Video Interleave) movie format was developed by Microsoft. Nuke's AVI support is dependent on the FFmpeg open-source audio/video codec library. If an AVI file fails to open, try adding `ffmpeg:` to the head of the path name (e.g., `ffmpeg:C:/Projects/test.avi`). For more information on the FFmpeg library, visit *ffmpeg.org*. On Windows systems, AVI support is also dependent on the DirectShow multimedia framework.

DPX and Cineon (`.dpx` **and** `.cin`**).** The DPX (Digital Picture Exchange) format is based on the Cineon file format, which was created for Kodak's early line of digital film scanners. Both formats use a 10-bit log architecture, which is well suited to capture the full exposure range of motion picture film stock. DPX is more flexible than Cineon in that it supports 8-, 12-, 16-, and 32-bit variations that may be linear or log. (Linear and log encoding is described in Chapter 3.)

MayaIFF (`.iff`**).** MayaIFF is native to Autodesk Maya. The format has the advantage of supporting alpha, depth, and motion vector channels. Nuke can read MayaIFF but cannot write it.

OpenEXR (`.exr`**).** The OpenEXR format was developed by Industrial Light & Magic and is currently available for public use. The format supports linear 16-bit half-float and linear 32-bit floating-point variations. OpenEXR can support an arbitrary number of custom channels, which makes it particularly useful for compositing. OpenEXR is quickly becoming the standard format for animation studios employing floating-point pipelines.

PNG (`.png`**).** The PNG (Portable Network Graphics) format was developed to replace the older GIF format. PNG carries an alpha channel and high-quality compression.

QuickTime (`.mov`**).** By default, the QuickTime movie format is supported by Windows and Mac OS X operating systems. Linux versions, however, can utilize the QuickTime format through the FFmpeg open-source library. If a QuickTime file fails to open, try adding `ffmpeg:` to the head of the path name (e.g., `ffmpeg:C:/Projects/test.mov`).

RAW. RAW image files contain data from the image sensor of a film scanner or DSLR (digital single-lens reflex) camera. Nuke can read a limited number of DSLR camera types.

REDCODE (`.r3d`**).** REDCODE is a proprietary format encoded by the Red One and Red EPIC digital video cameras. Because the Red cameras are often used to capture visual effects plates and shoot high-definition television

(HDTV) programs and feature films, Nuke's ability to read the format is currently evolving and expanding.

Targa (.tga). Targa was developed in the 1980s by Truevision. Common variations include 24-bit (8 bits per channel) and 32-bit (8 bits per channel with alpha).

TIFF (.tiff, .tif). The Tagged Image File Format was developed in the 1980s as a means to standardize desktop digital imaging. The format exists with various compression schemes and supports 16-bit and 32-bit floating-point architecture as well as an alpha channel.

Properties Bin

Each node you create is given a properties panel in the Properties Bin pane at the right side of the Nuke window. The properties panels are stacked vertically. Each properties panel carries the node's unique information—that is, unique parameters. The parameter values are set by string cells (cells that carry text), numeric cells, sliders, or dropdown menus (Figure 1.10). You can close a properties panel at any time by clicking the X button at the top right of the panel title bar. You can reopen a panel for a node by double-clicking the node in the Node Graph.

FIGURE 1.10 The properties panel for a Read node.

Using the Node Graph

The view within the Node Graph is not fixed. You can zoom closer to displayed nodes by scrolling with a middle mouse button (MMB) wheel or Opt/Alt+MMB-dragging. You can move the view left/right or up/down by MMB-dragging. You can automatically center a selected node or nodes by clicking the MMB while the mouse is in the Node Graph.

Creating Nodes

There are several ways to create a new node:

- Click a category icon on the toolbar and choose a node from the dropdown menu.
- RMB-click in the Node Graph and choose a node from the shortcut menu. For example, choose Image > Read (Figure 1.11). This is the method that is most often used in this book.

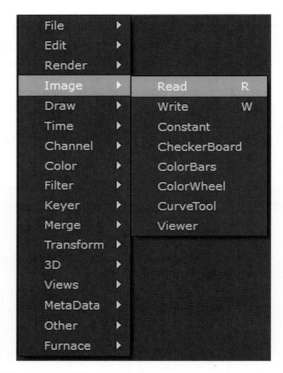

FIGURE 1.11 RMB node menu available in the Node Graph.

- Press the Tab key while the mouse is in the Node Graph. A shortcut dialog box opens (Figure 1.12). Type the first few letters of the node name. When the node appears in the dropdown menu, click its name.
- A few nodes have default hot keys. For example, pressing the B key while the mouse is in the Node Graph creates a Blur node. R pops up the File Browser window in anticipation of creating a Read node. To see a complete list of hot keys, choose Help > Key Assignments from the menu bar. You can customize the hot key assignments by editing the menu.py Python script; for a demonstration, see Chapter 10.

FIGURE 1.12 Shortcut dialog box activated by the Tab key in the Node Graph.

Connecting, Disconnecting, and Branching Pipes

To connect one node to another, LMB-drag an unconnected pipe and drop it on top of a different node. Nuke automatically distinguishes between inputs and outputs and makes a proper connection (Figure 1.13).

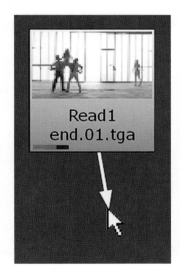

FIGURE 1.13 LMB-dragging an unconnected pipe.

To disconnect a pipe, LMB-drag either end of a pipe away from a node (Figure 1.14). When connected, the arrow end of a pipe is anchored to the input of a node while the nonarrow side of the pipe is anchored to the output of a node.

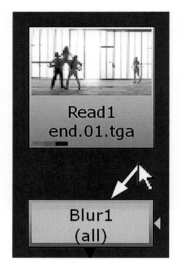

FIGURE 1.14 Disconnecting a pipe by LMB-dragging the output end.

To branch a node (to make an output go off in two directions), Shift+LMB-drag the arrow (input) side of the pipe and drop it on top of another node (Figure 1.15).

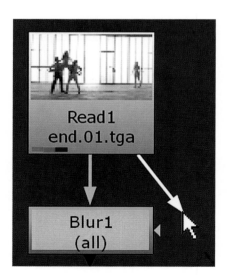

FIGURE 1.15 Branching a pipe by Shift+LMB-dragging the arrow (input) end of the pipe.

Selecting, Moving, Disabling, and Deleting Nodes

You can select a node by clicking it. A selected node turns pale orange. You can select more than one node by Shift-clicking. You can also LMB-drag a selection marquee around multiple nodes. To deselect nodes, simply click an empty area of the Node Graph.

Once a node is selected, you can reposition it within the Node Graph by LMB-dragging. Pipes automatically stretch and shrink to maintain connections.

You can temporarily disable a node by selecting it and pressing the D key. An X is drawn through the node icon (Figure 1.16). When a node is disabled, it has no affect on the input information (it's as if the node is skipped). To reenable the node, select it and press the D key again. Disabling a node is a good way to see what influence it has on the final output.

FIGURE 1.16 A disabled node.

To delete a node, press the Delete key while the node is selected.

Creating a Simple Composite

A simple composite includes at least three connected nodes: a Read node, some type of filter node to affect the Read node, and a Viewer node. For example, to apply a Blur node to an imported image, follow these steps:

1. With the mouse in the Node Graph, press the R key. This pops up the File Browser window. Locate an image file. An example file named `desert.tif` is included in the `Chapter1/Bitmaps/` folder on the DVD. Click the Open button.
2. A Read1 node is placed in the Node Graph. LMB-drag the dotted 1 pipe extending from the Viewer1 node and drop it on top of the Read1 node. The output of the Read1 node is thereby connected to the input of the Viewer1 node through a pipe. Alternatively, you can select the Read1 node and press the 1 key to automatically connect to Viewer1. The still image becomes visible in the Viewer1 panel of the Viewer pane. At this point, the image is sharply focused (Figure 1.17).
3. Select the Read1 node. The node turns pale orange. Click the Filter button in the toolbar (it features a solid circle). Choose Blur from the dropdown menu. A Blur1 node is inserted into the network between the Read1 node and the Viewer1 node (Figure 1.18).
4. Initially, there is no change, as the Blur1 node is essentially off by default. To apply a blur, you must raise the Size parameter value. Raise the value by dragging the Value slider, carried by the Blur1 properties panel, to the

FIGURE 1.17 The imported image, as seen in the Viewer pane.

FIGURE 1.18 A Blur node is added to the node network. Note the red, green, and blue channel lines, as well as the word (all), which indicates that those three channels are affected by the Blur node.

right (Figure 1.19). (If the properties panel is not visible in the Properties Bin pane, double-click the Blur1 node in the Node Graph.) For example, a Size value of 50 blurs the still significantly (Figure 1.20). The Size parameter determines the size of the convolution filter applied to the image. (Convolution filters are discussed in Chapter 6.)

FIGURE 1.19 The Blur1 node properties panel. The Size parameter is set to 50.

FIGURE 1.20 The result of the network. A sample Nuke script is included as `simple_composite.nk` in the `Chapters/Chapter1/Scripts/` directory on the DVD.

Inserting, Duplicating, and Cloning Nodes

To insert a node into an existing node network, LMB-drag the node and drop it on an existing pipe. The pipe is broken in two and reconnected to the node's input and output. You can also select an upstream node (one that provides an output) and create a new node through the toolbar. The new node is inserted downstream of the selected node. (The pipe arrows indicate the direction information is flowing; much like water in a river, information in Nuke flows downstream.)

To duplicate a node, select a node and choose Edit > Duplicate from the menu bar or press Opt/Alt+C. The properties of the duplicated node are copied from the original node. If the selected node is part of a node network, the duplicated node is freed from the network and is not connected to any other node.

To clone a node, select a node and choose Edit > Clone from the menu bar or press Opt/Alt+K. The cloned node possesses parameter values that are identical to the original. An orange clone line is drawn between the original and the clone (Figure 1.21). When the original node's properties are updated, the clone automatically updates to maintain an exact parameter match. If you alter the values of the cloned node, the original node is updated to maintain an exact parameter match.

To make a clone useful, its input and output must be connected to other nodes. For example, in Figure 1.22, a cloned Blur node is used to blur the

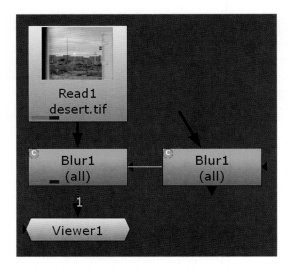

FIGURE 1.21 A cloned Blur node (right) is connected to the original Blur node (left) via an orange connection line. Both nodes sport a C symbol to further indicate the cloning.

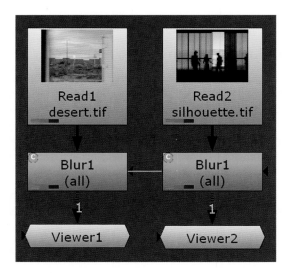

FIGURE 1.22 A cloned Blur node (right) blurs the output of a second Read node. A sample Nuke script is included as blur_clone.nk in the Chapters/Chapter1/Scripts/ directory on the DVD.

output of a second Read node. The output of the cloned Blur node is connected to a second Viewer node. You can create additional Viewer nodes at
any time by choosing Viewer > Create New Viewer from the menu bar or
pressing Ctrl+I.

Organizing the Node Graph

The Node Graph can quickly become unintelligible if there are a large
number of nodes and connections. The following sections contain a few tips
for keeping the graph organized.

Snapping and Arranging Nodes

When you LMB-drag a node close to another node in the same node
network, the node will vertically or horizontally snap. If you fail to "feel" the
snapping action, zoom in closer to the network.

You can select multiple nodes and force Nuke to arrange them in an automatic fashion by pressing the L key.

Creating a Backdrop

You can create a backdrop for a set of nodes. A backdrop is a colored rectangle that distinguishes the node set from other nodes (Figure 1.23). To
create a backdrop, select several nodes, RMB-click in the Node Graph, and

FIGURE 1.23 A backdrop is created for two nodes of a network. The backdrop color is changed from default
violet to red. The backdrop is renamed Read_and_Blur.

choose Other > Backdrop. Once you have a backdrop, you can manipulate it in the following ways:

- You can rename the backdrop by double-clicking its title bar and entering a new name in the name field of its properties panel.
- You can choose your own color for the backdrop by clicking the Tile_color button (to the immediate right of the name field in the properties panel) and selecting a new color from the Color Sliders/Color Wheel dialog box.
- You can resize a backdrop by LMB-dragging the triangular handle at the bottom right corner.
- To move a backdrop, LMB-drag the title bar. Note that any nodes that fall within the interior of the backdrop, whether they are connected to a network or not, are moved along with the backdrop. To move the backdrop without affecting the nodes, Cmd/Ctrl-drag the title bar.
- To delete a backdrop, move all the nodes out of the backdrop area, click the title bar, and press the Delete key.

Bending Pipes

You can create a right-angle bend in a pipe and thus avoid pipes running in a diagonal fashion. To do so, select an upstream node (one that provides the output), RMB-click, and choose Other > Dot. A dot is placed along the pipe. LMB-drag the dot downward, upward, or sideways until the pipe forms a right-angle bend (Figure 1.24). Alternatively, press the Cmd/Ctrl key while the mouse is in the Node Graph. Small yellow dots appear at the center of each pipe. Click on one dot to convert it to a permanent dot.

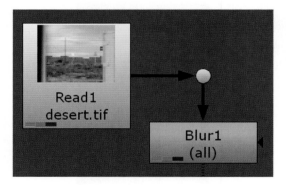

FIGURE 1.24 A right-angle pipe bend courtesy of a dot.

Exploring the Viewer Pane

Each Viewer node in the Node Graph has a Viewer panel with corresponding tab in the Viewer pane. Nuke provides Viewer1 by default, but you can create additional Viewer nodes at any time by choosing Viewer > Create New Viewer from the menu bar. Each new Viewer node is numbered consecutively. To switch between Viewer nodes, simply click the Viewer panel tabs (Figure 1.25).

FIGURE 1.25 Three Viewer nodes indicated by three tabs in the Viewer pane.

You can connect a Viewer node to the output of any node in the Node Graph. The corresponding Viewer tab displays the output result of all the nodes upstream of the Viewer node. Any nodes downstream of the Viewer node connection are ignored. You can connect multiple Viewer nodes to multiple nodes within a single node network (Figure 1.26).

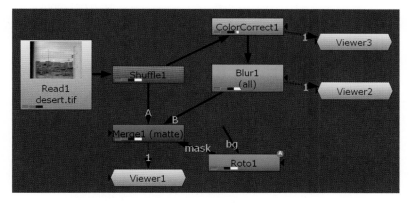

FIGURE 1.26 Three Viewer nodes connected to three different nodes in a single node network.

It's also possible to connect a single Viewer node to multiple node outputs. To do so, LMB-drag the output pipe of a node and drop it on top of the Viewer node. Each new connection to the Viewer node is numbered consecutively. (You can also select a node and press a number key to make a new connection between the node and the Viewer1 node.) To examine the various outputs in the Viewer1 tab, press the appropriate number key while no nodes are selected. For example, in Figure 1.27, Viewer1 is connected to the output of the Blur1 node and the Merge1 node. By pressing the 1 key, the Blur1 output is displayed in the Viewer1 tab. By pressing the 2 key, the Merge1 output is displayed in the Viewer1 tab.

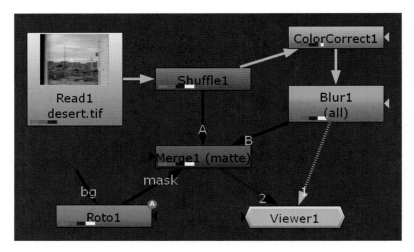

FIGURE 1.27 The Viewer1 node is connected to the outputs of two other nodes. When the 1 key is pressed, the output of the Blur1 node is displayed in the Viewer1 panel. In addition, the pipes involved in the display are colored orange.

Viewer panels include their own set of option buttons and cells. These are discussed throughout the book.

Resolutions, Frame Rates, and Frame Ranges

When Nuke is launched, it creates an empty project, which is known as a script. By default, the project resolution is set to 2048 × 1556, the project frames per second (fps) is set to 24, and the frame range is set to 1 to 100. You can change these settings by choosing Edit > Project Settings from the menu bar. The Project Settings panel opens in the Properties Bin pane (Figure 1.28).

FIGURE 1.28 Bottom of the Project Settings panel.

2048 × 1556, also known as full aperture, super 35, or 2K, is a resolution commonly used by the visual effects industry that matches a popular scan size for motion picture film. You can set the resolution to other commonly used sizes through the Full Size Format menu. Common video resolutions include HD (1920 × 1080 HDTV) and PC_Video (640 × 480 standard-definition TV). Resolution is measured as pixels and is written as pixel width × pixel height. In general, it's best to set the resolution to match the resolution of the image sequences, still images, or movies you'll import or the resolution you ultimately wish to render. Additional information on resolutions is discussed throughout this book.

You can change the project fps (or frame rate) through the Fps slider. This should be set before starting any keyframe animation. (Animation is discussed in Chapter 2.) The three most commonly used frame rates are 30 (NTSC video used in North America and Japan), 25 (PAL and SECAM video used widely outside North America), and 24 (motion picture film). Note that different flavors of HDTV support all three frame rates.

You can set the frame range, which affects the duration of the timeline, by changing the Frame Range start and end values.

You can create a new, empty script at any time by choosing File > New from the menu bar. The new script is opened in a new Nuke window.

Playing the Timeline

The timeline, which is included at the bottom of the Viewer pane, allows you to play back the output of a Viewer and thus show motion (Figure 1.29).

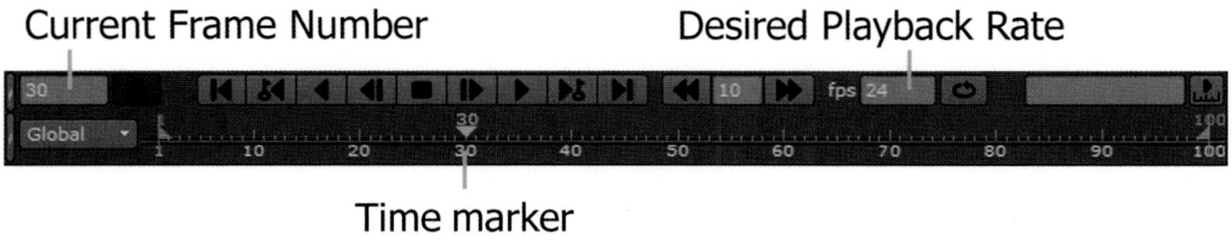

At present, Nuke offers a limited set of options for working with interlaced video. For more detail, see Appendix B. In contrast, image sequences are progressive, whereby each frame is whole and is not broken into two interlaced fields.

Current Frame Number   Desired Playback Rate

Time marker

FIGURE 1.29 The timeline.

The timeline includes a standard set of playback controls. In addition, it includes the following features:

Time marker The marker is an orange upside-down triangle that you can interactively LMB-drag left or right to "scrub" through a series of frames.
Current frame number You can jump to a specific frame number by entering a value into this cell.

Desired playback speed This cell, labeled Fps, sets the desired playback rate of the timeline and is independent of the Fps cell offered by the project settings. While the timeline is playing, however, the cell reports the actual playback rate. Nuke attempts to play back in real time. For example, if Desired Playback Rate is set to 30, Nuke attempts to play exactly 30 fps. This may be impossible to achieve if the project resolution is large or the displayed node network is complex. Hence, it may be necessary to render a flipbook. The FrameCycler program, which is designed to view flipbooks, is discussed in the last section of this chapter.

Opening and Saving Nuke Scripts

Nuke scripts are saved as ASCII text files and are given the `.nk` extension. To open a script, choose File > Open from the menu bar. Use the File Browser window to locate the file. To save a script, choose File > Save. To save a script under a new name, choose File > Save As. To import a script into an open script, choose File > Import. If you open a script while a script is already open, the program is relaunched and you will have two iterations of Nuke running; to avoid this, first close the open script by choosing File > Close.

Nuke automatically backs up an open script every 30 seconds after the program is idle for 5 seconds. If the script has never been saved, the backup is stored in the Nuke's Temp directory. For example, you can find the `.autosave` file in the `C:/users/userName/AppData/Local/Temp/nuke` directory on a Windows 7 system. If the script has been saved, the backup is stored in the directory where the script was previously saved. You cannot open the `.autosave` file through File > Open unless you rename it with an `.nk` extension. Otherwise, Nuke automatically retrieves the autosaved file if Nuke is launched after a program crash. You can change how often the script is backed up and where it backs up to by editing the properties in the Preferences tab of the Preferences window (Edit > Preferences from the menu bar).

Note that imported image sequences, stills, and movies are not stored within the script files. Instead, Read nodes carry an absolute path in the File field. For example, a file might be located at `C:/Projects/Footage/`. If the imported file is moved to a new location, Nuke will be unable to locate it. In such a situation, you must relocate the missing file by clicking the File field Browse button.

Rendering

To export a composite, you must write an image sequence or movie to disk through a Write node. (The process of writing files is often called *rendering*.) You can follow these steps:

1. Select the node you wish to render (do not select a Viewer node). Press the W key or RMB-click and choose Image > Write. A Write

node is inserted into the network. Open the Write node's properties panel.

2. Click the Browse button beside the File parameter. The File Browser window opens. Navigate to the directory where you want to write the files. Click the Save button. The File Browser closes and the directory path is written to the File field. Add the file name to the end of the directory path (Figure 1.30). If you are rendering an image sequence, you must add # symbols to represent the numeric placeholders. For example, you can enter test.###.ext, whereby Nuke names the files test.001.ext, test.010.ext, test.100.ext, and so on. In this case, the .ext extension represents the three-letter extension code for various file formats (.tga, .exr, and so on). If you enter a proper extension, Nuke automatically changes the File Type menu to match. (For a list of image formats and their extensions, see the "Supported Image Formats" section earlier in this chapter.)

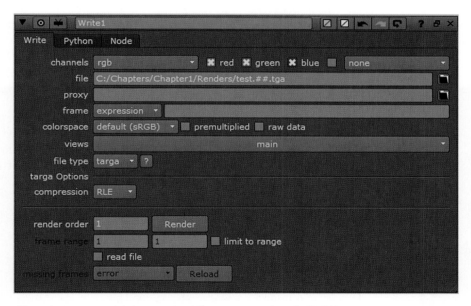

FIGURE 1.30 Write node properties panel. A directory path and file name are entered into the File field.

3. To write out a specific frame range, select the Limit To Range radio button and enter values into the Frame Range start and end cells.
4. Once you've adjusted the various Write properties, launch the render by clicking the Render button.

If you prefer to render a QuickTime or AVI movie, set the File Type menu to FFmpeg and add a .mov or .avi extension to the file name. For more information on the FFmpeg library, see the "Supported Image Formats" section earlier in this chapter.

Playing Back with FrameCycler

Although the playback controls provided by the timeline are convenient, their features are somewhat limited. In addition, playing back through the timeline does not necessarily guarantee that the sequence will achieve real-time speed. As a solution, Nuke offers FrameCycler, which is an advanced playback program that comes bundled with the software. To play back with FrameCycler, however, you must create a flipbook, which is a specially prepared, prerendered sequence of frames. To create a flipbook, follow these steps:

1. Select a node you wish to flipbook. It's not necessary to select a Write node. You can select any node in a network. Choose Render > Flipbook Selected from the menu bar or press Opt/Alt+F. The Flipbook dialog box opens. Enter a frame range into the Frame or Frame Range cell. For example, enter 1–30 to render frames 1 to 30. Press the OK button.
2. The flipbook renders. A Progress dialog box displays its namesake. When the render is finished, the FrameCycler window opens. The flipbook is loaded onto the timeline and is ready for playback.

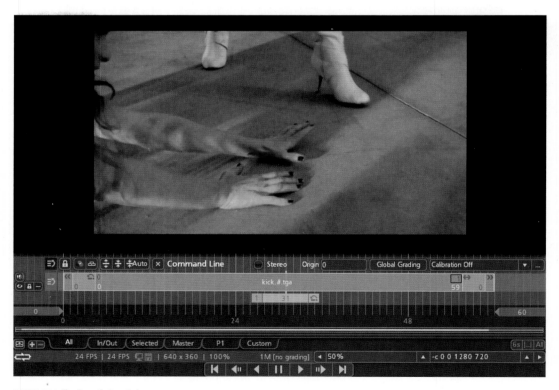

FIGURE 1.31 The FrameCycler window.

3. The FrameCycler offers a standard set of playback controls (Figure 1.31). The first time the program plays the flipbook, it's loaded into memory. Subsequent playbacks attempt to achieve real-time speeds.

4. To zoom in or out, change the Resample menu from Resample Off to a percentage such as 50%. To reposition the flipbook within the player, MMB-drag.

You can use the FrameCycler to review an image sequence or movie that is already written to disk. To do so, follow these steps:

1. You cannot launch the version of FrameCycler that's bundled with Nuke outside Nuke. Therefore, if FrameCycler is not already running, you must go through the Nuke's flipbook feature. To avoid wasting time on a complete flipbook render, you can select a random node, press Opt/Alt+F, and enter 0 into the Frames To Flipbook Frames cell. The first frame of the sequence is rendered as a one-frame-long flipbook. To delete the flipbook, click the X button at the top left of the FrameCycler timeline.

2. Once the FrameCycler window is open, click the Desktop button at the bottom left. (If you don't see the button, maximize the window.) The file browser opens. To display the directory tree, click the Tree button at the top left. Navigate to an image sequence or movie and double-click its icon. The sequence is placed on a new timeline. To return to the viewer, click the Desktop button once again. The sequence is ready to play back.

> FrameCycler is a complex program with numerous options that are beyond the scope of this book. For additional documentation, see the `FrameCycler_Pro_ User_Guide` PDF in the `NukeProgramDirectory /FrameCycler Windows/doc/` directory on the DVD.

Tutorial 1: Kicking a Heart
Part 1: Setting Up a New Script

Tutorial 1 carries you through the steps needed to add a rendered 3D still image to live-action video footage. Part 1 of the tutorial sets up a new script, imports the necessary files, adjusts the resolution through the addition of a Reformat node, and creates a simple composite through a Merge node.

1. Launch Nuke. Click the Image icon on the toolbar and choose Read from the dropdown menu. Alternatively, you can place the mouse in the Node Graph, RMB-click, and choose Image > Read from the shortcut menu. A new node, Read1, is placed in the Node Graph. Simultaneously, the File Browser window opens. Navigate to the `Tutorials/Tutorial1/Plates/kick/` directory. (See the Introduction for tips on working with files on the DVD.) Click on the `kick.###.tga 0 59` image sequence name (this may also appear as `kick.%02d.tga 0 59`). Click the Open button. The File Browser window closes and the image sequence is loaded into the Read1 node.

2. Note that the bounding box is set to a default resolution of 2048 × 1556, which is provided by the 2k_Super_35(full ap) resolution preset. To view the imported sequence, connect the Viewer1 node to the Read1 node. To do this, LMB-drag the dotted Viewer1 input

pipe and drop it on top of the Read1 node. Alternatively, you can click the Read1 node so that it becomes selected (selected nodes turn a pale orange) and press the 1 key on the keyboard. As soon as Viewer1 is connected, the sequence is visible in the Viewer1 panel and the bounding box is reset to 1280 × 720, which is the resolution of the sequence (Figure 1.32). The sequence features a character reaching for an unseen object, which in turn is kicked away by a second character.

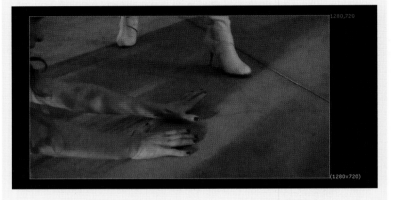

FIGURE 1.32 Kick sequence, as seen in the Viewer1 panel with the current frame set to 58. The resolution of the sequence is 1280 × 720.

3. Choose Edit > Project Settings from the menu bar. In the Project Settings panel, change the Fps parameter to 30. The image sequence was derived from a video shot at 30 fps. To ensure that the characters move at their original speed, the fps must be matched between the video and the project. Change the frame range to 0, 59. The image sequence is 60 frames long.

4. Create a new Read node. In the File Browser window, navigate to the `Tutorials/Tutorial1/Renders/heart/` directory. Click on the `heart.exr` file name and click the Open button. Disconnect the Viewer1 node from the Read1 node and connect it to the Read2 node. The new sequence features a still 3D render of a stylized heart. Black surrounds the heart, which indicates empty 3D space (Figure 1.33). You can check the render's alpha channel by placing the mouse in the Viewer panel and pressing the A key. White indicates opaque pixels, black indicates transparent pixels, and gray indicates semi-transparent pixels. Hence, when viewing the render's alpha channel, the heart appears white (Figure 1.34). To return to the RGB view, press the A key again. You can also

FIGURE 1.33 Heart render, as seen in the Viewer1 panel. The resolution of the sequence is 2048 × 1556. *(Heart modeled by Gerardo Perusquia Montes.)*

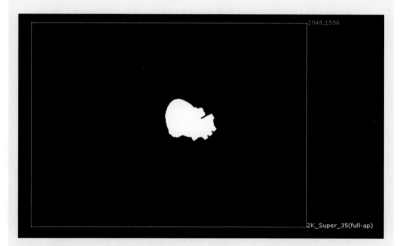

FIGURE 1.34 Alpha channel of same render.

switch between channels by changing the Display Style menu at the top of the Viewer pane; the menu is set to RGB by default, but may be changed to A for alpha. (Alpha channels are discussed in more detail in Chapter 4.) Note that the Read node's Colorspace menu is set to Linear by default. This prevents the node from converting the render with a color space look-up table (LUT). In this case, the Linear setting prevents the heart from taking on unnecessary contrast. Color spaces and LUTs are discussed in Chapter 3.

5. The resolution of the heart render is 2048 × 1556. The resolution mismatch between the kick sequence and the heart render will lead to problems unless addressed. There are two solutions in this situation: You can scale up the kick sequence or scale down the heart render. Assuming that a resolution of 1280 × 720 is sufficient for the final render, you will maintain better quality if you scale down the heart render. Scaling up requires the synthesis of new pixels, which leads to a softening of the image. (For more information on scaling, see Chapter 2.) To scale down the heart render, you can use a Reformat node. Select the Read2 node, RMB-click, and choose Transform > Reformat from the shortcut menu. In the Reformat1 node's properties panel, change the Output Format menu to 1280 × 720. The output is instantly scaled.

6. Because the render includes an alpha channel that stores transparency information, you can place the heart "on top" of the image sequence by creating a Merge node. To do so, press the M key or RMB-click in the Node Graph and choose Merge > Merge from the shortcut menu. A Merge1 node is added to the Node Graph. Connect the input B pipe of the Merge1 node to the output of the Read1 node. The input B pipe is designed to accept a background image or what might be considered the "lowest layer" or a layered composite. Connect the input A pipe to the output of the Reformat1 node. Connect the Viewer1 input pipe to the output of the Merge1 node. (See Figure 1.36 for the final node network layout.) The heart is composited on top of the video footage (Figure 1.35). For more information on node connection,

FIGURE 1.35 The heart is composited on top of the image sequence through the use of a Merge node.

see the "Connecting, Disconnecting, and Branching Pipes" section earlier in this chapter. Merge nodes are discussed in more detail in Chapter 4.

This concludes Part 1 of Tutorial 1. Choose File > Save As to save a copy of the script. A sample Nuke script is included as `Tutorial1.1.nk` in the `Tutorials/Tutorial1/Scripts/` directory on the DVD. In Chapter 2, we'll continue to refine the composite by keyframe animating the transformations of the heart render. As an extra step, you can spend time refining the current node network layout. For example, you can add dots to create right-angle bends in the pipes and/or add backdrops to define particular areas of the network. For example, in Figure 1.36 a dot is added to the pipe running between the Read1 node and the Merge1 node. You can add a dot by selecting the Read1 node, RMB-clicking, and choosing Other > Dot from the shortcut menu. To add a backdrop, Shift-click the Read2 node and Reformat1 node, RMB-click, and choose Other > Backdrop from the shortcut menu. For more information on dots and backdrops, see the "Organizing the Node Graph" section earlier in this chapter.

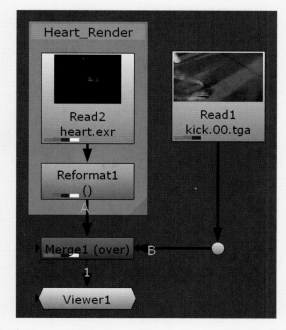

FIGURE 1.36 The final node network for Part 1 of Tutorial 1. A dot and backdrop are added for additional network clarity.

CHAPTER 2

Transforming and Keyframing

Compositing programs differ from digital imaging programs in that they are designed for animation. As such, it's necessary to place keyframes that define the values of parameters at different frames along the timeline. The keyframes define transformations, such as translate, scale, and rotate, and allow various filters to change their qualities over time.

This chapter includes the following critical information:

- Working with bounding boxes
- Transforming outputs
- Keyframing parameters
- Editing animation curves

Bounding, Reformating, and Cropping

The bounding box, visible in the Viewer panels as a dotted white box, defines the area of the frame that the program considers to have valid data. Initially, the bounding box fits itself to the project resolution. The resolution of the bounding box is indicated by an X,Y readout at the top right of the box (Figure 2.1).

FIGURE 2.1 The X,Y readout of a bounding box. The resolution is 2048 pixels wide × 1556 pixels high.

Scaling an Output to the Project Resolution

If an output is connected to the current Viewer, the bounding box snaps to the resolution of the output. If you prefer to maintain the project resolution, you can add a Reformat node to the network. To do so, select the Output node, RMB-click, and choose Transform > Reformat from the Shortcut menu. The output is automatically scaled to fit the project resolution. The output's original aspect ratio is maintained so that the image is not unduly distorted. For example, applying a Reformat node to a 1920 × 1080 output in a 2048 × 1556 project causes the output to be scaled to 2048 × 1355 (Figure 2.2). In this situation, the top and bottom rows of pixels from the output are streaked vertically to fill the empty areas within the bounding box; you can avoid this, however, by selecting the Reformat node's Black Outside checkbox.

You can alter the Reformat node's behavior by changing the Resize Type menu in the properties panel. You can force the rescale to snap vertically by

FIGURE 2.2 A 1920 × 1080 output is snapped to a 2048 × 1556 project resolution with a Reformat node. A sample Nuke script is included as reformat.nk in the Chapters/Chapter2/Scripts/ directory on the DVD.

setting the Resize Type to Height or force the output to fit perfectly by changing the Resize Type to Distort. The Reformat node also offers a convenient means to flip an output. Select the Flip checkbox to flip vertically, select the Flop checkbox to flip horizontally, or select the Turn checkbox to rotate the output 90 degrees.

Trimming an Output

You can trim the edges of an output by adding a Transform > Crop node. If you raise Box X and Box Y above 0, the left edge and bottom edge are respectively cropped. If you lower Box R and Box T below the default value (which corresponds to the bounding box resolution), the right edge and top edge are respectively cropped (Figure 2.3). The cropped area receives black pixels in the RGB channels and black pixels in the alpha channel, which corresponds to 100% transparency. You can soften the resulting edges by raising the Softness slider. You can snap the resulting cropped output to the bounding box by selecting the Reformat checkbox.

FIGURE 2.3 A 1920 × 1080 output is trimmed with a Crop node. 100 pixels are trimmed from each edge by setting X to 100, Y to 100, R to 1820, and T to 980. A sample Nuke script is included as `crop.nk` in the `Chapters/Chapter2/Scripts/` directory on the DVD.

Translating, Rotating, and Scaling

You can translate, rotate, or scale any node output by connecting the output to a Transform node. You can create a Transform node by RMB-clicking in the Node Graph and choosing Transform > Transform or pressing the T key.

Once a Transform node is connected, a circular handle appears at the center of the output in the Viewer panel (Figure 2.4). You can interactively translate, scale, and rotate the output by LMB-dragging the handle. LMB-dragging the center of the circle translates the output. LMB-dragging the dots lying on

FIGURE 2.4 The circular handle provided by a Transform node.

the circle scales the output in that direction. LMB-dragging the long line at the right of the circle rotates the output.

The manipulation of the transform handle remotely changes the parameter values of the Transform node (Figure 2.5). The parameters include Translate X and Translate Y where X runs left/right and Y runs up/down; 0,0 for the translation equates to the default position of the output. You can change what is considered 0,0 and thereby where the handle rests by changing the Center X and Center Y parameters.

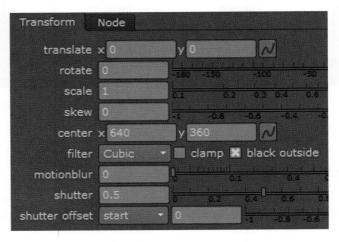

FIGURE 2.5 The parameters of a Transform node.

If an output is translated left/right or up/down without reducing its scale, it overhangs the Viewer bounding box. The Viewer bounding box, which is

FIGURE 2.6 An output is transformed so that it overhangs the edge of the Viewer bounding box. The portion that overhangs is cropped.

indicated by a solid line, determines what section of the Viewer output is rendered when a flipbook or a Write node is employed. The resolution of the Viewer bounding box matches the resolution of the transformed output. As such, the overhanging output is cropped.

The Transform node also carries Rotate and Scale parameters. In addition, a Skew parameter is provided. Changing the Skew to a nonzero value skews the output into a trapezoidal shape (even through the bounding box remains rectangular).

By default, the Scale parameter carries a single cell and slider, named W (width). If you move the Scale slider, the width and height remain equal, preventing the output from elongating in one direction. If you interactively scale the output, however, the Scale parameter is broken into separate W and H (height) cells. At that point, W and H can carry different values. You can force Scale to carry W and H cells at any time by clicking the Switch Between Single Value And Multiple Values button to the right of the slider (the button features a "2").

Using Specialized Transform Nodes

Aside from the Transform node, there are several nodes that create unique transformations. They are available through the Transform menu.

> **CameraShake** adds its namesake by moving the output in a seemingly random fashion. The movement is based on a procedural noise. You can add rotation and scale to the shake by raising the Rotate and Scale parameters above 0. To increase the strength of the shake, raise the Amplitude slider. To adjust the "coarseness" of the shake, adjust the Frequency. Lower Frequency values make the individual movements large and slow. Higher Frequency values make the movements small and rapid. To increase the complexity of the movements (where

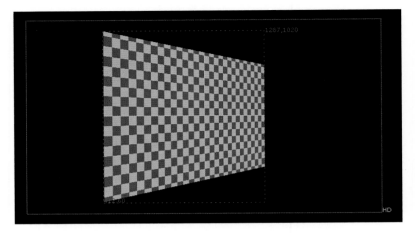

FIGURE 2.7 A checkerboard is rotated with a Card3D node as if it was a 2D card in a 3D space. A sample Nuke script is included as `card3d.nk` in the `Chapters/Chapter2/Scripts/` directory on the DVD.

higher-frequency motion is laid over lower-frequency motion) raise the Octaves parameter.

Card3D creates the illusion that the output is a 2D card within 3D space. Hence, the node offers transform parameters that allow you to transform, rotate, and scale the output along X, Y, and Z axes. The output always remains flat, as if it's a photo postcard (Figure 2.7). (Nuke offers a full 3D environment through specialized camera nodes; these are discussed in Chapter 9.)

Tile allows you to repeat and output in the X and Y directions, much like the UV tiling controls available to a texture in a 3D animation program. You can "zoom" into an output by lowering the Rows and Columns parameters below 1.

Several nodes offer redundant transform control. These include Mirror, which allows you to flip or flop an output, and Position, which allows you to move the output in the X and Y directions. Additional nodes are designed for specialized tasks (UV remapping, lens distortion, motion tracking, spline deformation, and HDRI mapping) and are covered in the remaining chapters.

Filter Considerations

Any node that applies a transform includes a Filter parameter (see Figure 2.5). The Filter parameter drives the node's filter interpolation, which is necessary when the output is rotated, enlarged (*upscaled*), or reduced (*downscaled*). The interpolation determines the color values of the resulting pixels. You can roughly divide the filter interpolations into the following three categories:

Nearest neighbor copies the color value of the nearest original pixel. The interpolation is very efficient, but leads to blockiness and stairstepping, whereby diagonal edges are stepped (Figure 2.8). To apply a nearest-neighbor style of interpolation in Nuke, set Filter to Impulse.

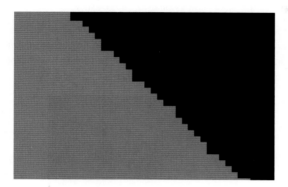

FIGURE 2.8 A red, solid-color bitmap is rotated by 45 degrees with a Transform node. The Filter is set to Impulse, creating stairstepping along the edge.

Bilinear is a type of filter that uses a triangular-shaped curve function. Bilinear filters are able to average the color values of surrounding original pixels by weighting the values based on the distance to the new pixel. Bilinear filters are more accurate than nearest-neighbor filters and produce more subtle transitions between pixels. Bilinear filters are sometimes referred to as tent or Bartlett filters.

Cubic filters build upon bilinear filters by using a bell-shaped curve function. The default Filter setting in Nuke is, in fact, Cubic, which offers the best combination of quality (smooth edges with relatively sharp detail) and efficiency (Figure 2.9).

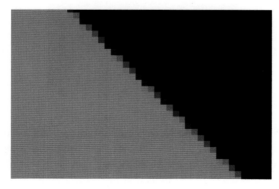

FIGURE 2.9 Filter is set to Cubic, creating a smoother edge. A sample Nuke script is included as `cubic.nk` in the `Chapters/Chapter2/Scripts/` directory on the DVD.

When examining the results of a particular filter, note the Viewer panel's zoom setting. For example, in Figures 2.8 and 2.9, the Viewer is set to a ×9 zoom so that individual pixels are easily seen. To view an output without any zoom and thus judge it in its native size, set the Zoom dropdown menu at the top right of the Viewer panel to ×1. You can interactively zoom in or out by pressing the + or − keys or using a mouse scroll button.

In addition to Cubic, Nuke provides six filter types that use subtle variations of the standard bell-shaped curve. These include Keys, Simon, Rifman, Mitchell, Parzen, and Notch. Of these, Rifman produces the sharpest edges and Notch produces the softest edges (Figures 2.10 and 2.11).

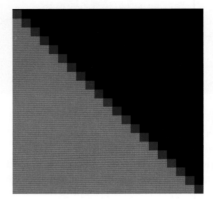

FIGURE 2.10 Filter set to Rifman.

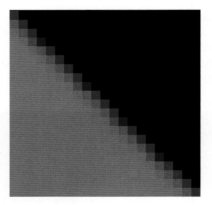

FIGURE 2.11 Filter set to Notch.

When an image is upscaled, new pixels are synthesized and inserted between the original pixels (i.e., the original pixels are *padded*). When an image is downscaled, pixels must be discarded. To ensure that new or surviving pixels retain accurate colors that represent the original pattern, interpolation filters must be applied. Once again, the cubic family of filters creates the most accurate results.

Bilinear and cubic filters are variations of convolution filters. A *convolution filter* multiplies the values within an image or output by the values contained in a kernel matrix. A *kernel matrix* features rows and columns of numbers. Convolution filters are discussed in more detail in Chapter 6.

Keyframing

With traditional, handdrawn animation, a *keyframe* is a drawing that represents a critical position or pose for a character or object moving through a shot. The phrase includes the word "frame" because that animation requires *n* number of individual drawings per second and a second is composed of *n* number of film or video frames. For example, a traditional project might be shot on motion picture film, which operates at 24 frames per second (fps). If the project is animated on 1's, 24 drawings per second are required, with each drawing exposed for one frame. If the project is animated on 2's, 12 drawings per second are required, with each drawing exposed for two frames.

In the realm of digital animation, a *keyframe* is a stored value of a particular parameter of a node at a specific frame on a timeline. This is often referred to as a *key* and the process of creating keys is *keyframing*. The keyframe value might take the form of a transformation, whereby the translation, rotation, or scale value along one or more axes (X, Y, Z) is stored. The value might determine the particular intensity of a filter, such as the strength of a blur.

In-betweening

Digital animation offers the advantage of automatic in-between generation. An *in-between* is a drawing, position, or pose that falls between keyframes. With traditional animation, the addition of an in-between requires an additional drawing. With digital animation, the program provides the in-between values. For example, if you set a keyframe at frame 1 and 10 in Nuke, Nuke creates in-between values for frames 2, 3, 4, 5, 6, 7, 8, and 9. In-between values are created by plotting curves through existing keyframes. Animation curves are discussed in the "Editing in the Curve Editor" section later in this chapter.

Keyframe Theory

Although keyframes are easy to create in Nuke, it may be a challenge to decide *where* on the timeline a keyframe should be created. The following are several approaches you can take:

Extremes. One common approach to keyframing is to determine the extreme positions of the character, object, or element that is being animated. For example, you may choose to animate a clock pendulum

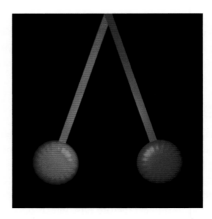

FIGURE 2.12 Two extreme positions for a swinging pendulum. The left extreme is colored red and the right extreme is colored blue.

swinging back and forth; if the pendulum is a still image, you would have to create all the motion within Nuke. There are two extreme positions for the pendulum swing: where the pendulum is at its farthest point on the left and where the pendulum is at the farthest point on the right (Figure 2.12). Once the extremes are identified, determine where on the timeline the associated positions occur. The distance between the keyframes determines the speed of the swing. If the pendulum requires 30 frames to move from one extreme to another, it's moving fairly slow. If the pendulum requires 4 frames to move from one extreme to another, it's moving fast. Extreme positions for characters often involve the extensions of the appendages (such as arms and legs).

Story points. Imagine that you are telling a story, even if you are only animating a single shot. Ask yourself what the critical story points are and convert those into keyframe poses or positions. For example, you may choose to animate a ball bouncing; if the ball is a still image, you would have to create all the motion within Nuke. Critical story points for a bouncing ball would include where the ball starts, where it hits the ground at the start of each bounce, where the peak of each bounce is, and where the ball comes to rest (Figure 2.13). Once the critical story points are identified, determine where on the timeline the associated positions occur.

Bisecting. One method that ignores any inherent story is bisecting. Bisecting requires you to set a keyframe at the start and end of the timeline, then at the midpoint, then at halfway points between existing keyframes. For example, with a 100-frame animation, you would set keyframes at 1, 100, 50, 25, 75, and so on. Bisecting can work well when

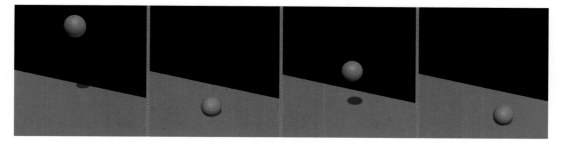

FIGURE 2.13 Critical story points for a bouncing ball. From left to right: where the ball starts, where it hits the ground, the peak of the bounce, and where it comes to rest.

motion of an output is simple or the value change of a parameter is regular and predictable.

Creating and Deleting Keyframes in Nuke

To create a keyframe, follow these steps:

1. Move the time marker to the frame at which you'd like to place a keyframe. Alternatively, you can enter a frame number in the Current Frame Number cell. (For more information on the timeline, see Chapter 1.)
2. Choose the parameter you wish to keyframe. The parameter might be a transform of a Transform node or a specialized parameter of a filter node. Click the Animation Menu button to the right of the parameter and choose Set Key (Figure 2.14). The Animation Menu button features a small, N-shaped curve. The parameter cell turns deep blue to indicate the existence of a keyframe. In addition, a blue line is placed on the timeline at the current frame (Figure 2.15).

FIGURE 2.14 Animation Menu button and its Set Key option.

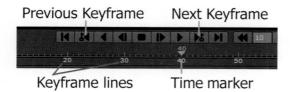

FIGURE 2.15 Previous and Next Keyframe buttons, plus blue keyframe lines, as seen on the timeline.

41

3. Move the time marker to a different frame. Change the parameter value by entering a new number into the number cell, moving the slider, or interactively using the handle of a Transform node. As soon as the value changes, a new keyframe is placed automatically at the current frame. Once two keyframes exist, an animation curve is created for the parameter.

You can update an existing keyframe by placing the time marker at the keyframe's frame number and updating the parameter value. You can delete a keyframe by placing the time marker at the keyframe's frame number, clicking the corresponding Animation Menu button, and choosing Delete. To remove all the keyframes and corresponding animation curve from a parameter, choose No Animation from the Animation Menu. You can use the Next keyframe and Previous Keyframe buttons available with the playback controls to jump to keyframes (Figure 2.15).

Editing in the Curve Editor

Once a parameter has two or more keyframes, you can edit the resulting animation curve in the Curve Editor. To do so, click the Animation Menu button beside a keyframed parameter and choose Curve Editor. The Curve Editor tab is activated and the corresponding animation curve or curves is displayed.

Curve Editor Overview

The left side of the editor displays a parameter tree (Figure 2.16). The tree includes the node name at the top with each animated parameter and associated channel below. Some parameters, such as Translate, carry two

FIGURE 2.16 The Curve Editor with two animation curves visible.

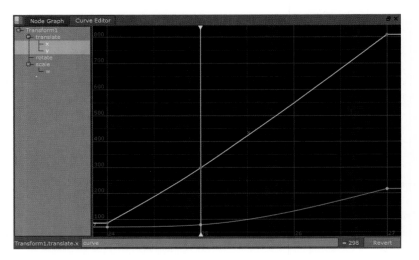

channels: X and Y. (A *channel* is an attribute that can carry a single animation curve.) Other parameters, such as Rotate, carry a single channel; thus, no additional channels are listed. Even if a parameter carries more than one channel, only the channels that are animated are displayed in the tree.

The right side of the editor features the curve graph. Here, animation curves for selected channels are displayed. Each keyframe is represented by a small dot along a curve. The vertical axis of the graph (the Y direction) represents the value of a parameter channel. The horizontal axis (the X direction) represents time as measured in frames. The curves are threaded through the keyframes; hence, the "curviness" of the curves is dependent on the location of the keyframes.

You can display a single curve in the editor by clicking on the parameter or channel name in the parameter tree. To display multiple curves, Shift-click multiple names. If you switch between curves, you may find that a curve is suddenly out of view. This is due to the values carried by the curves existing in different areas of the graph. You can automatically frame a selected curve, however, by clicking an empty area of the graph and pressing the F key.

To scroll the graph view left/right or up/down, Opt/Alt+LMB-drag. To scale the graph view, Opt/Alt+MMB-drag. To zoom in or out, press the + or − key or use a MMB scroll wheel.

Transforming Keyframes

You can move a keyframe in the Curve Editor graph by LMB-dragging the keyframe point. By default, the keyframe snaps to the nearest whole value along the X axis. To defeat this trait, RMB-click the keyframe point and choose Edit > Frame Snap.

To move multiple keyframes, LMB-drag a selection marquee around the keyframe points. Each selected keyframe point turns white and its associated tangent handles are displayed (tangent handles are discussed in the next section). A transform box is also added (Figure 2.17). You can move the box and keyframes by LMB-dragging the central crosshair. You can also scale the keyframes relative to each other by LMB-dragging any edge of the box. Alternatively, you can Shift-click multiple keyframe points to select them.

When a single keyframe is selected, its values are displayed to the right of the keyframe and take the form of x*FrameNumber*, y*ParameterValue* (Figure 2.18). You can change the frame number or parameter value in a precise manner by LMB-clicking either readout and entering a new value into the number cell that appears. In addition, the slope value of the tangent handle is indicated by a θ (Theta) value, which is listed beside one

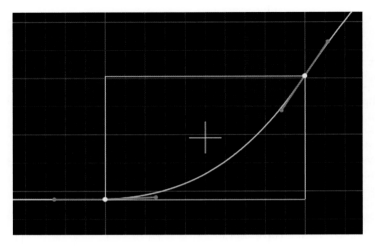

FIGURE 2.17 Two keyframes are selected. Their tangent handles are drawn as red lines. A white transform box surrounds the keyframes.

FIGURE 2.18 A single keyframe is selected. The frame value (x) and parameter value (y) carried by the keyframe are listed to the right of the keyframe point.

or two ends of the tangent handle. For information on tangent manipulation, see the next section.

To delete a keyframe, select the keyframe and press the Delete key. To add a new keyframe, select a curve by clicking on it so it turns yellow and Cmd/Ctrl+Opt/Alt-click on the curve. A new keyframe is added where your mouse arrow is positioned. The curve is replotted so that it threads its way through the new keyframe. Adding additional keyframes allows for greater control over the shape of the curve and the resulting animation.

Manipulating Tangents

When a keyframe is selected, its tangent handle is displayed. The tangent determines how the curve flows through the keyframe. Once again, in-between frame values are determined by the program by plotting animation curves. Thus, the shape of an animation curve affects the resulting animation. Hence, the ability to fine tune the tangent handles gives you greater control over the animation process.

You can move a tangent handle by LMB-dragging the dot at either end of the handle. By default, the handle moves like a see-saw. However, you can break the handle into two separate handles, by RMB-clicking over an associated keyframe and choosing Interpolation > Break from the shortcut menu. Once the tangent is broken, you are free to move either side of the handle (Figure 2.19). A broken tangent allows sharp corners to be formed on the curve, which may be useful for creating a sudden change of value (e.g., a transformed output may suddenly change direction). You can "unbreak" a handle by choosing Interpolation > *tangent type*.

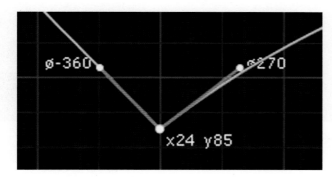

FIGURE 2.19 A broken tangent handle, once manipulated, forms a sharp corner on the curve.

Changing the Tangent Type

By default, Nuke creates curves that smoothly thread through keyframes. You can adjust the way in which the curve flows, however, by changing the interpolation type of one or more of the tangents. To do so, select one or more keyframes, RMB-click in the Curve Editor, and choose Interpolation > *tangent type*. The following are descriptions of the tangent types:

Smooth is the default tangent type.
Linear forces the curve to move in a perfectly straight line between keyframes (Figure 2.20). This creates abrupt changes in the speed of the parameter value change.

45

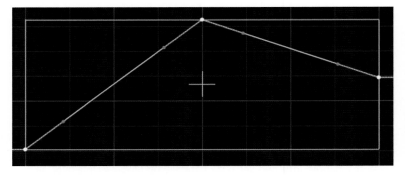

FIGURE 2.20 Three keyframes with Linear tangent interpolation.

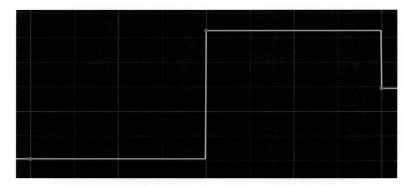

FIGURE 2.21 Same keyframes from Figure 2.20 with Constant interpolation.

Constant creates a stepped curve, where there is no change in the parameter Y value until the next keyframe is encountered (Figure 2.21). If this style of tangent is applied to Translate parameters, the animated element would appear to suddenly jump from one position to the next.

Catmull-Rom, Cubic, and Horizontal offer variations of the Smooth tangent type. Catmull-Rom takes into consideration the Y values of the nearest left and right keyframes; this creates subtle variations in the "curviness" of the curve as it passes through closely spaced keyframes. Cubic matches the tangent slope to the steepest side of the curve as it runs to previous of next keyframes; this can cause the curve to peak at a higher point in Y than the keyframes that lie on its path. (Figure 2.22).

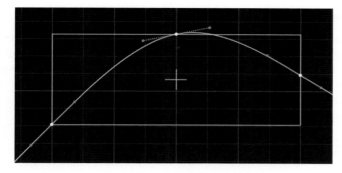

FIGURE 2.22 Same keyframes from Figure 2.20 with Cubic interpolation.

Horizontal forces the tangent handles to maintain 0 slope, where the left and right side of the tangent handle has the same position in the Y direction.

Using the Dope Sheet

The release of Nuke v6.2 introduced the Dope Sheet, which offers an alternative means to adjust *when* keyframes occur on the timeline. The Dope Sheet appears in its own tab to the right of the Curve Editor. Keyframes are added automatically to the Dope Sheet as they are added to the Curve Editor.

To see specific keyframes in the Dope Sheet, click the Animation Menu button for an animated parameter and choose Dope Sheet from the shortcut menu. The left side of the Dope Sheet contains a parameter tree much like the Curve Editor (Figure 2.23). However, channels are automatically hidden in the tree; to show these, click the + symbol beside each parameter name. For example, clicking the + beside Translate reveals the X and Y channels. The right side of the Dope Sheet contains a keyframe field, where keyframes are indicated as gray markers. The keyframe field indicates time in frames from left to right. There is no Y direction, however, as parameter values are inaccessible in the sheet.

FIGURE 2.23 The Dope Sheet. A Transform1 node is listed with animated Translate X, Translate Y, Rotate, and Scale W (width) parameters. Translate X and Translate Y have three keyframes each, while Rotate and Scale only have two keyframes each.

47

Manipulating Keyframes

You can select a keyframe marker by clicking it. To move the marker to a different frame, LMB-drag the marker left or right. Note that the parent marker travels with the one you have selected. For example, if you move the W (width) keyframe marker, the parent marker for Scale, as well as the parent marker for the node (such as Transform1) moves in unison (Figure 2.24).

FIGURE 2.24 A Scale W keyframe is selected and moved. The selection is indicated by the white keyframe markers and the yellow frame readout. When the W marker is moved, the parent markers for Scale and Transform1 follow automatically.

To change the view with the keyframe field, use the same key and mouse combinations as you would for the Curve Editor (see the "Curve Editor Overview" section earlier in the chapter). You can select multiple keyframes by Shift-clicking or LMB-dragging a marquee box. You can delete a keyframe by selecting it and pressing the Delete key. You can insert a new keyframe by Cmd/Ctrl+Opt/Alt-clicking in an empty area of the keyframe field.

Adjusting Read Nodes

The Dope Sheet offers the ability to adjust the duration and timeline location of image sequences or video imported through a Read node. To view a Read node in the Dope Sheet, open its properties panel and switch to the Dope Sheet tab. For example, in Figure 2.25, a Read1 node is displayed. The Read1 node carries an image sequence that is numbered 0 to 59 for a total of 60 frames. The parameter tree displays the node name and the File channel. In the keyframe field, the image sequence is represented by a gray horizontal line surrounded by open and close brackets.

You can reposition the sequence/video line by LMB-dragging it left or right. Moving the line to the right causes the sequence/video to occur later on the

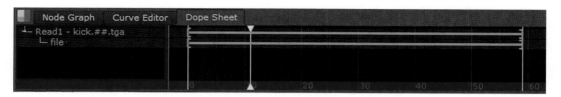

FIGURE 2.25 A 60-frame image sequence is featured in the Dope Sheet. The sequence is numbered 0 to 59, which corresponds to the frame range of the project. The vertical gray lines indicate the frame range start and end.

FIGURE 2.26 The sequence line is moved to the right so that the sequence is not utilized until frame 10 of the timeline. The brackets are moved inwards so only a portion of the sequence is used.

timeline (Figure 2.26). For example, moving the line so that the open bracket rests at frame 10 means that the sequence/video will not be visible until frame 10. By default, the empty gap on the timeline is filled with a held copy of the first frame of the sequence/video. To avoid this, change the Read node's Before menu (beside the Frame Range First cell) and After menu (beside the Frame Range Last cell) from Hold to Loop, Bounce, or Black. Loop cycles the sequence/video to fill any timeline gaps. Bounce also cycles the footage, but reverses the frame order with each iteration. Black simply inserts a black frame and does not search for any file; the black frame is given 100% transparent alpha.

You can trim the sequence/video line so that only a portion is used by the program. To do so, LMB-drag the open bracket to the right and/or LMB-drag the close bracket to the left. In this situation, the frame that rests at the open bracket is repeated to fill the gap between the start of the line and the open bracket. At the same time, the frame that rests at the close bracket is repeated to fill the gap between the end of the line and the close bracket. To alter this behavior, change the Read node's Before and After menus to Loop, Bounce, or Black.

If the Read node carries a still image, the open and close brackets are provided but no horizontal line appears. The brackets determine how many frames the image is held for on the timeline.

Activating Motion Blur

Motion blur is the streaking of an object as it moves during the exposure of one frame of film or video. If an object moves one foot during the exposure of one frame, the motion blur streak appears one foot long.

By default, animating the transforms of an output in Nuke will not produce motion blur. You can add motion blur, however, by raising a Transform node's Motionblur parameter above 0. Motionblur sets the sampling rate of the blur, whereby the output is repeated along its motion path (the path drawn in the Viewer that indicates the motion of the output) for the duration of a virtual shutter. The higher the Motionblur value, the smoother and more realistic the blur. In the real world, a *shutter* is the physical or electronic mechanism of a camera that controls the duration that one frame of film or video is exposed to light. The virtual shutter within Nuke is controlled by the Transform node's Shutter parameter. By default, Shutter is set to 0.5, which forces the program to start at the current frame and go forward in time 0.5 frames to determine the output's start and end position along its motion path. The motion blur streak is thus drawn between the start and end position (Figure 2.27).

You can offset the start and end position of the blur by changing the Shutter Offset menu and Shutter Custom Offset cell. For example, if you set Shutter Offset to Centred (centered), the program goes back in time 0.25 frames and forward in time 0.25 frames to determine the start and end position. If you set Shutter Offset to Custom and Shutter Custom Offset to 2, the program goes forward in time two frames to determine the start position. Note that Shutter Custom Offset only functions if Shutter Offset is set to Custom.

FIGURE 2.27 A Transform node has its Motionblur and Shutter parameters set to 1. The transformed spaceship render is blurred along its motion path.

Tutorial 1: Kicking a Heart

Part 2: Keyframing Transforms

In Part 1 of this tutorial, we set up a new script, imported an image sequence of two characters interacting with an unseen object, imported a 3D render of a stylized heart, adjusted the resolution of the heart render with a Reformat node, and created a simple composite through a Merge node. Part 2 adds keyframe animation to the 3D render, allowing the heart to be kicked out of the frame. In addition, we'll activate motion blur.

1. Open the Nuke script you saved after completing Part 1 of this tutorial. A sample Nuke script is included as `Tutorial1.1.nk` in the `Tutorials/Tutorial1/Scripts/` directory on the DVD.

2. In the Node Graph, select the Reformat1 node. Press the T key or RMB-click and choose Transform > Transform from the shortcut menu. A Transform1 node is inserted between the Reformat1 node and Merge1 node.

3. Move the time marker to frame 24. This is the frame on which the character wearing the white boots makes contact with the heart during a kick. However, the heart is to too far left to make a solid connection with the boot. While the Transform node is selected and the circular transform handle is visible in the Viewer, interactively move the heart up and to the right. Note that the Transform X and Transform Y parameter cells of the Transform node's properties panel automatically update with new values. To make the movement more precise, enter 85 in the Transform X cell and 70 into the Transform Y cell. Because the heart render is surrounded by transparent alpha, the bounding box overhang does not matter (Figure 2.28).

4. In the Transform1 node's properties panel, click the Animation Menu button beside Transform X and Y and choose Set Key. The cells turn deep blue to indicate a keyframe. A blue keyframe line is also placed on the Timeline at frame 24. Move the time marker to frame 27. This is the frame where the kicking boot crosses the corner of the frame. With the Transform1 node selected, interactively move the heart so that it is ahead of the kicking boot and out of frame. While you move the heart, it will remain visible (Figure 2.29); however, when you release the mouse to end the transform, the heart disappears because it is beyond the edge of the frame. A keyframe is set automatically for frame 27. In addition, an motion path line is drawn in the Viewer between the frame 24 position and frame 27 position.

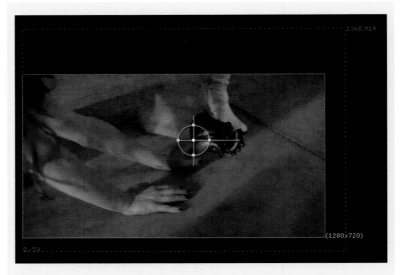

FIGURE 2.28 The heart is transformed to 85,70 in X,Y to better line up with the boot kick.

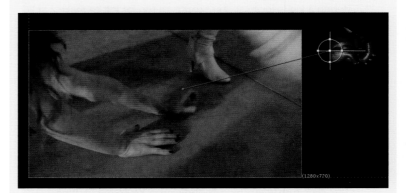

FIGURE 2.29 The heart is moved past the edge of the bounding box and out of the frame.

5. Play back the timeline. The heart is "kicked" out of frame by the boot. To avoid playing back all 60 frames, you can narrow the timeline by clicking the Frame Range Lock button so that its corners turn red, and enter a new range, such as 20-30, into the Frame Range cell (Figure 2.30). The frame range indicators, which appear as orange triangles on the timeline, move from the default start and end positions to the new range (Figure 2.31). Play back the timeline. The playback is now restricted to the frame range. You can change the Frame Range cell values at any time.

FIGURE 2.30 The Frame Range Unlock button, in an unlocked state (right) and the Frame Range cell (left).

FIGURE 2.31 The frame range indicators (orange) are positioned at frames 20 and 30, while keyframes remain at frames 24 and 27.

6. At this stage, the heart moves in a perfectly straight line due to the existence of two keyframes. You can add an arc to the heart's animation path by adding a third keyframe. To do so, move the time marker to frame 25. Interactively move the heart so the motion path forms a slight, down-pointing arc (Figure 2.32).

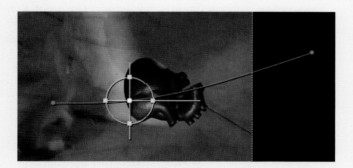

FIGURE 2.32 Close-up of motion path. A third keyframe, at frame 25, allows the path to form a down-pointing arc.

7. When animating, you are not limited to Translate X and Translate Y. In fact, animating the Scale and Rotate parameters can help create more believable motion. To add such animation, return to frame 24 and open the Transform1 node's properties panel. Click the Animation Menu button beside Scale and choose the Set Key. Do the same for the Rotate parameter. Move the time marker to frame 27. Change the Scale cell to 1.5. Note that the cell changes from a pale blue to a deep blue. While a deep blue color

indicates the presence of a keyframe, a pale blue color indicates that the values are derived as an in-between by plotting values on the associated animation curve. Change the Rotate cell to 70. Note that the rotation occurs from the center of the transform handle and not the logical center of the rendered heart. If you wish to rotate the heart from its center, change the Center X and Center Y to 720 and 380, respectively. Ideally, changes to the Center X and Center Y should be applied *before* setting any keyframes on the node; otherwise, the motion path may be shifted in an undesirable fashion.

8. At this point, there is no motion blur present. You can add blur to the heart by raising the Transform1 node's Motionblur slider to 1. This significantly slows the playback, at least for the first play through. However, a believable motion blur is created for an otherwise static image (Figure 2.33). To see the result more clearly, you can temporarily hide the various overlays present in the Viewer. To do so, RMB-click in the Viewer and choose Overlay from the shortcut menu. The first time you choose the option, only the motion paths are hidden. The second time you choose this option, all overlays, including bounding boxes and transform handles, are hidden. The third time you choose this option, the overlays return. You can also press the O key.

This concludes Part 2 of Tutorial 1. Save a copy of the script. A sample Nuke script is included as `Tutorial1.2.nk` in the `Tutorials/Tutorial1/Scripts/` directory on the DVD. In Chapter 3, we'll match the heart to the background through color grading.

FIGURE 2.33 Detail of motion-blurred heart, as seen on frame 25. The Viewer overlays have been hidden.

Tutorial 2: Flying a Spaceship

Part 1: Adjusting Curves

Tutorial 2 allows you to adjust previously created animation curves in the Curve Editor. The animation features a 3D render of a spaceship floating over a photographic background.

1. Open the following script on the DVD: `Tutorials/Tutorial2/Scripts/Tutorial2.start.nk`. The script features two Read nodes. Read1 carries a 60-frame, OpenEXR render of a spaceship. Read2 carries a still photo of an industrial location on the edge of a desert. The spaceship is repositioned through a Transform1 node connected to Read1's output (Figure 2.34). The output of Transform1 is merged on top of the output of Read2 with a Merge1 node. The result is sent to Viewer1. The project resolution is set to 2048 × 1556. If the output of Merge1 is fit into the Viewer1 panel so that the entire bounding box is visible, the background and spaceship may appear rough. For example, the telephone lines may appear stairstepped. To view the true quality of the output, you must set the Viewer1 panel's Zoom menu to ×1. If you are zoomed in, you can scroll left/right and up/down in the panel by MMB-dragging. You can refit the output image to the Viewer1 tab by changing the Zoom menu to Fit.

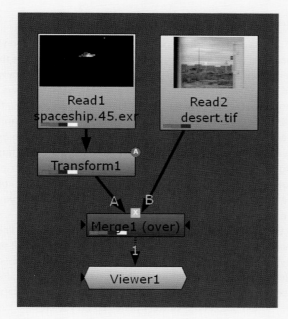

FIGURE 2.34 The node network.

2. Play back the timeline. The spaceship moves right to left, finally moving past the edge of the bounding box at the end of the timeline. Select the Transform1 node to display the motion path in the Viewer1 panel (Figure 2.35). Although the 3D render allows the spaceship to slowly rotate in place, the right-to-left motion is provided by the Transform1 node. Examine the Transform1 node's properties panel. The Translate X, Translate Y, Rotate, and Scale parameters are keyframed animated, as is indicated by the blue number cells.

FIGURE 2.35 Close-up of spaceship render with motion path provided by the Transform1 node.

3. At this stage, the motion path is linear, making the motion of the spaceship very rigid. To alter this motion, you can adjust the animation curves for the Translate X and Translate Y parameters. Click the Animation Menu button beside these parameters and choose Curve Editor from the shortcut menu. To examine the X and Y curves more closely, Shift-select the X and Y channels in the parameter tree of the Curve Editor, click in the curve graph area, and press the F key. The curves are automatically framed (Figure 2.36). The X curve is marked with a small x. The Y curve features a small y. Each curve has three keyframes. (The colors of the curves may vary depending on the version of Nuke you are running.)

4. At this point, the tangent interpolation of the keyframes is linear. To change the interpolations, draw a marquee box around all six keyframes, RMB-click in the curve graph, and choose Interpolation > *interpolation type*. Try each interpolation type and note the affect the type has on the shape of the animation curves and the shape of the motion path in the Viewer1 panel. When you create a new keyframe, it's automatically assigned a Smooth tangent

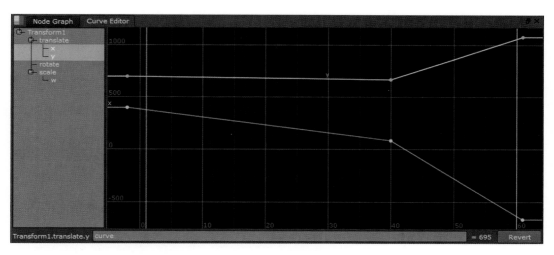

FIGURE 2.36 The Translate X and Y animation curves.

interpolation. You can derive the smoothest motion for the spaceship with Smooth, Catmull-Rom, or Cubic interpolation. Catmull-Rom and Cubic will cause the animation path to dip between the first and second keyframes (Figure 2.37). You can adjust the resulting shape, however, by moving the individual X and Y tangent handles.

5. Adjust the tangents of the X and Y curves by selecting a keyframe in the curve graph, clicking the dots on either end of a tangent handle, and LMB-dragging. The goal is to create an animation path that allows the spaceship to smoothly move offscreen

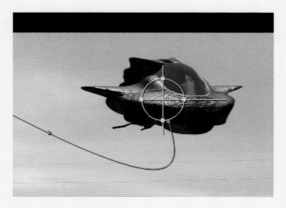

FIGURE 2.37 The Cubic tangent interpolation causes the motion path to dip between the first and second keyframes.

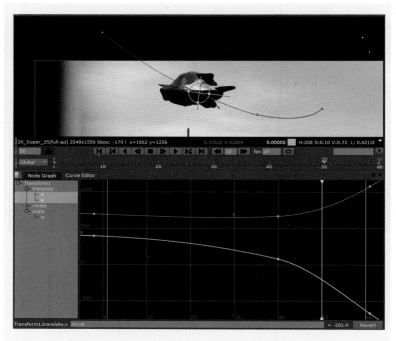

FIGURE 2.38 The adjusted X and Y curves and the resulting motion path.

(Figure 2.38). Play back the timeline. To see the motion more clearly, hide the motion path and transform handle by pressing the O key twice. (To bring the overlays back, press O a third time.) Due to the large project resolution, the playback will not reach real-time speeds until the second time it loops on the timeline. For more accurate real-time playback, you can create a flipbook. To do so, return to the Node Graph, select the Merge1 node, choose Render > Flipbook Selected from the menu bar, enter 1-60 in the Frame/Frame Range cell of the Flipbook dialog box and proceed to play the timeline of the FrameCycler window. (For more information on the FrameCycler program, see Chapter 1.)

6. Although the spaceship exists as a rendered image sequence, it does not include motion blur. Although 3D programs such as Auotdesk Maya can create motion blur, it must be activated (in this case, it wasn't). Because the right-to-left motion of the spaceship is provided by the Transform1 node, you can add motion blur in the composite by raising the Transform1 node's Motionblur parameter to 1. Although the resulting blur is relatively subtle, it will help with the realism of the scene (Figure 2.39).

FIGURE 2.39 Motion blur is activated for the Transform1 node.

This concludes Part 1 of Tutorial 2. Save a copy of the script. A sample Nuke script is included as `Tutorial2.1.nk` in the `Tutorials/Tutorial2/Scripts/` directory on the DVD. In Chapter 3, we'll adjust the elements though color grading.

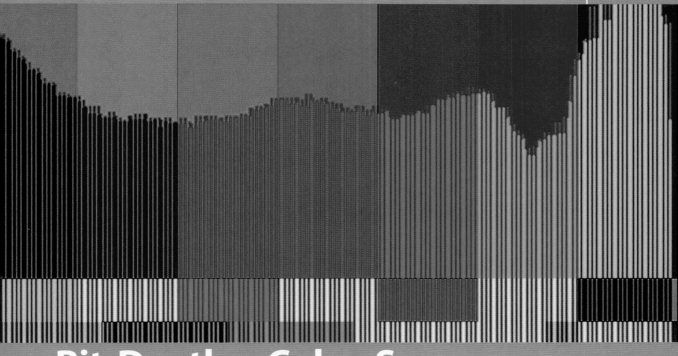

Bit Depths, Color Spaces, and Color Grading

A critical component of digital compositing is the proper selection and conversion of color spaces. Failure to take color space into account can lead to composites with mismatched color values or color artifacts. In addition, image formats vary in their fundamental mathematical makeup, leading to additional concerns as files are imported into Nuke and written out to disk. Once the technical aspects of color space and image format conversion are mastered, aesthetic color adjustments remain. Such adjustments fall under the auspice of color grading. Nuke offers a wide range of color filter nodes that allow you to undertake color grading within the program.

This chapter includes the following critical information:

- Understanding bit depth, color space, and look-up tables
- Converting between color spaces in Nuke
- Differentiating among linear, logarithmic, integer, and floating-point image formats
- Color grading with Nuke color filter nodes

Understanding Bit Depth

Digital images carry three channels: red, green, and blue (RGB). (Other specialized channels, such as alpha, are carried by a limited number of file formats and are discussed throughout this book.) Each channel's bit depth establishes how many potential colors (or *tonal steps*) that channel can carry. Bit depths are expressed as a number, such as 1-bit, 2-bit, and so on. The number represents an exponent where the base is 2. For example, 1-bit equates to 2^1 or simply 2. 8-bit equates to 2^8 or 256; hence, an 8-bit image has 256 potential colors per channel for a total of 16,777,216 potential colors ($2^8 \times 2^8 \times 2^8$). The number 2 is used as the base because a single bit has two potential states (0/1 or off/on). A *bit* is a discrete unit of digital data.

Bit Depth and Color Space in Nuke

When you import a bitmap, image sequence, or video file into a Nuke script, it's automatically converted to Nuke's internal color space, which is linear 32-bit floating-point RGB. All operations within Nuke are calculated within the linear 32-bit floating-point RGB color space. A *color space* is a gamut that uses a particular color model. A *gamut* is a subset of colors that a particular device can display. A *color model* employs specific primary colors, combinations of which create all other possible colors. For example, RYB (red-yellow-blue) and RGB (red-green-blue) are two color models. Digital images use the RGB model, while traditional art forms, such as oil painting, use the RYB model.

The color space conversion is carried out by the Read node. To interpret the imported file's native format correctly, and thus guarantee an accurate conversion, the Read node's Colorspace menu must be set correctly (Figure 3.1). The menu offers multiple look-up table (LUT) settings, each of

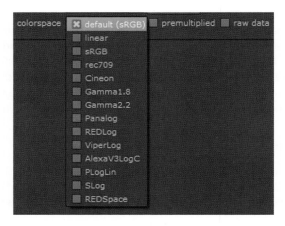

FIGURE 3.1 The Colorspace menu and Raw Data parameter of a Read node (as seen in Nuke v6.3).

which converts the file data using a specific color space. (A *LUT* is an array that remaps input values.) Nuke automatically chooses a proper LUT by reading the imported file's header. However, you have the option to change the menu to a different LUT.

The following are descriptions of each LUT:

Default defers to the Default LUT Settings, found in the LUT tab of the Project Settings panel. See the next section for more information.

Linear does not convert the file data, but uses it as is.

sRGB applies the standard sRGB IEC6 1966-2.1 color space conversion. sRGB is widely used for digital image processing. For example, the default color space in Photoshop is sRGB.

Rec709 applies a standard HDTV color space conversion.

Cineon and **PLogLin** apply two variations of a 10-bit log-to-linear color space conversion. (For more information on log files, see the "Log and Linear Formats" section later in this chapter.)

Gamma 1.8 and **Gamma 2.2** apply a specific gamma curve to the incoming image. (See the "Understanding Gamma" section later in this chapter.)

SLog, Panalog, REDLog, ViperLog, and **AlexaV3LogC** apply specific log-to-linear conversions designed for various camera systems, such as the Sony F35 CineAlta, Viper Filmstream, and Arri Alexa. The REDSpace LUT, on the other hand, bases the conversion on a curve provided by the RED camera manufacturer.

Depending on the version of Nuke you are running, several LUTs may be missing (e.g., new LUTs were introduced with version 6.3v1). It's possible to avoid the color space conversion altogether by selecting the Read node's Raw Data checkbox (see Figure 3.1). This may be necessary if other nodes in the node network are handling color space conversion. (See the "Using the Colorspace Node" later in this chapter.)

Default LUT Settings

If a Read node's Colorspace menu is set to Default, it uses the Default LUT Settings section of the LUT tab of the Project Settings panel to determine the type of conversion it applies to the imported file. (You can bring up the Project Settings panel by choosing Edit > Project Settings from the menu bar.) The conversions are divided into four categories: 8-Bit Files, 16-Bit Files, Log Files, and Float Files (Figure 3.2). Thus, if the Read node imports an 8-bit file, the conversion is determined by the 8-Bit Files menu, which is set to sRGB by default. Nuke can identify whether a file is 8-bit, 16-bit, linear, or float by reading the file's header. Although the menus settings are logical in most situations, you can change them for a specialized result. For example, you can change 8-Bit Files to Linear so that the 8-bit data is read as-is and no conversion is applied.

FIGURE 3.2 The Default LUT Settings section of the LUT tab of the Project Settings panel.

Additionally, the Default LUT Settings section provides a Monitor menu, which determines the conversion that is applied before sending the output to any non-Viewer display, such as a broadcast or television monitor.

The LUT tab includes a LUT curve editor. This offers a convenient way to see what a particular LUT is doing to the values of an imported image. The available LUTs are listed in the graph's left column (Figure 3.3). If you click on a particular LUT name, its curve is displayed in the graph. For example, if you click the word "sRGB," the sRGB curve is displayed. The up/down Y axis of the graph represents the raw input values as read from the imported file. The left/right X axis represents the values output by the Read node. Thus, if an input value is 0.5 and the sRGB LUT is applied, the output value is approximately 0.2. If you switch to the Linear LUT, you can see that an input of 0.5 leads to an output of 0.5.

FIGURE 3.3 The sRGB LUT curve, as displayed in the LUT tab graph.

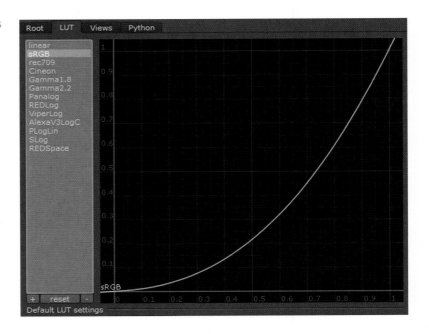

You can make a custom LUT by clicking the + sign at the bottom left of the LUT list, entering a LUT name into the New Curve Name dialog box, clicking OK, and editing the curve. You can edit a LUT curve the same way you would an animation curve in the Curve Editor. For more information on the Curve Editor, see Chapter 2.

Writing Out a Specific Color Space

The Write node includes the Colorspace menu, which allows you to apply a LUT to the output before it is written to disk. The Default option uses the Default LUT Settings section of the Project Settings LUT tab. The Linear option disables the Colorspace menu and the output values are written out as is. In general, the most suitable option for linear 8- and 16-bit files is sRGB. The most suitable option for generic log files is Cineon.

Understanding Gamma

Computer monitors operate in a nonlinear fashion. That is, the relationship between voltage and brightness is not 1-to-1. This relationship is represented by a gamma curve, whereby the voltage is raised by the power of gamma to increase the brightness. This gamma is often referred to as native gamma.

Human perception of light produces its own gamma curve, where the there is less sensitivity to bright areas of an image or scene and more sensitivity to dark areas (the inverse of native gamma).

Computer operating systems generally employ an inverse gamma curve in a process known as gamma correction. However, gamma correction is not designed to neutralize the native gamma curve. Instead, gamma correction is designed to efficiently distribute the tonal range across a limited number of bits in a manner suitable for human perception. If gamma correction is not applied by the operating system, digital images appear to have improper contrast.

Gamma correction is represented by a single number. On a Windows operating system, the gamma correction value is 2.2 by default. On a Macintosh system, the gamma correction value is 1.8. Large animation or visual effects studios may create custom gamma settings for specific projects. Nevertheless, any gamma correction applied by Nuke happens in addition to the system gamma correction.

There are several ways to apply gamma curves within Nuke (whereby the node output is affected by the gamma curve, but the system gamma correction is unaffected). The Read and Write nodes offer Gamma 1.8 and Gamma 2.2 Colorspace menu options. In this case, the gamma curve is applied before those values are output or written by the nodes. In addition, the Grade and ColorCorrect nodes carry Gamma parameters. These nodes are discussed in more detail in the "Color Grading" section later in this chapter.

Bit Depth Output Issues

Various output devices and output formats are unable to match the 32-bit color space of Nuke. As such, it's important to be aware of ramifications of such bit depth disparity. A few of these are:

- Most computer monitors, whether they are CRTs, flat screens, or built-in displays on laptops, operate in 8-bit color space. That is, they offer 8 bits per channel. Hence, when viewing a Nuke output, you are not seeing the full 32-bit color range. The disparity is lessened, to some degree, by using a 10-bit monitor, such as the HP DreamColor or Eizo ColorEdge. To lessen the impact even further, you can use a custom Viewer Process LUT and apply monitor calibration. These approaches are discussed in the next two sections.

- Many output formats, such as various digital video formats, require 8- or 10-bit color space to produce sufficient quality. Hence, the loss of bit depth is not overly detrimental. On the other hand, film recorders, which record digital images to motion picture film stock, can operate in 10-, 12-, and 16-bit modes.

- Even though it's not possible to view the full 32-bit color space on a monitor, the 32-bit architecture of Nuke does provide more accurate calculations. For example, applying filters in an 8-bit color space is significantly less accurate than applying the same filters within a 32-bit color space. The inaccuracy may lead to such artifacts as posterization, where transitions between color form harsh bands.

Using the Viewer Process Menu

The Viewer Process menu allows you to apply a custom LUT to the displayed output *before* it reaches the Viewer. (The Viewer Process menu is located at the top right of the Viewer panel, as seen in Figure 3.4.) This offers a means to emulate a specific output format without affecting the node network. Keep in mind that all calculations within Nuke are carried out in linear 32-bit color space. That is, no LUT is applied *until* a Write node writes the output to disk. A Read node will apply a LUT to an imported image; however, the output of the Read node is linear. Hence, the Viewer Process menu converts Nuke's linear color space using one of its offered

FIGURE 3.4 Viewer Process menu (left) and the Input Process button (right).

LUTs. For example, if you set the Viewer Process menu to Rec709, the Viewer emulates HDTV color space. By default, the menu only offers None, sRGB, and Rec709. The None option is equivalent to Linear, whereby no output values are altered. You can add additional LUTs to the menu list; this is discussed in Chapter 10.

Monitor Calibration Overview

Proper monitor calibration ensures that a correct gamma correction curve is applied. In addition, monitor calibration aids in the adjustment of the system's brightness, contrast, and color temperature settings so that they are optimal for the environment in which the monitor is located. Accurate monitor calibration requires calibration software and a colorimeter (a physical sensor that temporarily attaches to the screen). The software is able to output known values to the screen, compare those values to the reading taken by the colorimeter, and prepare a custom monitor profile. The monitor profile includes a LUT for each color channel. The LUT contains gamma correction information, as well as the system white point. A *white point* is a coordinate in color space that determines what is considered "white." The white point is affected by the system's color temperature, which is measured in the Kelvin scale (such as 6500 K). Calibration software offers the user the ability to choose a color temperature and thus determine the white point. Once a monitor profile is in place, the values of a digital image are remapped by the monitor profile LUT before they are sent to the screen. If no custom monitor profile is present, a default profile is provided by the operating system.

Calibration software and hardware ranges in price and complexity. While some models are targeted at casual users, others are aimed at professional digital artists. Calibration manufacturers include Pantone, X-Rite, and Monaco. Depending on the type of monitor used, it may be necessary to apply calibration on a regular basis; as monitors age, they are prone to color "drift."

Integer and Floating-Point Formats

Common image formats, such as GIF, BMP, JPEG, PNG, and Targa, store values as integers. Integers are numbers that are written without a fractional or decimal competent. Hence, the red pixel value of a JPEG file might be stored as 98, even though the value provided by the software calculation might be 98.6252. The use of integers leads to rounded values, which in turn leads to loss of accuracy.

In contrast, floating-point image formats avoid this loss, and thereby increase accuracy, by storing decimal information. The format takes a fractional number and multiples it by a power of 10. For example, a floating-point number may be encoded as 1.432e−4, where e−4 is the same as $\times 10^{-4}$. Thus, 1.432 is multiplied by $\times 10^{-4}$ or 0.0001, producing 0.0001432. Large numbers can also be stored. For example, a number may be encoded as 1.432e+6, where e+6 is the same as $\times 10^6$. Thus, 1.432 is multiplied by $\times 10^6$ or 1,000,000, producing 1,432,000. Once again, all calculations within Nuke are made within a 32-bit floating-point space, making the software highly accurate. As for image formats, OpenEXR, TIFF, and HDR support floating-point architecture.

Log and Linear Formats

Nuke operates in a linear color space. The linear calculation breaks the color range into equal increments. For example, an 8-bit RGB scale of 0 to 255 has 256 equal steps. Hence, each increase in intensity happens in a predictable and equal fashion. For example, changing the intensity of pixels from 1 to 2 requires one step, which is the same as increasing the pixel from an intensity of 100 to 101.

In contrast, logarithmic calculations are inherently nonlinear. This is due to the use of a logarithmic formula, which follows $\log_{base}(\text{intensity}) = \text{exponent}$ or $\text{base}^{\text{exponent}} = \text{intensity}$. Thus, each incremental increase in the exponent leads to large leaps in intensity. For example, $10^2 = 100$ while $10^3 = 1000$; in this case, 100 is 10 times greater than 10. A logarithmic curve naturally matches the characteristic curve of motion picture film stock. A *characteristic curve* plots the optical density (successful exposure) of the film stock over the exposure duration. To increase the optical density in an incremental fashion, the exposure must increase logarithmically. Hence, log (logarithmic) image formats are favored when scanning or recording back to motion picture footage. Cineon and DPX are two log formats that are supported by Nuke. In addition, Nuke supports various camera-specific log formats, including Slog, PanaLog, REDLog, ViperLog, and AlexaV3LogC.

Working with Log Files

The main disadvantage of log files is their inability to be viewed correctly in Nuke's linear color space. Nuke tries to solve this by converting a log file to linear space as it's loaded into a Read node. If Nuke detects a log format, it sets the Colorspace menu to Cineon or one of the camera-specific menu options. If the log-to-linear conversion does not occur, the image appears washed out (see the next section).

Converting Log Files

If you wish to control the log-to-linear conversion, you can select the Raw Data parameter of the Read node and connect the Read node's output to a Color-space node. See the "Using the Colorspace Node" section later in this chapter.

You can also undertake a log-to-linear conversion using the Log2Lin node. To do so, follow these steps:

1. Use a Read node to import a log bitmap or image sequence. A sample file is included as `log.cin` in the `Chapters/Chapter3/Bitmaps/` directory on the DVD. Select the Raw Data parameter so that it is checked. Raw Data prevents the program from applying a LUT conversion. Connect a Viewer to the Read node. To gauge the result without adding an additional viewer LUT, set the Viewer Process menu to None. The image appears washed-out (Figure 3.5).

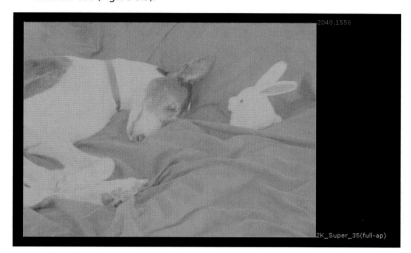

FIGURE 3.5 Log file viewed with the Raw Data parameter selected.

FIGURE 3.6 Same file after the connection of a Log2Lin node.

2. With the Read node selected, RMB-click and choose Color > Log2Lin. The image will immediately regain its lost contrast (Figure 3.6).
3. Open the Log2Lin1 node's properties panel. Adjust the Black, White, and Gamma parameters. Black sets the black point, which is the value found in the log file that is considered 0-value "black" in Nuke's linear color space.

White sets the white point, which is the value found in the log file that is considered 1-value "white" in Nuke's linear color space. Note that the parameter values are on a 10-bit scale that runs from 0 to 1023 for a total of 1024 tonal steps. Gamma applies a gamma correction curve to the input. A sample Nuke script is included as `log2lin.nk` in the `Chapters/Chapter3/Scripts/` directory on the DVD.

The Log2Lin node operates in the opposite direction and will apply a linear-to-log conversion if you set the Operation parameter to Lin2Log. This may be necessary for preparing an output for a film recorder. (The Write node is also able to carry out the conversion if the Colorspace menu is set to a linear space.)

You can also apply a log-to-linear conversion by connecting a PLogLin node (Color > PLogLin with Nuke v6.3). The PLogLin node uses the "Josh Pines" conversion method. The method trades the white and black points for a midtone value. This value is identified by matching a single value in the linear color space (through the Linear Reference Value menu) to a single value in the log space (through the Log Reference Value menu).

Note that Nuke also offers the Truelight node (Color > Truelight), which makes the log-to-linear conversion using a Truelight profile file. Truelight is a color calibration standard developed by FilmLight, which manufactures film scanners.

Writing Floating-Point and Log Files

OpenEXR, TIFF, and HDR formats support floating-point architecture. OpenEXR offers 16-bit "half" and 32-bit "float" variations. TIFF supports 8-bit integer, 16-bit integer, and 32-bit float variations. HDR is a 8-bit floating-point format. When rendering a sequence through a Write node, you can choose to render a floating-point format by changing the File Type menu to Exr, Tiff, or Hdr. Exr and Tiff provide an additional Datatype menu that allows you to choose a specific bit depth. For example, you can choose between 16-Bit Half or 32-Bit Float when writing out an OpenEXR file (Figure 3.7).

FIGURE 3.7 Write node bit depth options when File Type menu is set to Exr.

Cineon is a 10-bit log format. DPX is also logarithmic, but supports 8-, 10-, 12-, and 16-bit variations. You can render these formats by changing the Write node's File Type menu to Cin or Dpx. You can change the DPX bit depth through the Write node's Datatype menu.

Using the Colorspace Node

You can convert Nuke's linear color space by connecting a Colorspace node to the network. The node's properties panel contains two rows of menus (Figure 3.8). The In row sets the incoming color space, illuminant, and primaries. The Out row determines the outgoing space, illuminant, and primaries. *Illuminants* are standardized profiles that allow images to be compared under different lighting conditions with consistency. Illuminants are identified by a letter and number, such as D65. Illuminant profiles determine a white point by using a specific color temperature. *Color primaries* are coordinates within a Yxy color space that define primary colors, such as red, green, and blue. (With Yxy color space, Y is luminance and x/y are coordinates that identify the hue/chroma component.)

FIGURE 3.8 The In and Out menus of the Colorspace node.

As an example, if you wish to convert Nuke's linear color space to an HDTV color space, you can follow these steps:

1. Select the node with the color space you wish to alter. RMB-click and choose Color > Colorspace. Open the new Colorspace node's properties panel. As a test, you can use a ColorBars node (Image > ColorBars). (Color bars are used to calibrate broadcast monitors and televisions.)
2. Set the Colorspace_out menu to Rec709(~1.95). Rec709 is HDTV color space with a 1.95 gamma. Leave the Illuminant_out menu set to D65. The D65 illuminant operates at 6500 K (Kelvin), which is a standard color temperature for HDTV televisions. Leave the Primaries_out menu set to sRGB. HDTV utilizes sRGB coordinates.
3. Connect a Viewer to the Colorspace1 node. To accurately gauge the result of the Colorspace node, set the Viewer Process menu, in the Viewer panel, to None. To judge the effect of the Colorspace node, select the node and press the D key to toggle it off and on (Figures 3.9 and 3.10). A sample Nuke script is included as `colorspace.nk` in the `Chapters/Chapter3/Scripts/` directory on the DVD.

71

FIGURE 3.9 A Colorspace node converts the output of a ColorBars node to HDTV color space.

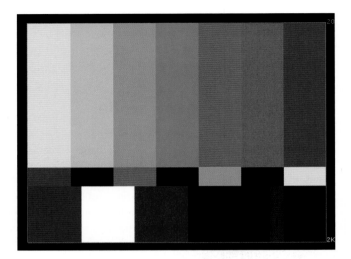

FIGURE 3.10 Same output with the Colorspace node disabled. Note the difference in intensity of the pluge bar—the gray bar at the bottom right.

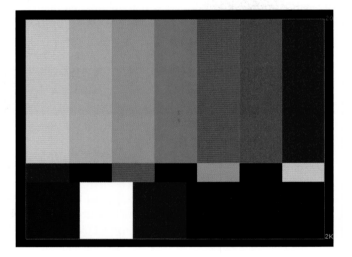

One advantage of the Colorspace node is its ability to convert to more esoteric color spaces. For example, you can switch to a space that separates lightness (also referred to as *value*) from hue and saturation. This may be useful for creating mattes based on lightness while ignoring color. HSV and HSL color spaces offer two variations of the hue-saturation-lightness model. L*a*b* color space also separates lightness, where a* and b* are color coordinates. *Hue* is the degree to which a color can be identified as unique when compared to primary colors such as red or blue; different hues are visible on a color wheel. *Saturation* is the intensity of a specific color, such as red. YCbCr is a digital video format that separates luminance (Y) from the blue (Cb) and red (Cr) components. *Luminance* is brightness balanced for human perception. YPbBr is an analog variation of YCbCr.

Note that switching to a lightness-based color space will alter the way in which the Viewer displays channels. Normally, pressing the R, G, and B keys while your mouse is over the Viewer panel will cause the red, green, and blue channels to be displayed individually; these will appear as grayscale versions of the output. If you switch to HSV, the R key will show the hue channel, the G key will display the saturation channel, and the B key will display the value channel (Figure 3.11). The hot keys are a shortcut for the Display Style For Selected Layer's Channels menu (the third menu for the top left of the Viewer panel, which is set to RGB by default).

FIGURE 3.11 A saturation channel, displayed by pressing the G key in the Viewer panel. The image is included as `mirror.tif` in the `Chapters/Chapter3/bitmaps/` directory on the DVD.

Examining individual channels, whether they are red, green, and blue, or hue, saturation, and lightness, can often reveal compression artifacts and noise that are not otherwise visible in the RGB display. Nuke allows you to apply filters to individual channels to tackle such problems; for more information, see Chapter 6.

Color Grading

Color grading is the process by which the color balance of a shot is adjusted to appear optimal on a specific output format, such as broadcast video, and consistent across a multishot project, such as a feature motion picture. A *shot* is an image sequence or video that is derived from a single camera placement (wide shot, two shot, close-up, and so on). You can apply color grading to an entire frame of a shot, or apply the grading to specific areas of the frame using a matte or mask.

Although dedicated color grading software exists (Autodesk Lustre, Assimilate Scratch, and Da Vinci Resolve to name a few), it's possible to apply color grading techniques inside Nuke. This involves the application of various color filter nodes or the use of more advanced 3D LUTs.

Employing a Histogram

The effect of a color filter parameter can be described in relation to its impact on the color distribution of the input. That is, the parameter changes the distribution so that the color intensity of various pixels changes. You can visualize such a change by connecting a Histogram node to the color filter node (Color > Histogram). A *histogram* is a graphic representation of color distribution, where the percentage of pixels or the number of pixels (as in Nuke) that possess a specific color value, such as 0.5, are indicated by a vertical bar in the graph. With the graph, the horizontal scale runs from 0 to the total number of value steps and the vertical scale indicates the percentage of pixels that share the same color value. For example, if you connect a Histogram node to a Constant node (Image > Constant), which produces a solid color, a single vertical bar appears in the histogram graph (Figure 3.12). This is because *all* the pixels within a single channel of the Constant output share the same color value. (The Histogram node combines the red, green, and blue channel values when building vertical bars.)

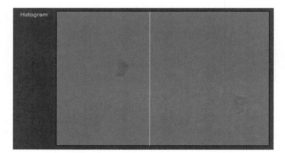

FIGURE 3.12 The output of a Constant node, which is set to a green, is connected to a Histogram node. The histogram graph displays a single vertical bar, indicating that all the pixels of the Constant node share the same value. A sample Nuke script is included as constant_histogram.nk in the Chapters/ Chapter3/Scripts/ directory on the DVD.

Note that the horizontal scale of the graph is often referred to as a *tonal range*, where there are a specific number of *tonal steps* available to the color space. For example, 8-bit color space is limited to 256 tonal steps. That is, there can only be 256 different values for a single color channel. With 32-bit floating-point color space, however, the number of tonal steps is virtually unlimited. However, to successfully create a graph, the Histogram node reduces the tonal range to roughly 300 vertical bars.

If you connect the Histogram node to a more complex output, the graph is filled by many vertical bars with differing heights (Figure 3.13). If the bars at

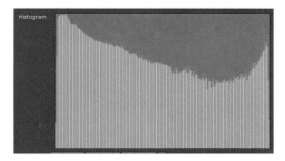

FIGURE 3.13 The output of a Read node is connected to a Histogram node. A sample Nuke script is included as `bitmap_histogram.nk` in the `Chapters/Chapter3/Scripts/` directory on the DVD.

the left end of the graph are the highest, then the output contains many dark or shadowy areas. If the bars at the right end of the graph are the highest, then the output contains many bright, well-lit areas. If the bars are the highest in the center of the graph, then the output is biased toward midtones.

Common Color Filter Parameters

You can access a number of color filter nodes through the Color menu. The following parameters are shared between these nodes:

Gamma applies gamma correction. If Gamma is set to 1, the parameter has no effect on the input.

Brightness, if positive, biases the color distribution toward the high end of the color range. If negative, Brightness biases the distribution toward the low end.

Contrast, if positive, stretches the current color distribution toward the low end and high end (Figure 3.14 and 3.15). Thus, colors with extremely low values, such as 0, are more likely to exist along with colors with extremely high values, such as 1. Negative Contrast values have the opposite effect, reducing the contrast and "washing out" the output.

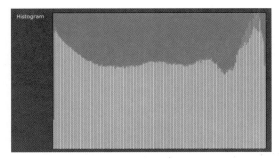

FIGURE 3.14 Histogram showing a number of peaks and valleys.

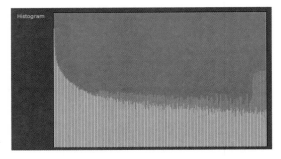

FIGURE 3.15 Same histogram after the insertion of a ColorCorrect node with Contrast set to 3. Note the flattened midtone area and the small peaks at the far left and far right. A sample Nuke script is included as contrast.nk in the Chapters/Chapter3/Scripts/ directory on the DVD.

Gain, if set above 1, stretches the distribution toward the high end. If set below 1, Gain slides the distribution toward the low end; this empties an area to the right of the slid distribution (Figure 3.16). Ultimately, Gain offers an additional means to add or remove contrast to or from an output.

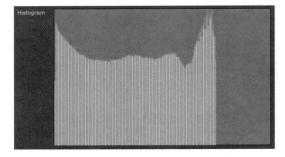

FIGURE 3.16 A 0.75 Gain value slides the color distribution to the left (low end) of the histogram. A sample Nuke script is included as gain.nk in the Chapters/Chapter3/Scripts/ directory on the DVD.

Lift and **Offset**, if positive, slide the current color distribution toward the high end. This empties an area to the left of the slid distribution (i.e., there are no pixels with low-end values). For Lift, negative values stretch the distribution toward the low end. For Offset, negative values slide the distribution toward the low end. Ultimately, Lift and Offset offer an alternate means to adjust the brightness or darkness of an output. **Saturation**, if given a high value, increases the contrast between RGB channels. Channels with high values are pushed closer to the maximum value (1). Channels with low values are pushed closer to the minimum value (0). This increases the likelihood that a single channel, such as red, will dominate various areas of the output.

Common Color Filter Nodes

Of all the color filter nodes, ColorCorrect, Grade, HueShift, Saturation and HueCorrect, are perhaps the most useful for common color manipulation tasks. These are detailed as follows:

ColorCorrect offers Saturation, Contrast, Gamma, Gain, and Offset parameters. The parameters are repeated so that you can affect the entire output, or only the shadows (low end), midtones, or highlights (high end) of the output. The node provides a convenient means to adjust saturation, brightness, and contrast of an image.

Grade, as its name infers, is designed for color grading tasks. It includes Lift, Gain, Offset, and Gamma parameters (Figure 3.17). In addition, the

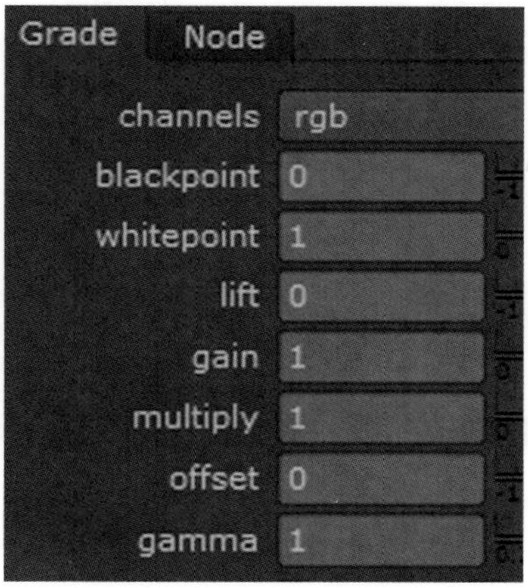

FIGURE 3.17 Grade node parameters.

node includes Multiply, Whitepoint, and Blackpoint. The Multiply value is a constant that all the values of the input are multiplied by. For example, if Multiply is set to 2, all the values are multiplied by 2. Note that values within Nuke can exceed the standard threshold of 1. Values above 1 are referred to as *superwhite*. Superwhite values cannot be written out to an 8- or 16-bit integer image format (they are clamped to 1). However, you can write superwhite values to a floating-point format such as OpenEXR. The Whitepoint parameter determines what value is considered "white." For example, if you set the slider to 0.5, the output values are remapped so that 0.5 is pushed to 1. This brightens the output. Whitepoint values above 1 have the opposite effect.

The Blackpoint parameter determines what value is considered "black." For example, if you set the slider to 0.5, the output values are remapped so that 0.5 is pushed to 0. This darkens the image. Negative Blackpoint values have the opposite effect.

HueShift, as its name infers, allows you to shift the output hues through a CIE Yxy color space. With CIE Yxy, Y is luminance and x and y are color coordinates within a "sole-shaped" color diagram. You can rotate the Yxy color space around the Y axis with the Hue Rotate parameter. This shifts all the colors of the output. For example, a value of 180 causes red to become cyan, green to become pink, and blue to become a goldish-brown (Figure 3.18). The node also provides

FIGURE 3.18 A Hue Rotate value of 180 changes skin tone to cyan. The image is included as `smile.tif` in the `Chapters/Chapter2/Bitmaps/` directory on the DVD.

a standard Brightness parameter. Saturation, however, is divided into Overall Saturation and Saturation Along Axis. Overall Saturation adjusts the contrast between color channels, causing colors with high intensity to become even more intense. Saturation Along Axis adjusts the values along a single axis in the xy plane of the Yxy color space. The axis is defined with the Color Axis RGB cells. R, G, and B respectively correspond to red, green, and blue, each of which have their own axis that runs from one corner of the Yxy diagram toward the diagram center (which holds the white point). For example, if Color Axis RGB is set to 0, 1, 0, and Saturation Along Axis is set to 4, the green axis values are scaled. This causes the green pixels within the output to become very intense (Figure 3.19).

FIGURE 3.19 Color Axis RGB is set to 0, 1, 0, and Saturation Along Axis set to 4. As a result, the greens within the output become more intense than reds and blues. A sample Nuke script is included as hueshift.nk in the Chapters/Chapter3/ Scripts/ directory on the DVD.

Saturation offers a simple means to adjust its namesake through a Saturation slider. It offers the advantage, however, of including a Luminance Math parameter. When the node separates the luminance information from the hue and saturation, it uses the Luminance Math formula to weight the luminance. For example, Rec709 uses the formula $Y = 0.2126$ red $+ 0.7152$ green $+ 0.0722$ blue. In other words, the luminance is biased toward the green channel. In the realm of computer graphics, *luminance* is the brightness of a channel as balanced for human perception, which is more sensitive to brightness than color variation (among the colors, there is greater human sensitivity toward green). Of the Luminance Math options, Ccir 601 (a digital video standard) places less emphasis on the green channel and Maximum inserts the maximum amount of contrast between channels. To convert the output to grayscale, set Saturation to 0.

HueCorrect

The HueCorrect node is unique in that it allows the manipulation of saturation based on a range of hues through an interactive graph. The left column of the graph lists a series of suppression curves you can adjust. The horizontal axis of the graph maps incoming saturation values. The axis displays hues on a scale that runs from 0 to 6. Red, green, and blue primaries rest at 1, 3, and 5, respectively. The vertical scale of the graph runs from 0 to 2 and represents outgoing saturation. Each saturation curve has seven points. To see the curve, click on the suppression curve name in the left column. You can move any curve point by LMB-dragging. You can move the entire curve up or down by drawing a selection marquee around all the points and LMB-dragging. In its default state, a suppression curve does not alter the saturation; the curve points all lie at 1.

For example, if you wish to alter the saturation of a particular hue in an image without changing the remaining hues, follow these steps:

1. Connect a HueCorrect node to the output you wish to manipulate. Place the mouse pointer over the hue you want to change in the Viewer. A yellow crosshair appears in the HueCorrect node's graph that indicates where the hue lies. For example, using the bitmap illustrated in Figure 3.20, the blue of the t-shirt lies at 4.5 on the horizontal incoming saturation axis and roughly 0.6 on the vertical outgoing saturation axis. Note the position of the crosshair (Figure 3.21).

FIGURE 3.20 The blue of a t-shirt is targeted for manipulation by a HueCorrect node. A sample bitmap is included as sweep.tif in the Chapters/Chapter3/Bitmaps/ directory on the DVD.

2. If you wish to reduce the saturation of the selected hue, select the word "Sat" in the left column, and LMB-drag the point closest to the value straight down (Figure 3.22 and 3.23). If there is no point where the hue is, you can insert a new point by Cmd/Ctrl+Opt/Alt-clicking on the curve. To increase the saturation, LMB-drag straight up. The vertical axis serves as a multiplier for the incoming saturation. For example, if a point sits at 2, the incoming saturation is doubled. If a point is dragged to 0, the hue loses all saturation. Note that the repositioned point creates slopes on the curve. This causes similar hues to lose some saturation. For example, the blue jeans, blue spill on the floor, and blue contained within the green broom change slightly.

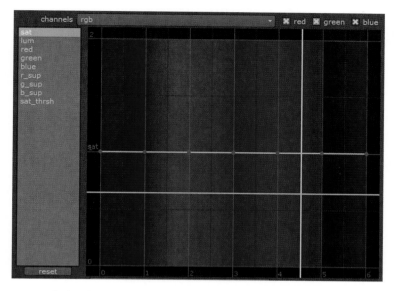

FIGURE 3.21 The hue of the t-shirt is indicated by the yellow/white crosshair in the HueCorrect graph. The Saturation suppression curve is displayed.

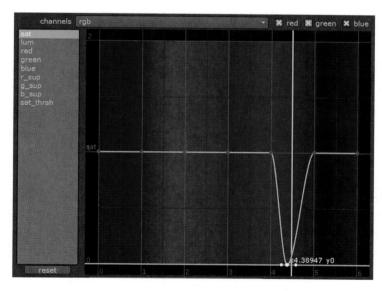

FIGURE 3.22 A new point is inserted on the Saturation suppression curve and dragged down to 0.

Note that the Saturation suppression curve affects the red, green, and blue channels equally. You can adjust the Lum (Luminance) suppression curve to change the luminance of the hue on all three channels. (Luminance is biased toward the green channel to match human

FIGURE 3.23 The t-shirt is desaturated in the resulting output without unduly affecting other hues. A sample Nuke script is included as huecorrect.nk in the Chapters/Chapter3/Scripts/ directory on the DVD.

perception.) If you choose the Red, Green, or Blue curve, the namesake channel component of the hue is isolated. If you choose R_sup, G_sup, or B_sup, the vertical axis of the graph no longer serves as a multiplier; instead, the vertical axis indicates the degree of suppression of the red, green, or blue channel.

The HueCorrect node is particularly useful for reducing the color spill found in greenscreen footage. This is explored further in Chapter 5.

Specialized Color Filter Nodes

Additional color filter nodes provide specialized color adjustments, some of which create stylized results. These are briefly discussed here.

Clamp allows you to "clamp" values within an input. For example, if the input contains superwhite values of 2, the addition of a Clamp node automatically changes all the superwhite values to 1. Any value below 1 is unaffected. The node's Minimum and Maximum parameters determine the minimum and maximum allowable values. Any values below the minimum or above the maximum are changed to the Minimum and Maximum values.

Exposure multiplies each channel by a constant. The constant is defined by the Red, Green, and Blue parameters. The scale of the Red, Green, and

Blue sliders is determined by the Adjust In parameter. The Adjust In menu includes Stops, Lights, Densities, and Cineon, each of which are specific to motion picture film exposure (whereby film density is related to exposure duration). The node provides an additional means to adjust a log input as it can operate in Cineon color space through the Colorspace menu.

HistEQ equalizes the histogram of an input by spreading the color distribution across the full tonal range. This offers an additional means to adjust contrast. The Histogram Entries parameter controls the number of steps employed by the equalization; low values create posterization (color banding).

Invert inverts the input with the following formula: 1 – color value. Hence, blacks become whites and colors with high intensities receive low intensities (Figure 3.24).

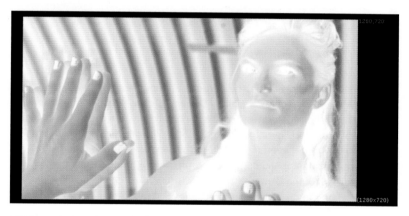

FIGURE 3.24 An image is inverted with an Invert node. The image is included as `mirror.tif` in the `Chapters/Chapter3/Bitmaps/` directory on the DVD.

MinColor determines the difference between the lowest value of the input and the Target parameter value and adds the result to the entire input. To activate the node, you must set the Target value and then click the Find Pixel Delta button.

Posterize creates a stylized result by forcing a limited number of colors on the input. For example, if the Colors parameter is set to 2, only two colors are available to the entire image (not including 0-black and 1-white; see Figure 3.25). Posterization may occur naturally, without a Posterize node, when a calculation is inaccurate in a low bit depth environment. For example, applying a heavy blur in an 8-bit composite can create the color banding associated with posterization in low-contrast areas, such as skies.

RolloffContrast allows you to control contrast by fine-tuning the contrast curve. A contrast curves carries an S shape, whereby the low end

FIGURE 3.25 An image is stylized with a Posterize node. A sample Nuke script is included as `posterize.nk` in the `Chapters/Chapter3/Scripts/` directory on the DVD.

possesses a shallow slope, the midtone area possesses a steep slope, and the high end possesses a shallow slope. With the RolloffContrast node, you adjust the set "softness" of the transition between the low-end, high-end, and mid-tone area by setting the Soft Clip value. Higher values make the transition between dark and light values more subtle. The overall strength of the applied contrast is controlled by the Contrast parameter. You can offset the center of the contrast curve by changing the Center value. High Center values darken the result. Low Center values brighten the result (Figure 3.26 and 3.27).

FIGURE 3.26 A RolloffContrast node adds contrast to an image. Contrast is set to 1.5 and Center is set to 0.2.

FIGURE 3.27 Same output with Center set to 0.6 and Softness set to 0.2. A sample Nuke script is included as `rolloffcontrast.nk` in the `Chapters/Chapter3/Scripts/` directory on the DVD.

SoftClip is designed to compress superwhite values into a 0-to-1 range (or a custom range defined by the Softclip Min and Softclip Max parameter values). SoftClip provides several mathematical modes for the compression, which are set by the Conversion menu. You can choose to maintain the hue and brightness (with a loss of saturation), maintain hue and saturation (with loss of brightness), or apply a logarithmic compression curve (Figure 3.28 and 3.29). Thus, the node provides greater control than the Clamp node, which simply tosses away value ranges above the Maximum value or below the Minimum value.

FIGURE 3.28 An output with superwhite values is compressed with a SoftClip node. The Conversion menu is set to Preserve Hue And Brightness.

FIGURE 3.29 Same output with Conversion set to Preserve Hue And Saturation. Note the loss of highlights on the cheeks. A sample Nuke script is included as `softclip.nk` in the `Chapters/Chapter3/Scripts/` directory on the DVD.

Additional Histogram Functionality

The Histogram node offers a means to examine what's happening with the color distribution of the input. However, you can also use the node to remap the distribution of the input. The node includes an Input and Output Range (Figure 3.30). The Input Range establishes what values are accepted from the input. The Input Range includes three cells. From left to right, they establish the black point of the input, the midtone of the input, and the white point of the input. For example, if you set the cells to 0.1, 1, and 0.9, values between 0 and 0.1 are clamped to 0, values between 0.9 and 1 are clamped to 1, and values between 0.1 and 0.9 are remapped to fill the entire 0-to-1 range. If the midtone cell is left set to 1, it has no effect on the image. If the midtone cell is set to a non-1 number, a gamma correction curve with that value is applied. For example, a midtone value that is less than 1 reduces the contrast while brightening the image.

FIGURE 3.30 The Input Range and Output Range section of a Histogram node.

The Output Range determines the range in which the Input Range is remapped in preparation for output. The left cell sets the black point of the range. The right cell sets the white point of the range. For example, if the right cell is set to 0.8, the entire color distribution is remapped to fit within the 0-to-0.8 range, regardless of the Input Range settings. This leaves the 0.8-to-1 range empty. This may be useful if you are preparing an output for broadcast video, where values above a certain threshold are not permitted.

Grading a Single Channel

Thus far, color filters have been applied to the red, green, and blue channels equally. It's possible, however, to affect fewer channels with a color filter node. To do so, deselect the Red, Green, or Blue checkboxes at the top of a filter node (Figure 3.31). For example, if you wish to apply a node to the red channel without affecting the green or blue channels, deselect Green and Blue. The node icon indicates the preference by including the affected channel names in parenthesis, drawing long channel lines for affected channels, and drawing short channel lines for unaffected channels (Figure 3.32). In addition, you can force the node to affect the alpha channel, by itself, by switching the Channels menu to Alpha. You can also affect specialized channels, such as Depth or Motion, by switching the Channels menu to Other Layers > *channel name*. You can add a channel to those already affected by setting the Additional Channels menu, to the far right of the node, to a channel name.

FIGURE 3.31 Channels menu (left); Red, Green, and Blue checkboxes (center); and Additional Channels menu (right). With this example, red, green, and alpha channels are affected by the node.

FIGURE 3.32 Grade node. The red and alpha channels are affected, as is indicted by the text within parentheses and the long channel lines drawn at the bottom left of the node icon.

Using 3D LUTs

Thus far, the LUTs discussed in this chapter have been 1D LUTs. The LUTs provided by Nuke's Read and Write nodes' Colorspace menus are one dimensional. That is, they are 1D arrays of values designed to remap an input. If a 1D LUT is applied to an RGB input, the same array is applied three times. In contrast, a 3D LUT defines colors as triplets (three values corresponding to RGB). Three-dimensional LUTs are often represented as a color cube where three corners of the cube correspond to red, green, and blue, while the other three corners correspond to the secondary colors yellow, cyan, and magenta. Any given color has a X, Y, Z coordinate within the cube. When a 3D LUT is applied, it essentially deforms the color space of the input to fit the color space occupied by the LUT's color cube. Because the deformation affects all the color coordinates within the cube, it's able to emulate color crosstalk, which is a natural artifact of motion picture film stock. In comparison, applying a 1D LUT to a red channel has no effect on the blue or green channels. The 3D LUT's color space deformation is carried out by deformation lattice. The lattice resolution is represented by a single number, such as 17 (a $17 \times 17 \times 17$ lattice is thereby applied). The higher the lattice resolution value, the more accurate the 3D LUT deformation.

Creating a Custom 3D LUT

You can convert a network of Nuke nodes into a custom 3D LUT. A custom LUT allows you to apply a complex color grading process with a single step or quickly apply a color grading process to multiple nodes or node networks. To create a LUT, you must use CMSTestPattern and GenerateLUT nodes. You can follow these steps:

1. In the Node Graph, RMB-click and choose Color > 3D LUT > CMSTestPattern. Connect the new node to Viewer1. The CMSTestPattern generates a color calibration pattern. Open the CMSTestPattern1 node's properties panel. The node carries a single parameter, RGB 3D LUT Cube Size, which determines the resolution of the LUT's deformation lattice.
2. Insert one or more color correction filter nodes between the CMSTestPattern1 and Viewer1 nodes. You can add a single node, such as Colorspace, or multiple nodes, such as Grade, ColorCorrection, Saturation, and so on. Adjust the parameters of the filter nodes. For example, set the Colorspace parameters to convert one color space to another (linear-to-log, linear-to-Rec709, and so on). Alternately, adjust the series of color filter nodes to apply a specific color grading that may be useful across an entire series of shots.
3. Insert a GenerateLUT node between the last filter node and the Viewer1 node by choosing Color > 3D LUT > GenerateLUT. See Figure 3.33 for an example network. Open the GenerateLUT1 node's properties panel. Choose a style of LUT through the File Type menu. Nuke supports .vf (Nuke Vectorfield), .cms (generic color management format), .cube (Iridas), .cub (Truelight), .3dl (Autodesk/Scratch), .csp (CineSpace), and .blut (Houdini). To use the 3D LUT within Nuke, choose the .vf format. (If you plan to use the LUT in an external color grading program, choose the matching format.) Set a file name and file location by using the Output

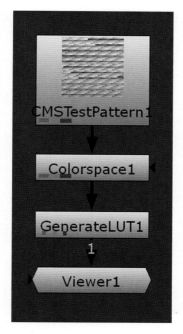

FIGURE 3.33 A custom 3D LUT network.

File cell. Click the Generate And Write LUT File button. The LUT file is written to disk.

Applying a Custom 3D LUT

To apply a custom 3D LUT to a node network, you can use a Vectorfield node. To do so, select the node that you wish to apply the custom LUT to, RMB-click, and choose Color > 3D LUT > Vectorfield. Then locate the LUT file by using the node's Vectorfield File Browse button. You can choose a LUT created by a GenerateLUT node or a LUT created by an external program. When the Vectorfield's File Type menu is set to Auto, the node will identify the file format.

Alternatively, you can apply the 3D LUT to the Viewer input, regardless of what input might be displayed. To do so, create a new Vectorfield node, load a 3D LUT file, select the Vectorfield node, and choose Edit > Node > Use As Input Process from the menu bar. (It's not necessary to connect the Vectorfield to any other node.) Press the IP (Input Process) button so that it turns red (see Figure 3.4 earlier in this chapter). The 3D LUT is applied (Figure 3.34). To toggle off the LUT, click the Input Process button so that it turns gray.

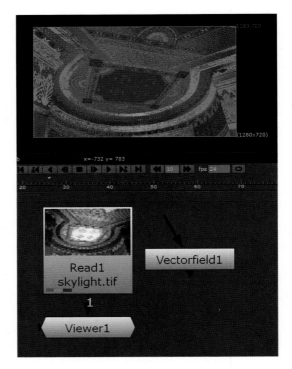

FIGURE 3.34 A Vectorfield node is linked to the Input Process button. When the button is activated, the 3D LUT is applied to the Viewer (in this case, the 3D LUT applies a linear-to-HSV color space conversion). A sample Nuke script is included as `input_process.nk` in the `Chapters/Chapter3/Scripts/` directory on the DVD. A 3D LUT file is included as `3dlut.vf` in the same directory.

Note that it's possible to apply any node to the Input Process button. In that situation, the node is duplicated, removed from the network, and linked to the Input Process button.

Examining Color Values

One important aspect of color grading is gauging the values within various sources. This is often required when matching blacks and whites. If you match blacks between different sources, you're matching black points. That is, you're matching the pixels with the lowest values. On a more practical level, you want to make sure that shadows are equally dark between sources. For example, the shadows within a CG render should match the shadows within live-action video footage if the two sources are to be composited together. If you match whites between different sources, you're matching white points.

You can read the value of any pixel or group of pixels displayed in the Viewer by placing your mouse pointer over pixel(s) and noting 2D Image Information readout along the bottom of the Viewer panel (Figure 3.35).

| 1280x720 bbox: 0 0 1280 720 channels: rgb | x= 993 y= 150 156x456 | 0.12002 0.06990 0.04234 0.00000 | H: 26 S:0.40 V:0.38 L: 0.07856 |

| A | B | C | D | E | F | G | H | I |

FIGURE 3.35 The 2D Image Information readout area of the Viewer panel: (A) resolution; (B) bounding box coordinates; (C) channels; (D) position of mouse pointer; (E) sample area x, y size (if any); (F) sample pixel or sample area average red, green, and blue values on 0-to-1 scale; (G) color swatch with sample color; (H) alternative color space readout; (I) Alternative Colorspace dropdown menu.

You can sample a single pixel by Cmd/Crtl+clicking. You can define a sample area by Cmd/Ctrl+Shift-dragging in the Viewer. The Alternative Colorspace menu includes Spotmeter (display F-stops based on 1/48 second exposure), 8-bit (0-to-255 scale), 8-bit Hex (8-bit scale converted to hexadecimal code), Log (10-bit 0-to-1023 scale), HSVL (0-to-1 scale where V [value] and perception-balanced Luminance are both provided).

Tutorial 1: Kicking a Heart
Part 3: Color Grading for Better Integration
In Part 2 of this tutorial, we added keyframe animation to the 3D render of the heart, allowing it to be kicked out of the frame. Part 3 adds color grading to better match the render to the background image sequence.

1. Open the Nuke script you saved after completing Part 2 of this tutorial. A sample Nuke script is included as Tutorial1.2.nk in the Tutorials/Tutorial1/Scripts/ directory on the DVD.
2. Move the time marker to frame where the heart is not in motion, such as frame 20. This prevents the program from slowing down to calculate the motion blur.
3. Select the Read1 node. RMB-click in the Node Graph and choose Color > Grade. You can also press the G key. A Grade1 node is inserted between the Read1 and Merge1 nodes. (See Figure 3.39 later in this section for the final node network.) In the Grade1 node's properties panel, change Whitepoint to 0.5. This brightens the image sequence by stretching the color distribution between 0 and 0.5 so that it fills the entire 0-to-1 range.
4. You can see the numeric result of the Grade1 node on any given area of the image by placing your mouse pointer over the image in the Viewer1 panel and noting the RGB values in the 2D Image Information readout. While Whitepoint is set to the

91

default 1, a highlight on the white boot might have RGB values of roughly 0.25, 0.2, and 0.15. After Whitepoint is set to 0.5, the same area of the image produces values around 0.5, 0.4, and 0.3. If you wanted to make the highlight peak near 1, set the Whitepoint to 0.2 (this will make the image sequence appear overexposed). If you are used to working with an 8-bit 0 to 255 color scale, you can change the Alternative Colorspace menu to 8-bit.

5. Change the Grade node's Gamma to 0.7. This increases the contrast within the midtone range. Note that a lower Gamma value increases the saturation of the image. To defeat this, select the Grade1 node, RMB-click, and choose Color > Saturation. A Saturation1 node is inserted between the Grade1 and Merge1 nodes. In the Saturation1 node's properties panel, change the Saturation parameter to 0.6 (Figure 3.36).

FIGURE 3.36 The brightness and saturation of the image sequence are adjusted with a Grade and Saturation node.

6. In the Viewer, Cmd/Ctrl+Shift-drag a selection marquee around the darkest section of the ground shadow directly below the character's left hand. The values are roughly 0.004, 0.003, and 0.002 (or 14, 11, and 9 in 8-bit). Make a note of the values as the image sequence's black point. Cmd/Ctrl+Shift-drag a selection box around the darkest section of the heart render (Figure 3.37). The values are roughly 0.003, 0.001, and 0.02 (or 10, 5, and 38 in 8-bit). Make a note of the values as the render's black point.

FIGURE 3.37 A selection box is drawn around a dark region of the heart render. The values are displayed in the 2D Image Information readout.

7. Select the Reformat1 node, RMB-click, and choose Color > ColorCorrect. You can also press the C key. A ColorCorrect1 node is inserted between the Reformat1 and Merge1 nodes. In the ColorCorrect1 node's properties panel, click the Switch Between A Single Value And Multiple Values button beside Master Contrast (the button is labeled with a 4). The parameter slider is converted to individual numeric cells for the red, green, blue, and alpha channels. Adjust the red, green, and blue cells while watching the readout update. (The selection box is left in the Viewer until you draw a new selection box or Cmd/Ctrl-click.) The goal is to produce values close to the image sequence's black point, which is roughly 0.004, 0.003, and 0.002. Set the red, green, and blue cells to 0.8, 0.7, and 1.7. The render is so heavily biased toward the blue channel that the Master Contrast blue cell must be raised significantly to sufficiently lower the blue values.

8. Although there's a better match between the blacks, the render remains extremely saturated. To better match the saturation, click the Switch Between A Single Value And Multiple Values button beside Master Saturation. Enter 0.6 into the blue cell. The blue saturation is lowered (Figure 3.38).

   This concludes Part 3 of Tutorial 1. As an optional step, organize the Node Graph to maximum clarity. For example, add a second backdrop behind the Read1 node and the new Grade1 and Saturation1 nodes (Figure 3.39). A sample Nuke script is included as `Tutorial1.3.nk` in the `Tutorials/Tutorial1/Scripts/` directory on the DVD. In Chapter 4, we'll further integrate the heart by rotoscoping the character's hand and adding a ground shadow.

FIGURE 3.38 The heart render is adjusted with a ColorCorrect node.

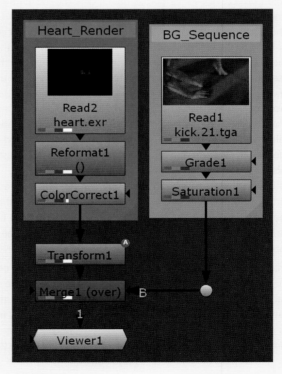

FIGURE 3.39 The organized node graph.

Tutorial 2: Flying a Spaceship

Part 2: Color Grading for Sunset

In Part 1 of this tutorial, we refined the keyframe animation to the 3D render of the spaceship, allowing it to move smoothly across the frame. Part 2 adds color grading to change the apparent time of day.

1. Open the Nuke script you saved after completing Part 1 of this tutorial. A sample Nuke script is included as `Tutorial2.1.nk` in the `Tutorials/Tutorial2/Scripts/` directory on the DVD.

2. Open the properties panel for the Transform1 node. Set Motionblur to 0 to temporarily turn off motion blur. This will speed up the display while making color grading adjustments.

3. Open the properties panel for the Merge1 node. Note that the Mix parameter is set to 0.99. This means that the dissolve value for input A of the Merge1 node is 99%. In other words, the spaceship render has 1% transparency; it's as if the spaceship's alpha channel has a maximum value of 0.99 on a 0-to-1 scale. Return the Mix value to 1. Note that the blacks found within the spaceship render become much darker. Return the parameter to 0.99. By setting Mix to 0.99, the blue from the sky is allowed to show through. As a result, a spaceship appears to take on a slight atmospheric haze. The Mix parameter, along with the Merge node, is discussed in more detail in Chapter 4.

4. Select the Merge1 node, RMB-click, and choose Color > HueCorrect. A HueCorrect1 node is inserted after the Merge1 node. The HueCorrect1 node affects the output of the Merge1 node and thereby affects the net output of all the upstream nodes. (For maximum control, you can insert separate HueCorrect nodes after the Read1 and Read2 nodes; this would allow you to adjust the outputs of Read1 and Read2 separately.) Open the HueCorrect1 node's properties panel. Click the word "Red" in the curve suppression list on the left side of the panel. The red curve is displayed. LMB-drag a selection marquee around the entire curve so that all the points on the curve are selected. LMB-drag the selected points upward until the curve sits at 1.5 in the Y direction of the graph. The output takes on a red cast, which shifts the apparent time of day toward sunset or sunrise (Figure 3.40).

You can toggle the HueCorrect1 node's influence by selecting the node and pressing the D key several times. Moving the red curve upward multiplies the original intensities of the red channel by 1.5, which skews the overall color balance of the output toward red. To make the curve point position more accurate, you can enter 2 into the y number cell of an x,y point readout. If you don't

FIGURE 3.40 The output of the Merge1 node is given a red cast with a HueCorrect node.

see the x,y readout, select a single point. To activate either the x or y number cell, click the white x or y.

This concludes Part 2 of Tutorial 2. A sample Nuke script is included as `Tutorial2.2.nk` in the `Tutorials/Tutorial2/Scripts/` directory on the DVD. In Chapter 4, we'll create the illusion that the ship is applying a cloaking device by manipulating the render's alpha channel.

Alpha Mattes, Merging, and Rotoscoping

Compositing necessitates the combination of bitmaps, image sequences, videos, and/or procedurally-generated patterns. Whereas a layer-based program simply stacks layers with preference to upper layers, Nuke combines inputs through various "merge" nodes. Regardless of the compositing program used, a layer or input's alpha channel must be considered as it carries pixel transparency information. In Nuke, if an input does not carry an alpha channel, you can synthesize one by creating an alpha matte. You can generate such a matte by manipulating RGB information, targeting a specific color with a chroma key node, or drawing a mask with a rotoscoping node.

This chapter includes the following critical information:

- Working with alpha
- Combining inputs with merge nodes
- Generating mattes
- Rotoscoping masks

Understanding Alpha and Premultiplication

In the realm of digital image manipulation, *alpha* is a channel that stores transparency information. The transparency information is often referred to as a *matte,* where the matte carries grayscale values. The values run from 0-black (equal to 100% transparency) to 1-white (equal to 100% opaqueness). Alpha is necessary when compositing various elements on top of each other without having higher elements completely obscuring the lower ones. With a Nuke Merge node, the input A pipe is the "higher" input, while the input B pipe is the "lower" input.

You can examine an alpha channel in Nuke by pressing the A key while the mouse is over the Viewer panel (Figure 4.1). While some image formats carry an alpha channel, others do not. By the same token, image formats that support alpha may not include the alpha information. For example, a Targa render generated by Autodesk Maya will most likely include an alpha channel. However, a TIFF scan of motion picture film will not include alpha. Nevertheless, you can add an alpha channel to any output within Nuke at any time. For more information on image formats and whether they support alpha, see Chapter 1.

FIGURE 4.1 Close-up of the alpha channel carried by the spaceship render used for Tutorial 2. The majority of pixels are 0-black or 1-white with a few pixels along the ship edge carrying midrange values such as 0.5. The render was generated with Autodesk Maya.

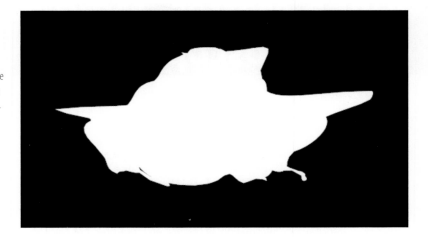

Premultiplication Overview

Premultiplication is an optional process whereby the RGB values of a digital image are multiplied by the alpha values within the same image. For example, if a pixel in the red channel has a value of 0.8 and the alpha value of the same pixel has a value of 0.5, the resulting premultiplied red channel value for the pixel is 0.4. Ultimately, premultiplication speeds up compositing calculations. If premultiplication is interpreted correctly by a compositing program, matte edges appear clean. (Matte edges occur along the edges of objects where the transparency transitions from 100% transparency to 100% opaqueness.) If premultiplication is incorrectly interpreted, a gray line often appears in RGB along the object edge; this is particularly evident when motion blur is present.

For example, in Figure 4.2, a render of a 3D primitive is merged over a white background. The Premultiplied parameter carried by the render's Read node remains deselected. The motion-blurred edge of the render picks up a gray cast, which interferes with the texture detail along the edge. In this situation, an empty 3D background influences the semi-transparent pixels along an object edge. 3D programs, such as Autodesk Maya or 3ds Max, assign the black RGB values to empty space (although you can change the color if you wish). The programs also offer the option to render an alpha channel in addition to the RGB channels; the renders are automatically premultiplied.

FIGURE 4.2 Close-up of 3D render in Nuke with alpha left in a unpre-multiplied state. The motion-blurred edge picks up a gray cast. A sample script is included as unpremultiplied.nk in the Chapters/Chapter4/Scripts/ directory on the DVD.

Premultiplying and Unpremultiplying in Nuke

Nuke automatically recognizes the alpha channels of imported images. However, premultiplication is not recognized unless you select the Read node's Premultiplied checkbox. The Premultiplied parameter adds the following steps to the Read node interpretation:

1. Divides the color values by alpha values (unpremultiplies).
2. Applies the color space conversion as determined by the Colorspace parameter.
3. Remultiplies the color values by alpha values.

The extra steps guarantee the proper color values appear along the matte edges.

Additionally, Nuke supplies Premult and Unpremult nodes (in the Merge menu) to premultiply or unpremultiply any output. Occasionally, you will need to manually premultiply or unpremultiply an output so that the alpha values are correctly interpreted. For example, the Erode node requires pre-multiplication to function properly. This is demonstrated in "Tutorial 3: Removing an Imperfect Greenscreen" at the end of Chapter 5. Additional examples are included throughout this book.

Using the Merge Node

The Merge node is tasked with merging inputs. Whereas a layer-based compositing program, such as After Effects, recognizes a dominate layer by its top-most position in the layer stack, the Merge node gives preference to input A. Therefore, you may consider Input A the "top" and Input B the "bottom."

A Merge node can accept more than two inputs (Figure 4.3). When you connect an additional input, the input pipes are relabeled; input A becomes input A1 and any additional inputs are labeled A2, A3, A4, and so on (input B remains the same). The input with the highest A number, such as A4, is given preference and becomes the "top" input. Note that the input pipe stub at the left side of the node icon carries the next highest input A; for example, if three input connections exist, the input pipe becomes A3.

FIGURE 4.3 A merge node with three input connections. In this example, A2 is the "top" input, A1 is the "middle" input, and B is the "bottom" input.

Choosing a Math Operation

The way in which inputs are combined is determined by the Merge node's Operation menu. The Operation menu applies a specific mathematical operation to determine how the pixel values of the various inputs are added, subtracted, multiplied, or averaged. The Operation menu is set to Over by default. If you are working with premultiplied inputs, you can write the Over operation as

$$A + (B \times (1 - a)) = C.$$

If the inputs remain unpremultiplied, the formula changes to

$$(A \times a) + ((B \times b) \times (1 - a)) = C.$$

In this case, A is the red, green, or blue value of a pixel in input A; B is the red, green, or blue value of the matching pixel in input B (the operation is applied to one color channel at a time); a is the alpha value of the same pixel in input A; b is the alpha value of the same pixel in input B; and C is the output value of the merged pixel. Hence, A occludes B unless a is less than 1. For example, if A is 0.5, a is 0.5 (50% transparency), B is 0.8, and b is 1 (0% transparency), the following math occurs:

$$(0.5 \times 0.5) + ((0.8 \times 1) \times (1 - 0.5)) = 0.65.$$

There are 30 operations available through the Operation menu. To display the mathematical formula for each, hold your mouse over the parameter name until the help dialog appears (Figure 4.4). Of the Operations, Over is used the most often. Other common operations include Screen, Multiply, Min, and Max. Various operations are demonstrated through the remainder of this book. To see the result of a particular operation, you can change the Operation menu at any time.

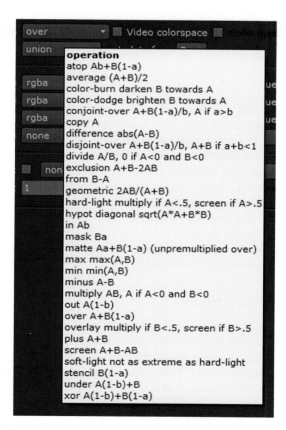

FIGURE 4.4 The Operation parameter help dialog. Mathematical formulas for each option are written out (* is the same as ×).

Mix Slider and Channel Menus

The Mix slider, located along the bottom of the Merge node's properties panel (Figure 4.5), determines the contribution strength of input A (and A1, A2, A3, and so on). In essence, input A's alpha value is multiplied by the Mix value. Hence, if Mix is set to 0.5, an otherwise opaque input A receives 50% transparency.

FIGURE 4.5 Merge node properties panel with Channels parameter sets and Mix slider.

Input A, input B, and the node output each receive a Channels parameter set in the Merge node properties panel (Figure 4.5). By default, the RGBA channels of the inputs are accepted by the node. By default, the node outputs RGBA. However, you can pick and choose which channels are accepted as input or as output by changing the Channels menu (the left menu that defaults to Rgba); selecting or deselecting the Red, Green, or Blue parameter checkboxes; and/or changing the Additional Channel menu (the right menu). For example, you can deselect Red, Green, and Blue and leave the Additional Channel menu set to Rgba.alpha; thus only the alpha channel is processed. Note that all A inputs (A1, A2, A3, and so on) are affected equally by a single A Channels parameter set.

Chaining Merge Nodes

As an alternative to connecting more than two inputs to a Merge node, you can chain two or more Merge nodes together. For example, in Figure 4.6, two spaceship renders are added to a background with the aid of two Merge nodes. The output of Merge1 is connected to the input B of Merge2. This offers the immediate advantage of providing two Mix sliders and two A Channels parameter sets. Therefore, the opacity and utilized channels of each render is independent. If the renders are connected to input A1 and input A2 of a single Merge node, they would share a single Mix slider and a single A Channels parameter set.

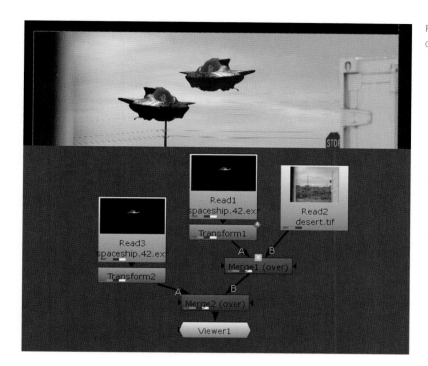

FIGURE 4.6 Two Merge nodes are chained together.

Hooking Up a Mask

Many nodes in Nuke, including the Merge node and various filter nodes, carry a Mask input (Figure 4.7). Initially, the input is drawn as a pipe stub at the right side of the node icon. With a Merge node, the Mask input determines where input A will appear. The node carries this out by multiplying the alpha values within the Mask input by the alpha values within input A. If a pixel in the Mask input has a value of 0, the corresponding pixel within the input A alpha channel receives a value of 0; this causes the input A pixel to become 100% transparent. With a filter node, such as Blur, the Mask input limits where the filter effect occurs. For example, you can limit a blur to a small area of the frame. Note that the Mask input affects all A inputs equally (A1, A2, A3, and so on).

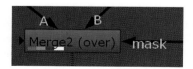

FIGURE 4.7 Merge node Mask input pipe.

Whereas an alpha channel is often referred to as an *alpha matte* or a channel that carries matte information, a *mask* is a device that generates a matte. The device may take the form of a bitmap, a procedural texture, or a bezier shape drawn within the compositing program. If a bitmap is used as a mask, it need not contain shades of gray. In fact, you can reuse the RGB information of a bitmap to control where a filter node has the greatest impact. For an example, follow these steps:

1.   Create a new Nuke script. Create a Read node. Import a bitmap or image sequence that features an area with a saturated color, such as red. You can use the `lipstick.tif` bitmap included in the `Chapters/Chapter4/Bitmaps/` directory on the DVD. The included bitmap features an actress wearing bright red lipstick (Figure 4.8). Connect a Viewer to the Read1 node.

FIGURE 4.8 The `lipstick.tif` bitmap features an actress with bright red lipstick.

2.   With the Read1 node selected, choose Color > Saturation. Change the Saturation parameter to 0. The image turns grayscale. Create a new Read node. Import the same bitmap into the Read2 node. Connect the Mask input of the Saturation1 node to the output of the Read2 node. You can do this by LMB-dragging the pipe stub at the right side of the Saturation1 node icon and dropping it on top of the Read2 icon. Use Figure 4.9 as a reference for the final node network.

3.   At this point, a red error message appears at the top of the Viewer tab: *Nonexistent channel used for mask.* By default, any node that carries a Mask channel takes information from the input's alpha channel. Because the `lipstick.tif` bitmap does not carry an alpha channel, there is no information to read. To solve this, open the Saturation1 node's properties panel and change the Mask Channel menu to a channel that exists, such as Rgba.red (Figure 4.10). Once a valid channel is selected, the

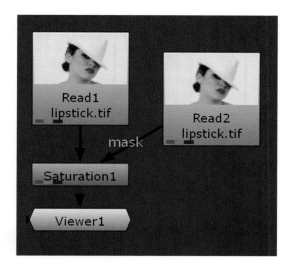

FIGURE 4.9 Node network with Saturation1 node utilizing the Read2 output as a mask.

error message is removed. The heaviest areas of desaturation thus occur in areas of the Mask input that carry the highest values. If the Mask Channel menu is set to Rgba.red, the lips are thus desaturated and lose their redness (Figure 4.11). Change the Mask Channel menu to Rgba.green and Rgba.blue channels for differing results. A sample script is included as mask.nk in the Chapters/Chapter4/Scripts/ directory on the DVD.

FIGURE 4.10 Saturation1 node's Mask Channel menu changed from default Rgba.alpha to Rgba.red.

FIGURE 4.11 The lips are desaturated as the desaturation is targeted at areas with intense red through the red channel mask.

Note that the presence of an input A alpha channel may affect the resulting merge. For example, in Figure 4.12, input A (a photo of a field) is masked with a black-and-white bitmap featuring a squiggled line. The Merge node's Mask Channel menu is set to Rgba.red. Input A carries a solid-white alpha channel. Hence, input A is cleanly masked. The Merge node merges the cut-out input A over a solid red color provided by a Constant node. If input A is switched to an input that does not possess an alpha channel, cut-out input A becomes semi-transparent (Figure 4.13). Nevertheless, it is possible to avoid the transparency by changing the Merge node's Operation. For example, setting the menu to Copy returns the opaqueness to Input A.

FIGURE 4.12 Input A (a photo of a field) carries an alpha channel and thereby is cleanly masked over a red Constant. A sample script is included as alphamask.nk in the Chapters/ Chapter4/Scripts/ directory on the DVD.

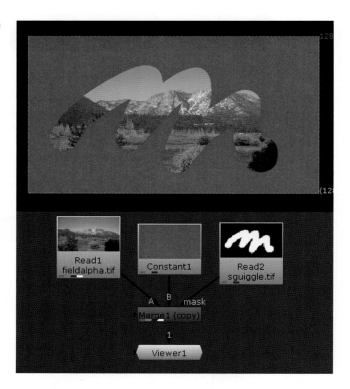

The Merge node's Mask parameter is selected automatically when a Mask input is connected to another node. You can invert the Mask input by selecting the Invert parameter (see Figure 4.10). Bezier shapes, used as masks, are detailed in the "Rotoscoping" section later in this chapter. Step 3 of Tutorial 2, featured at the end of this chapter, uses a procedural Noise node as a mask.

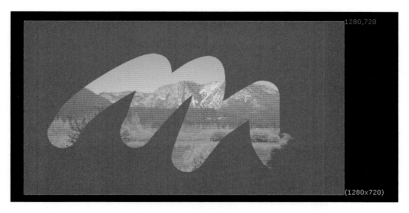

Pulling a Matte

In many situations, the output that requires a matte contains all the necessary information needed to create that matte. This approach is often called *pulling a matte*. Although you can utilize red, green, and blue channel information, as is demonstrated earlier in the section "Hooking Up a Mask," you can also use luminance information. Such a pulled matte is often referred to as a *luma matte*. For example, in Figure 4.14, a matte is pulled from a bitmap photo featuring silhouetted dancers against a bright set of windows.

With this example, the following steps occur:

FIGURE 4.14 A matte is pulled from the luminance information contained within a bitmap photo of silhouetted dancers. As a result, the red of a Constant node appears in the darkest areas.

1. The color space of the bitmap is interpreted as Linear through the Read1 node.
2. The color space is converted to L*a*b* through the Colorspace1 node (Figure 4.15).
3. The contrast of the luminance channel is increased by the ColorCorrect1 node.

FIGURE 4.15 The node network that creates the luma mask.

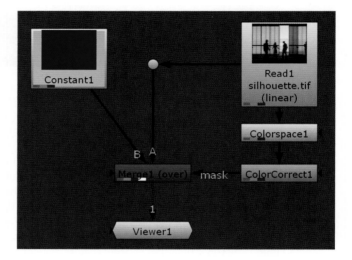

4. The luminance channel is used as matte information through the Mask connection of the Merge1 node.
5. The original bitmap is merged with a dark red color provided by the Constant1 node. The dark red appears in the silhouetted areas of the bitmap but does not affect the bright areas of the windows or the doorway. To ensure that the Mask input uses the luminance information, the Mask Channel menu of the Merge1 node is set to Rgba.red. (When the color space conversion is carried out, L* [luminance] is carried by the red channel; for more information on L*a*b* color space and the Colorspace node, see Chapter 3.)

If you wish to see what the luma matte looks like, connect Viewer1 to the ColorCorrect1 node and press the R key in the Viewer panel. A sample script is included as luma.nk in the Chapters/Chapter4/Scripts/ directory on the DVD. The chroma key process, whereby you convert a specific color to matte information, is a form of matte pulling and is discussed in Chapter 5.

Specialized Merge Nodes

In addition to the Merge node, Nuke provides several nodes designed for specialized merging. These are described briefly here.

Blend outputs the weighted average of two or more inputs. Each input pipe is consecutively numbered and receives a matching weight slider in the node's properties panel. The higher the slider value of an input, the more biased the weighting is toward it and the more opaque the input appears.

Dissolve also outputs the weighted average of two or more inputs (numbered 0, 1, 2, and so on). The Which parameter determines the weighting and runs from 0 to the highest input value. For example, if there are three inputs, the parameter runs from 0 to 2. If the Which slider is set to 0, the 0 input occludes the other inputs. If the slider is set to 1.5, the 1 and 2 inputs are averaged.

TimeDissolve, in contrast, only accepts two inputs (A and B). The two inputs are averaged. However, the weighting is controlled by an interactive curve (Figure 4.16). Time runs along the left/right X axis of the curve graph; the time range uses a normalized 0-to-1 scale, where you control the start and end frame through the In and Out parameters. The up/down Y axis also runs from 0 to 1 and represents the weighting. If a curve point sits at 1, input B occludes input A. If a curve point sits at 0.5, a 50% mixture of both inputs results. You can edit the curve as you would any other curve in the Curve Editor.

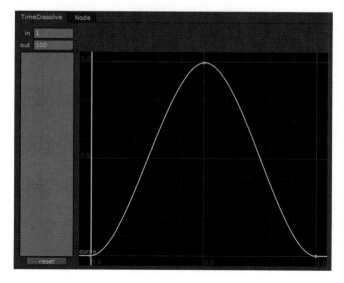

FIGURE 4.16 The curve graph of a TimeDissolve node. A new curve point is inserted at 0.5 in X. The curve is reshaped so that the node dissolves from input A to input B to input A once again. A sample script is included as timedissolve.nk in the Chapters/ Chapter4/Scripts/ directory on the DVD.

FIGURE 4.17 A 3D render is merged over a background with an AddMix node.

FIGURE 4.18 The AddMix A curve is bowed upward to give the A alpha channel midrange greater intensity. The B curve remains in its default state.

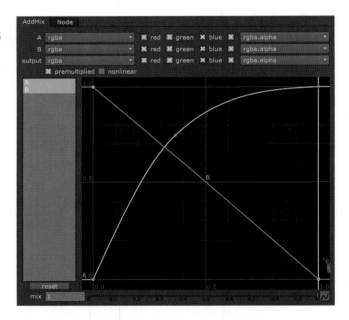

AddMix provides two interactive curves. The input A alpha is multiplied by the A curve and the input B alpha is multiplied by the B curve before the two inputs are added together. The interactive curves allow you to wield greater control over the edges of the output alpha matte. For example, in Figure 4.17, a render of a moving 3D primitive is merged over a background sky. If the A curve of the AddMix node is altered so that the midrange of the input A alpha is given reduced values (Figure 4.18), the motion-blurred edge of the primitive becomes more transparent and thus more subtle (Figure 4.19). Moving an A curve point upward in the graph causes an alpha value reduction, while moving a point downward has the opposite result. You can edit the curve as you would any other curve in the Curve Editor. Note that the AddMix node carries a Premultiplied parameter, which is deselected by default. A sample script is included as `addmix.nk` in the `Chapters/Chapter4/Scripts/` directory on the DVD.

FIGURE 4.19 The altered A curve has greater transparency along the motion-blurred edge.

CopyRectangle cuts a rectangular hole into input B, thus allowing input A to show through. You can interactively move and scale the rectangle in the Viewer.

KeyMix cuts a hole into input B, allowing input A to show through. However, KeyMix requires that you connect a mask to its Mask input to define the cut region.

MergeExpression allows you to write an expression for specific channels. The properties panel appears identical to the Expression node (Color > Math > Expression). However, the MergeExpression node carries two input pipes (A and B), which you can reference within the expressions. Expressions are explored in Chapter 10.

Rotoscoping

Rotoscoping is any process that generates an animated mask, whereby the mask is converted to an alpha matte. The mask changes with each frame and thus follows the contours of a specific object. For example, you might rotoscope an actor to separate him or her from the background. With a digital compositing program, rotoscoping may take the form of an animated spline or hand-painted mask shapes. Rotoscoping is an important compositing technique; in fact, it's often used in combination with other matte-generation approaches, such as chroma keying (discussed in Chapter 5). Before the advent of digital image manipulation, rotoscoping required the tracing of motion picture film frames on paper. Nuke provides two nodes for the purpose of rotoscoping: Roto and RotoPaint.

Roto Node

The Roto node is designed for the specific task of rotoscoping. The node allows you to interactively create spline-based shapes, which are filled automatically to create matching alpha mattes. To apply the node, follow these general steps:

FIGURE 4.20 Roto node toolbar.

1. With no nodes selected, choose Draw > Roto (or press the O key in the Node Graph). A Roto node is created and a special Roto toolbar is added to the left side of the Viewer panel. From top to bottom, the toolbar includes a selection tool set, a points tool set, and a shape tool set (Figure 4.20).

2. With the Bezier tool selected (the Bezier tool is selected by default when a new Roto node is created), draw a bezier shape in the Viewer by clicking around the contour of the object you wish to separate. (If the Viewer does not display the output you wish to rotoscope, temporarily connect the Viewer to that output.) Each time you click, a point is deposited. In the same way the points of a curve in the Curve Editor define the curve's shape, the points of a Roto bezier define the bezier shape. For the bezier to create a functioning alpha matte, the bezier must be closed. That is, the last point must be placed where the first point lies. When you position the mouse pointer over the first point, the pointer displays a small circle, indicating that an additional click will close the bezier. Alternatively, you can press the Enter key to force a closure; Nuke automatically adds a bezier segment between the first point and the last point deposited.

3. Once the bezier shape is closed, it's filled with white in the RGB and alpha channels. To avoid obscuring the RGB channels with the white fill, you can temporarily reduce the Roto node's Opacity parameter to 0. (The Opacity parameter affects the RGB and alpha channels equally; to utilize the alpha channel as an alpha matte, Opacity must be left at 1.) If the Roto node is connected to a Viewer, you can examine the alpha channel by placing the mouse in the viewer and pressing the A key. The interior of the shape receives an alpha value of 1 (opaque), while the space around the shape receives an alpha value of 0 (transparent). You can connect the output of the Roto node to any other node that may benefit from the alpha matte. For example, you can connect the Roto output to the Mask input of the Merge node. The Merge node's input A is thus cut by the matte (Figure 4.21).

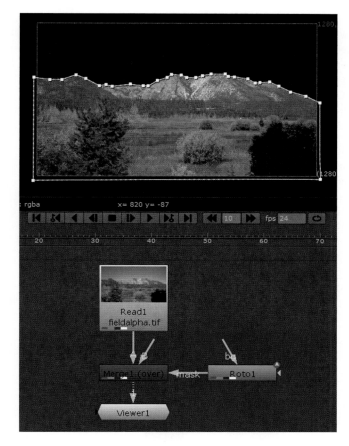

FIGURE 4.21 An alpha matte, generated by a Roto node, is connected to the Mask input of a Merge node. The Merge node's input A is thus cut by the matte; this maintains the field and mountain but removes the sky. A sample script is included as `roto.nk` in the `Chapters/Chapter4/Scripts/` directory on the DVD.

For a working example of the Roto node, see Tutorial 1 at the end of this chapter.

Editing a Bezier and Using B-Splines

You can edit an existing bezier shape in the following ways:

- To add a point to an existing bezier shape, click the bezier so that the existing points are visible and Cmd/Ctrl+Opt/Alt-click a bezier segment. Alternatively, switch to the Add Points tool available through the center Roto tool set.
- To delete a point, select the point with the Select All tool (available through the top Roto tool set) and press the Delete key; a selected point is indicated by a small line running perpendicular to the surrounding segments. Alternatively, switch to the Remove Points tool available through the center tool set.
- To curve a point by inserting a tangent handle, select the point with the Select All tool and press the Z key. Alternatively, switch to the Curve Points

tool available through the center tool set. You can rotate the tangent handle by LMB-dragging either tangent end. You can lengthen or shorten the tangent handle by dragging a tangent end in or out. To move one tangent end independent of the other, Cmd/Ctrl-drag.

- To cusp a point and thereby create a sharp corner, select a point and press Shift+Z. Cusped points are created by default when you draw the bezier shape. Alternatively, switch to the Cusp Points tool available through the center Roto tool set.

By default, the Roto node creates bezier shapes. However, you can also create B-spline, ellipsoid, or rectangular shapes. To create an ellipse or rectangle, switch the bottom Roto tool set to the namesake shape and LMB-drag in the Viewer. The resulting ellipse or rectangle is closed and carries four points that are either smoothed or cusped. You can edit the ellipse and rectangle as you would any other bezier shape. To create a B-spline shape, switch the bottom tool set menu to B-Spline and click in the Viewer. B-splines differ from beziers in that their points lie *off* the segments (much like a NURBS curve in Maya). You can add or delete points in the same way you would with a bezier shape. However, B-spline points generate smooth shapes that cannot maintain sharp corners (Figure 4.22).

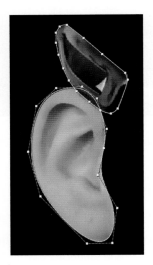

FIGURE 4.22 A B-spline shape (bottom, around ear) is combined with a bezier shape (top, around clip). A sample script is included as bspline.nk in the Chapters/Chapter4/Scripts/ directory on the DVD.

Combining Multiple Shapes

You can draw multiple shapes while using a single Roto node. To add an additional shape, click a shape tool, such as Bezier, in the Roto node toolbar and deposit points in the Viewer. Each shape is listed in the Curves section of

Visible
Locked
Handle Color
Render Color
Inverted
Blending Mode
Motion Blur

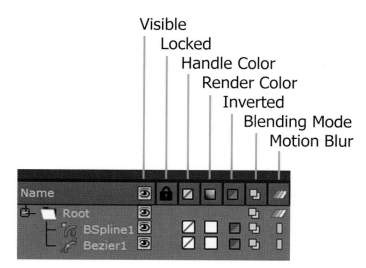

FIGURE 4.23 The Curves section of a Roto node's properties panel.

the Roto tab of the node's properties panel (Figure 4.23). The Curves section allows you to hide shapes, lock shapes (prevent edits), change the handle color (color of the shape curve), change the render color (the shape fill color), invert the alpha matte, choose a blending mode (the mathematical way in which shapes are combined), and activate motion blur for animated shapes.

By default, the Roto node's blending mode is set to Over. This is identical to the Over operation used by the Merge node. You can change the blending mode to other common operations by clicking the Blending Mode icon in the Curves section. (For more information on operations, see the "Choosing a Math Operation" earlier in this chapter.) For example, if you need to cut a hole into a shape, draw a smaller shape and set the new shape's blending mode to Exclusion (Figure 4.24).

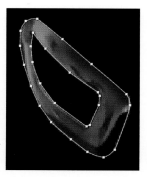

FIGURE 4.24 A hole is cut into a shape by setting a smaller shape's blending mode to Exclusion. A sample script is included as exclusion.nk in the Chapters/Chapter4/Scripts/ directory on the DVD.

You can delete, copy, or paste a shape by RMB-clicking the shape name in the Curves section. You can rename a shape by double-clicking the shape name and entering new text into the name field. The order in which the shapes appear in the Curves section affects the way in which the shapes are blended together. The top-most shapes win out over lower shapes much like a layer stack in Adobe Photoshop or After Effects. You can reposition a shape in the stack by selecting and LMB-dragging the shape name up or down. Selected shapes are indicated by an orange bar.

Feathering a Shape

Initially, the transition from 0-transparent pixels and 1-opaque pixels in the generated alpha matte is hard. You can soften this transition, however, by adjusting a point's feather. To do so, select the point. A small line appears perpendicular to the segments that lie to either side of the point. Click on the small line and drag outward. A feather point and dotted feather segments appear (Figure 4.25). (If the line is not visible, RMB-click over the point and choose Increase Feather from the menu.) The space between the feather segments and the original segments becomes a soft transition. You can pick and choose which points to feather; in addition, each point can carry a unique feather. The feather points carry their own tangent handles, which you can adjust separately. You can remove a feather from a point by switching to the Remove Feather tool through the center Roto tool set and clicking on the point in the Viewer. You can also remove a feather by RMB-clicking over the point and choosing Reset Feather from the menu. The ability to feather the shape is extremely useful when rotoscoping an object that is motion-blurred.

FIGURE 4.25 Close-up of a shape feather. The feather point (bottom) creates a 12-pixel transition from opaque alpha to transparent alpha at the widest span of the feather.

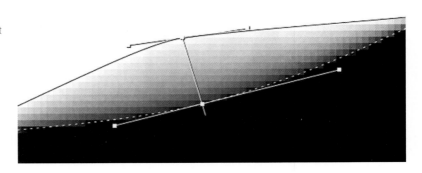

Adjusting the Matte Edge and Transforms

You can alter the overall quality of a shape's alpha matte edge by changing the Feather and Feather Falloff parameters. To do so, first select the shape name in the Curves section of the Roto node's properties panel. Feather controls the uniform softness, where higher values create a blurrier edge. Feather Falloff sets the rate of opacity change at the matte edge, where higher values create a more gradual transition from opaque alpha to transparent alpha.

You can change a shape's translation, rotation, scale, and skew through the Roto node's Transform tab. Once again, you must first select the shape name in the Curves section in the Roto tab. If you animate the shape, either through the Transform tab or by animating the positions of individual points (see the next section), you can adjust the resulting motion blur through the Shape tab.

Animating a Shape

When a bezier or B-spline shape is closed, it creates an alpha matte. The matte does not change over time. This is often useful for creating a matte for an object or objects that do not move. Such a matte often takes the form of a *garbage matte*, whereby unwanted objects in a shot are quickly deleted. For example, you might create a garbage matte to remove lighting equipment that appears along the edges of a greenscreen plate. In contrast, rotoscoping requires that the matte changes over time. This is necessary when creating a matte for a moving object, vehicle, or character. When using the Roto node, you can create an animated shape and matching animated matte with a few additional steps:

1. As soon as a shape is created with the Roto node, a keyframe for the shape is placed on the timeline for the current frame. This is indicated by a blue line. Move the time marker to a different frame. Interactively move points in the Viewer to match the contour of the object you are trying to rotoscope. Feel free to adjust tangents and feathering. As soon as a point is moved or adjusted, the Roto node creates a new keyframe. Note that each shape carried by a Roto node carries a unique set of keyframes. If you select a shape in the Viewer, the corresponding shape name is selected in the Curves section of the properties panel; if you select the shape name in the panel, the shape is selected in the Viewer.
2. Play back the timeline. The Roto node creates in-between positions for the shape so that it can successfully morph between the contours you defined. Continue to move the time marker to different frames and continue to adjust the shape. You can move all the points of the shape as a single unit by switching to the Select Points tool through the Roto toolbar top menu, LMB-dragging a selection marquee in the Viewer, and LMB-dragging the resulting transformation handle. You can delete

a keyframe by moving the time marker to the appropriate frame and clicking the Delete Key button in the properties panel (beside the Spline Key parameter). Note that the Spline Key cell appears dark blue when the timeline rests on a keyframe and appears light blue when the program is creating an in-between position for the shape. The total number of keyframes created for a shape is indicated by the cell to the right of the word "of."

In general, it's not necessary to create a keyframe for every single frame of the timeline. However, the number of keyframes required is dependent on the complexity of motion you are rotoscoping. In addition, it's not necessary to create a single shape for the rotoscope. You can break down an object into smaller, overlapping shapes to make the process easier. For example, if you are rotoscoping an actor, you can create one shape for the head, one shape for the neck and torso, and extra shapes for the arms and legs.

RotoPaint Node

FIGURE 4.26 Unique RotoPaint tool sets.

The RotoPaint node includes the functionality of the Roto node but adds the ability to interactively paint strokes. The strokes are based on a spline curve; however, you can determine the size, color, and softness of the stroke. When you create a RotoPaint node (Draw > RotoPaint), it adds its own toolbar to the left side of the Viewer tab. The top three tool sets are identical to the Roto node (see the "Roto Node" section earlier in this chapter). However, four new tool sets are added. From top to bottom, these are Brush/Eraser, Clone/Reveal, Blur/Sharpen/Smear, and Dodge/Burn (Figure 4.26).

Using the Brush

To use the Brush tool with the RotoPaint node, follow these steps:

1. Select the output you wish to rotoscope and choose Draw > RotoPaint. The output is connected to the Bg input of the new RotoPaint node. Connect the output of the RotoPaint node to a Viewer. The RotoPaint toolbar is added to the left side of the Viewer panel. In addition, a settings bar is added to the top of the view area.

2. Select the Brush tool through the left toolbar. The tool features a paintbrush icon. The settings bar updates to reveal controls that determine the color, blending mode, opacity, size, and hardness of the brush stroke (Figure 4.27). The right-most menu controls the lifespan

FIGURE 4.27 The RotoPaint settings bar, as seen when the Brush tool is selected.

and defaults to Single, which means that the stroke will only appear at the current frame. If you wish the stroke to last for the entire duration of the timeline, switch the menu to All. You can also choose a specific frame range by switching the menu to Range. LMB-drag in the Viewer to draw the stroke. When you release the mouse button, the stroke is completed and is listed in the Curves section of the RotoPaint node's properties panel as Paint*n*.

3. You can delete, copy, paste, change the stack order, change the blending mode, or invert the alpha matte of any stoke in the Curves section. To edit the stroke qualities of an existing stroke, select the stroke name in the Curves section and switch to the Stroke tab. The tab includes Brush Size, Brush Hardness, and Source parameters. Source controls the color of the stroke and has the same functionality as the Source parameter in the Shape tab. You can change the stroke's lifespan through the Lifetime Type menu of the Lifetime tab.

4. The stroke appears in the RGB and alpha channels. To see the alpha channel, disconnect the Bg pipe and press the A key while the mouse is in the Viewer. You can connect the output of the RotoPaint node to any other node that may benefit from the alpha matte. For example, you can connect the Roto output to the Mask input of the Merge node. The Merge node's input A is thus cut by the matte (Figure 4.28).

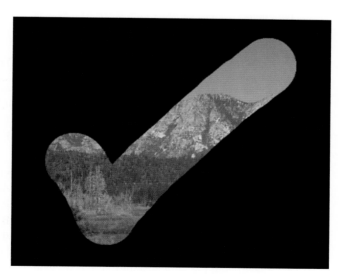

FIGURE 4.28 An alpha matte, generated by a RotoPaint node, is connected to the Mask input of a Merge node. The Merge node's input A is thus cut by the matte. A bitmap is thus cut into the shape of a stroke. A sample script is included as `rotopaint.nk` in the `Chapters/Chapter4/Scripts/` directory on the DVD.

FIGURE 4.29 A red stroke is composited directly over a background through a Merge node. A sample script is included as `rotopaintbg.nk` in the `Chapters/Chapter4/Scripts/` directory on the DVD.

Alternatively, you can composite the stroke directly over a background. For example, if you connect the RotoPaint output to the input A pipe of a Merge node while connecting the input B pipe to a background, the stroke appears on top of the background (Figure 4.29).

You can transform any stroke. To do so, activate the Select All tool (at the top of the toolbar), select the stroke name in the Curves section, switch to the Transform tab, and interactively move the stroke in the Viewer via its transform handle. You can keyframe animate any of the transformation parameters.

Repairing a Background with the Clone Tool

The Clone tool allows you to sample the pixels from one area of a background and paint them onto a completely different area. This makes the Clone tool ideal for covering up unwanted artifacts, such as dust, dirt, scratches, flares, labels, or small signs. To use the Clone tool, follow these steps:

1. Select the output you wish to rotoscope and choose Draw > RotoPaint. The output is connected to the Bg input of the new RotoPaint node. Connect the output of the RotoPaint node to a Viewer.
2. Select the Clone tool from the toolbar. Cmd/Ctrl+LMB-click in the Viewer over the area you wish to sample, drag the mouse to the point where you wish to start the stroke, and release the Ctrl key and LMB. A string is drawn from the sample point to the point where you released the key/button. LMB-drag to paint the stroke. The stroke takes on the color of the sampled area (Figure 4.30).

FIGURE 4.30 A Clone stroke covers the top of a lens flare. The flare appears as a vertical white stripe. The stroke is selected, revealing the stroke spline at the top of the figure. A sample script is included as `rotopaintclone.nk` in the `Chapters/Chapter4/Scripts/` directory on the DVD.

You can animate a Clone stroke's transformations through the Transform tab. The Clone tab, on the other hand, determines the Transform X, Transform Y, Rotate, Scale, and Skew of the sampled background. For example, if you increase the Scale to 2, the background is scaled by 200% before it is sampled for the stroke.

Using Specialized RotoPaint Tools

Aside from the Brush and Clone tools, you can use the Eraser, Blur, Sharpen, Smear, Dodge, and Burn tools to create specialized results. Brief descriptions of each follow.

Eraser "cuts" a stroke-shaped path into other brush strokes. This is achieved by setting the Source menu, in the Stroke tab, to Background. An Eraser stroke can only function if it is at the top of the stroke stack in the Curves section.

Blur utilizes the Bg input pipe color to create a blurred stroke. For the blur to function, the Source menu, in the Stroke tab, must be set to Foreground. The strength of the blur is determined by the Effect parameter in the Stroke tab. You can use the Blur tool to selectively blur a small section of an image (Figure 4.31).

FIGURE 4.31 A Blur tool stroke blurs a background in a confined area. A sample script is included as rotopaintblur.nk in the Chapters/Chapter4/Scripts/ directory on the DVD.

Sharpen functions in a manner similar to the Blur tool. However, the stroke area is sharpened through a process in which contrast is increased. The strength of the sharpen is determined by the Effect parameter in the Stroke tab.

Smear utilizes the Bg input pipe color. However, the pixels are offset in such a manner as to "push" the pixels ahead of the stroke.

Dodge and **Burn** utilize the Bg input pipe color. However, their blending modes are set automatically to Color-Dodge and Color-Burn. Dodging lightens the pixels and burning darkens the pixels. The Source menu must be set to Foreground for the Dodge and Burn strokes to function.

The FurnaceCore plug-in set includes the F_RigRemoval and F_Wire-Removal nodes. (The plug-ins appear in the Furnace or the Furnace-Core menu, depending on which version of Nuke you are running.) F_RigRemoval attempts to remove a rig (some type of a moving object) from an image sequence or movie and fill the void with the original empty background. Basic steps for its use are as follows:

1. Connect the F_RigRemoval's Src pipe to the output that carries the rig.
2. Open the F_RigRemoval properties panel. With the Rig Region menu set to Box, interactively place the red rig region box in the Viewer. The box should loosely cover the rig (moving object).
3. Expand the Rig Region Box section in the properties panel and set keys for the Rig Region BL (bottom left) and Rig Region TR (top right) corner values. Move ahead on the timeline and reposition the region box so that it covers the rig at all times.
4. Examine the node's output. If the rig is not completely removed, you can adjust the Num Frames parameter. Num Frames determines how many frames forward and backward the node will go on the timeline to seek data (image pixels without the rig) to fill the void left by the removed rig.

The F_RigRemoval includes a RigMask input pipe, which you can connect to a Roto node or other animated mask. To use the RigMask input, you must change Rig Region from Box to one of the alpha or luminance options.

In contrast, F_WireRemoval is designed to remove wires that may remain from physical stunt or light rigs used on a set. The node's basic workflow includes the following steps:

1. Connect the output containing the wire to the node's Source pipe. If a clean plate is available (same camera position without the wire), connect it to the CleanPlate pipe.
2. Identify the wire position by interactively moving the points of the node's wire widget in the Viewer. If the wire moves over time, activate the node's built-in wire tracker.
3. Once the wire tracking is successful for all the frames, choose a repair method through the Repair menu. Options include Spatial (current frame only), Spatial With Local Motion (motion estimation using previous and next frame), Spatial With Global Motion (motion estimation for entire sequence), and Clean Plate (if the CleanPlate pipe is connected).

For additional information on motion tracking (which uses controls similar to the F_WireRemoval's wire tracking), see Chapter 8. For information on motion estimation, see Chapter 6. For more information on the F_RigRemoval and F_WireRemoval nodes, see the "User Guide for Furnace" PDF available at The Foundry's website (www.thefoundry.co.uk).

Tutorial 1: Kicking a Heart
Part 4: Adding a Shadow and Rotoscoping a Hand

In Part 3 of this tutorial, we color graded the heart render and background image sequence to create better integration. Part 4 rotoscopes the character so that the heart can sit behind the hand. In addition, a shadow is created by duplicating the heart render output and applying filters to the duplicate.

1. Open the Nuke script you saved after completing Part 3 of this tutorial. A sample Nuke script is included as `Tutorial1.3.nk` in the `Tutorials/Tutorial1/Scripts/` directory on the DVD.

2. Move the time marker to frame 1 so that the heart is at rest on the ground. Open the Transform1 node's properties panel and temporarily set Motionblur to 0. This will speed up the Viewer as you update the node network.

3. In the Node Graph, RMB-click and select Transform > Transform or press the T key. LMB-drag the input pipe of the new Transform2 node and drop it on top of the Read2 node (see Figure 4.36 at the end of this section). Disconnect the Transform1 node from the Merge1 node. Connect the input A pipe of the Merge1 node to the output of the Transform2 node. Connect the A2 input pipe of the Merge1 node to the output of the Transform1 node. The A2 pipe is drawn as a pipe stub on the left side of the Merge1 node icon. If you cannot see the pipe stub (it may be covered by the A pipe connection), LMB-drag the Transform1 node output pipe and drop it on the Merge1 node. The A connection is relabeled A1 and the new connection between Transform1 and Merge1 is labeled A2. A Merge node can accept two or more connections. This series of connections allows a second iteration of the heart render to be placed over the background image sequence. The output of Transform2 is placed "under" the output of Transform1.

4. Open the Transform2 node's properties panel. Set Skew to 1, Rotate to −12, Translate X to −250, and Translate Y to −310. Click the 2 button beside Scale. This reveals the Scale W and Scale H cells. Set W to 0.7 and H to 0.8. This series of changes skews and elongates the heart so that it runs roughly in the same direction as other ground shadows contained in the image sequence.

5. Select the Transform2 node, RMB-click, and choose Color > Grade (or press G). Open the Grade2 node's properties panel. Change Blackpoint to 1. This turns the skewed heart to pure black (Figure 4.32). In this case, all values in the render equal to or less than 1 are converted to a value of 0.

6. With the Grade2 node selected, RMB-click, and choose Color > Grade (or press G). Open the Grade3 node's properties panel.

FIGURE 4.32 A second iteration of the heart render is scaled, rotated, and skewed with a Transform node. The result is darkened with a Grade node to emulate a shadow.

Change the Channels menu to Alpha. Change the Gain to 0.68. This decreases the intensity of the whites within the alpha channel. In turn, the heart render (now converted into a shadow) becomes less opaque. With the Grade3 node selected, RMB-click and choose Filter > Blur (or press B). Open the Blur1 node's properties panel and change Size to 22. This softens the shadow (Figure 4.33).

7. Move the time marker to frame 24. This is the last frame that features a static heart. Open the Trasform2 node's properties panel. Click the Animation Menu button beside Translate and choose Set Key. The X and Y cells turn blue. Move the time marker

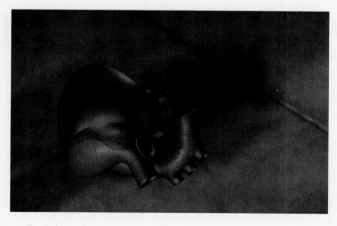

FIGURE 4.33 The shadow is made more transparent by darkening the alpha channel with an additional Grade node. The shadow is softened with a Blur node.

to frame 27. This is the frame where the heart render is kicked out of sight. With the Transform2 node selected, interactively move the shadow past the top-right corner of the bounding box. A new keyframe is placed on the timeline. This motion allows the shadow to move in correspondence with the heart.

8. Move the time marker to frame 22. This is the first frame where the heart render occludes the character's hand. To place the heart behind the hand, you will need to rotoscope. With no nodes selected, choose Draw > Roto. Connect the Roto1 node's Bg input pipe to the Read1 node. Create a new Viewer by choosing Viewer > Create New Viewer from the menu bar (Figure 4.34). Connect the output of the Roto1 node to Viewer2. Switch to the Viewer2 tab in the Viewer pane.

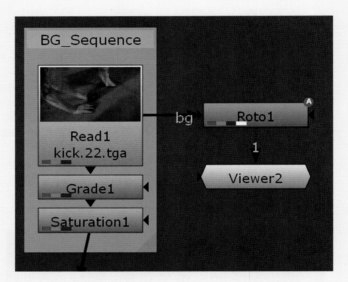

FIGURE 4.34 Initial rotoscope setup.

9. Click the Bezier tool in the Roto node toolbar. Draw a bezier shape by clicking in the Viewer. Close the shape so that it surrounds the fingers and palm. When the shape is closed, it's filled with white, which obscures the image sequence. Open the Roto1 node's properties panel and switch to the Shape tab. Change the Source menu to Background. This fills the shape with the original color found in the image sequence, which is connected to the Bg input pipe (Figure 4.35). Adjust the tangents and the feathers of the points (see the "Editing a Bezier and Using B-Splines" section earlier in this chapter for more information).

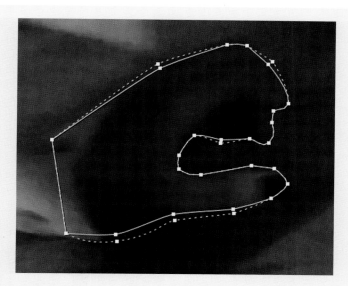

FIGURE 4.35 A bezier shape is drawn around the fingers and palm.

Move the time marker to frame 24 and readjust the shape contour to fit the hand. A new keyframe is laid down. Move the time marker to frame 23 and adjust the shape again.

10. Once you're satisfied with the rotoscoped bezier shape, switch back to the Viewer1 tab. Change the Roto1 node's Source menu back to Color. Disconnect the Bg pipe from the Read1 node. Connect the output of Roto1 to the Mask input of the Merge1 node (Figure 4.36). This causes the alpha matte of the Roto1 node to affect both the A1 and A2 inputs of the Merge1 node. Hence, a piece of the heart and shadow is cut out in the shape of the fingers. To invert the result, open the Roto1 node's properties panel, and select the Inverted checkbox beside the Bezier1 curve in the Curves section. The matte is inverted and a hole in the shape of the fingers is cut into the heart and shadow. Thus, the heart and shadow fits "behind" the hand (Figure 4.37). To increase the softness of the alpha matte edge, raise the Roto1 node's Feather parameter value. To temporarily hide the bezier curve in the Viewer, press O.

This concludes Tutorial 1. Reactivate motion blur by returning the Transform1 node's Motionblur parameter to 1. Render a test movie by selecting the Merge1 node and choosing Render > Flipbook Selected from the menu bar. As a bonus step, you can refine the transform animation of the heart so that the render matches the slight camera move present in the plate before the

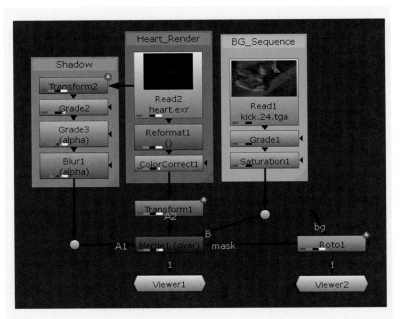

FIGURE 4.36 The final node network for Tutorial 1.

FIGURE 4.37 The Bezier shape is used as a Mask input for the Merge1 node, thus cutting a hole into the heart render.

kick. (It's also possible to apply motion tracking to the plate; motion tracking is discussed in Chapter 8.) A sample Nuke script is included as `Tutorial1.final.nk` in the `Tutorials/Tutorial1/Scripts/` directory on the DVD.

Tutorial 2: Flying a Spaceship
Part 3: Cloaking the Ship with a Procedural Matte
In Part 2 of this tutorial, we color graded the composite to create lighting suitable for a sunset or sunrise. Part 3 mattes the spaceship so that it's partially transparent (as if it carries a device that allows it to become invisible).

1. Open the Nuke script you saved after completing Part 2 of this tutorial. A sample Nuke script is included as `Tutorial2.2.nk` in the `Tutorials/Tutorial2/Scripts/` directory on the DVD.
2. In the Node Graph, RMB-click and choose Draw > Noise. With the Noise1 node selected, RMB-click and choose Color > Grade. Connect the output of the Grade1 node to the Mask input of the Merge1 node. Create a new Viewer by choosing Viewer > Create New Viewer from the menu bar. Connect Viewer2 to the Grade1 node. Use Figure 4.38 as reference for the final node network.

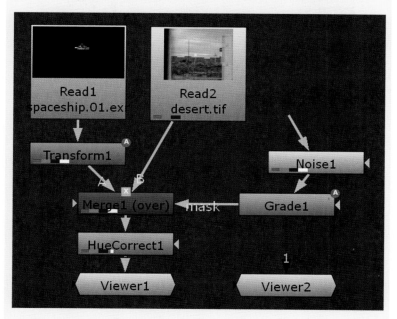

FIGURE 4.38 The final node network for Tutorial 2.

3. Switch to the Viewer2 tab. The Noise1 node creates a grayscale, procedural noise pattern (Figure 4.39). The same pattern appears in the RGB channels and the alpha channel. (The Noise node, along with other additional filter nodes, are discussed in more detail in Chapter 6.) Switch to the Viewer1 tab. The spaceship becomes partially transparent (Figure 4.40). Thanks to the Mask input, the values carried by the Read1 alpha are multiplied by the values of the Noise1 alpha. Areas of the spaceship render that carry

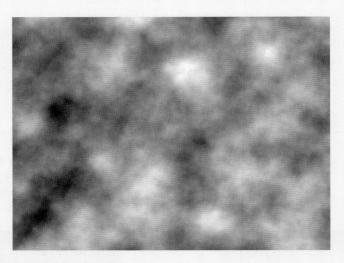

FIGURE 4.39 Pattern created by the Noise1 node.

FIGURE 4.40 Partially transparent spaceship, as seen on frame 42.

a 0 alpha value remain 0, while areas that carry a 1 alpha value are darkened.

4. Move the time marker to frame 1. Open the properties panel for the Grade1 node. Change the Channels menu from Rgb to Rgba. Place the mouse over the Lift numeric cell, RMB-click, and choose Set Key from the menu. A keyframe is laid down for the current Lift value, which is 0. (You can set a keyframe for any parameter in this fashion.) Move the time marker to frame 60. Change the Lift value to 1. Switch to the Viewer2 tab. Play back the timeline. Setting two keyframes on the Lift parameter causes the noise pattern to change from its default grayscale to pure white. Switch to the Viewer1 tab. Play back the timeline. The spaceship starts semi-transparent and becomes more opaque as it flies off.

This concludes Tutorial 2. A sample Nuke script is included as `Tutorial2.final.nk` in the `Tutorials/Tutorial2/Scripts/` directory on the DVD. Reactivate motion blur by returning the Transform1 node's Motionblur parameter to 1. Render a test movie by selecting the HueCorrect1 node and choosing Render > Flip-book Selected from the menu bar. As a bonus step, you can vary the noise pattern over time by keyframing the Z parameter of the Noise1 node.

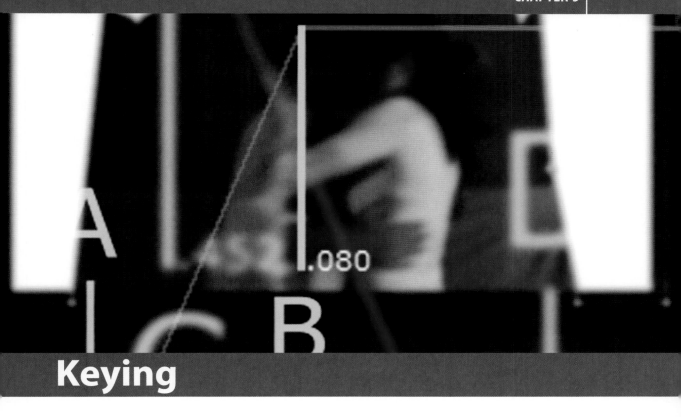

CHAPTER 5

Keying

Professional compositors often find it necessary to remove bluescreen or greenscreen from a live-action plate. Fortunately, a host of tools have been developed for such a task. The tools are generally called *chroma keyers*, as they target specific colors. You can use chroma keyers in a wide variety of ways to generate alpha mattes and thus impart transparency to a bitmap or image sequence that carried no alpha channel to begin with.

This chapter includes the following critical information:

- Chroma key basics
- Simple Nuke keyers
- Advanced Nuke keyers

Chroma Keying

Chroma keying is a critical part of professional compositing. As a process, chroma keying creates an alpha matte by targeting a specific color within a piece of film or video footage. This is necessary when shooting live action that utilizes a greenscreen or bluescreen. The screen may take the form of specialized fabric or a studio wall painted a specific shade of green or blue.

Although green and blue are the most common colors used for chroma keying, it's possible to use chroma key compositing tools to target other colors, such as black or red. In fact, you can use the tools to target colors in nature. For example, you can target the color of a sky, whether it's blue, gray, or orange.

Creating an alpha matte with a chroma key tool is called *keying* whereby the chroma key color is keyed out or keyed. The tools themselves are called *keyers*. Nuke offers eight keyers through the Keyer node menu. The part of the image you are trying to remove is often referred to as the *background*. The color of the background is often called the *screen color*, usually in reference to greenscreen or bluescreen. The part of the image you are trying to maintain is often referred to as the *foreground*. *Spill* represents background color that has reflected onto the foreground. For example, the green of a greenscreen may reflect onto an actor's white shirt.

Simple Keyers

You can break Nuke's keyers into two categories: simple and advanced. You can apply the simple keyers rapidly; however, they have a limited number of parameters with which to adjust the result. The Difference, Keyer, IBKGizmo, IBKColour, and HueKeyer nodes fall into this category. These nodes are discussed in this section.

Difference compares two inputs. Where the inputs carry identical pixel values in the RGB channels, the alpha matte is assigned a value of 0. Where the inputs carry different values, a value from 0 to 1 is assigned based on the degree of difference between the pixel values. The Difference node's input A is designed to accept a clean plate, which is a version of input B that lacks the foreground elements. For example, a clean plate may be created by shooting two shots with a locked-off camera. The first shot includes an actor and becomes input B. The second shot is missing the actor so that only the background remains; this becomes input A. For example, in Figure 5.1, a bitmap featuring the close-up of an actress is connected to input B, while a bitmap featuring the same background without the actress is connected to input A. The resulting matte removes the background and the whitest part of the hat (which carries values similar to the background). If the A and B inputs are reversed, the background is cut out in the shape of the actress's face.

The Difference node has two parameters, Offset and Gain. Offset darkens the resulting matte, while Gain brightens the resulting matte. In Figure 5.1, Offset is set to 0.15 and Gain is set to 3. Note that a Premult node is connected to the output of the Difference node. To use the alpha matte as part of a downstream process, such as a merge, the Difference node's output requires premultiplication.

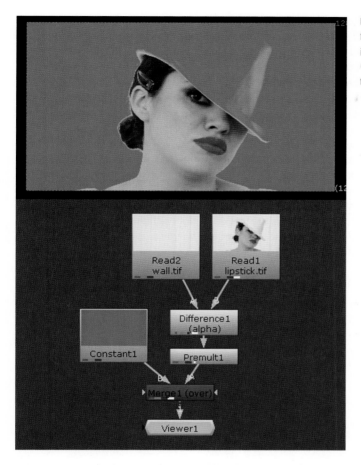

FIGURE 5.1 A Difference node is used to separate the face of an actress from a background. A sample script is included as `difference.nk` in the `Chapters/Chapter5/Scripts/` directory on the DVD.

Keyer provides standardized methods of creating an alpha matte based on color, luminance, or saturation. The mode of operation is set by the Operation menu. Targeted values are controlled by an interactive range graph. With the graph, the bottom-left yellow bar (the A handle) sets the low end of the range (Figure 5.2). The top-right yellow bar (the B handle)

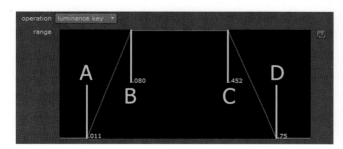

FIGURE 5.2 A range graph of the Keyer node. The A, B, C, and D handles are labeled.

sets the high end of the range. You can LMB-drag the A, B, C, and D handles. The C handle is revealed at the top right when the B handle is moved left. The D handle sits at the bottom right. Pixels with values to the left of the A handle are assigned a 0 (100% transparent) alpha matte value. The range between the B and C handles determines which pixels are assigned a 1 (100% opaque) alpha matte value. The range between the A and B handles establishes the taper at the matte edge; a greater slope between A and B produces a more gradual transition from transparency to opaqueness. The C and D handles allow you to offset the range that targets the foreground element (the part that receives a 1 alpha matte value). For example, if you move C and D handles to the left, the highest values within the input receive a 0 alpha matte value. In many cases, it's not necessary to move the C and D handles to generate an acceptable result.

As a working example, the black of a night sky is removed by moving the A handle to 0.0017 and moving the B handle to 0.01 (Figures 5.3 and 5.4). To create a softer edge transition, the B handle may be moved further to

FIGURE 5.3 A Keyer node removes the black of a night sky. The result is merged with the purple of a Constant node.

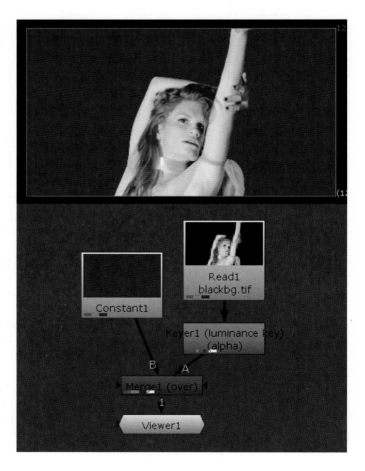

136

FIGURE 5.4 A Keyer properties panel, as used for Figure 5.3. A sample script is included as `keyer.nk` in the `Chapters/Chapter5/Scripts/` directory on the DVD.

the right. To create a harder edge transition, the A handle may be moved to the same value as the B handle. In this example, the Operation menu is set to Luminance Key. Alternatively, setting the menu to a color option causes the node to target the intensity of a particular color channel (R, G, or B) or a specific screen color (green or blue). Setting the Operation to Saturation Key causes the node to target pixels with high saturation. **IBKColour** and **IBKGizmo** work in conjunction and are designed specifically for greenscreen and bluescreen removal. You can follow these basic steps when using the nodes:

1. Create an IBKColour node and a IBKGizmo node. Connect the output of the IBKColour node to the C input of IBKGizmo node.
2. Connect the input of IBKColour node, along with the Fg input of the IBKGizmo node, to the output you wish to key. Optionally, attach the Bg input of the IBKGizmo node to the output you wish to use as a background. See Figure 5.5 as a reference for the node network.
3. Connect a Viewer to the output of the IBKColour node. This node attempts to isolate the screen color by removing all other colors. Open the node's properties panel. Change the Screen Type menu to Green or Blue to match the screen you are working with.
4. Connect a second Viewer to the output of the IBKGizmo node. This node takes the color information from the IBKColour node and creates the final alpha matte. Open the node's properties panel. Change the Screen Type menu to C-Green or C-Blue to match the IBKColour nodes Screen Type menu. The screen color is removed from the output. If noise persists within the matte, return to the IBKColour node and adjust the Size parameter. Size controls the color range that the IBKColour node targets when isolating the screen color. For example, in Figure 5.5, Size is set to 0.

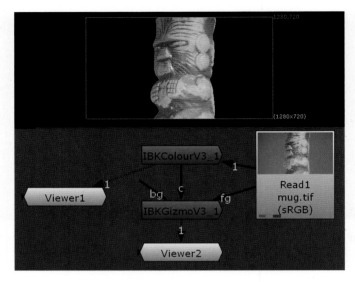

FIGURE 5.5 IBKColour and IBJGizmo are used to key a greenscreen. A sample script is included as `ibk.nk` in the `Chapters/Chapter5/Scripts/` directory on the DVD.

You can use the IBKGizmo node without the IBKColour node by setting the node's Screen Type menu to Pick and selecting a screen color through the Colour parameter.

HueKeyer identifies a screen color through an interactive graph. With the graph, hue is represented by the left/right X axis. The assigned alpha matte value for that hue is represented by the down/up Y axis. To use the HueKeyer, you can follow these basic steps:

1. Connect a HueKeyer node to the output you wish to key. Connect the output of the HueKeyer node to a Viewer.
2. Click the word "Amount" in the left column of the HueKeyer node's properties panel. Note that two of the curve points are set at 1 in anticipation of working with greescreen or bluescreen. Pull these two points back down to 0 by LMB-dragging. You can also click a point, click the Y readout number, and enter 0 into the number cell.
3. Identify the X axis position of the color you wish to key by placing the mouse over the color in the Viewer. A yellow/white crosshair moves to the corresponding location in the graph. Insert a new curve point at the X axis location by Cmd/Ctrl+Opt/Alt-clicking the curve. Move the new point up to 1 in Y (Figure 5.6). To see the resulting alpha matte, press the A key while the mouse is in the Viewer. The identified hue is keyed out and the corresponding alpha values are reduced to 0 black. Note that the HueKeyer's Invert parameter (at the bottom-right corner of the properties panel) is selected by default. This allows the Y axis

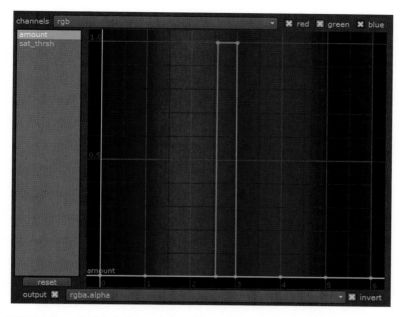

FIGURE 5.6 The graph of the HueKeyer node. Two of the Amount curve points are repositioned to 1 on the Y axis. The corresponding hues, which lie at 2.6 and 3 on the X axis hue scale, are thus targeted and are assigned a 0 alpha matte value. (The Invert parameter changes the 1 Y axis value to 0.)

values to be inverted; hence, the 1 values become 0 and 0 values become 1. To expand the hue range, insert additional points to the left or right of the new point, and move those up to 1. Interactively adjust the point positions in either the X or Y direction to refine the matte.

4. To remove noise from the foreground matte, click the word "Sat_thrsh" in the left column. A new curve appears. Identify the hue of noisy areas by dragging the mouse in the viewer. The yellow/white crosshair moves in the graph. Add a new point at the X axis position and move the point up in Y. The higher the point gets, the less intense the noise becomes. The Sat_thrsh curve establishes the required degree of saturation a pixel must possess to be keyed out.

5. To use the alpha matte as part of a downstream process, such as a merge, connect the HueKeyer node's output to a Premult node.

Beyond the interactive graph, the HueKeyer node offers no means to adjust the resulting matte. Hence, you may need to use additional filter nodes to address any remaining noise or rough matte edges. For example, in Figure 5.7, an Erode (Filter > Erode(Filter)) node is inserted between the HueKeyer and Premult nodes to soften the matte edge.

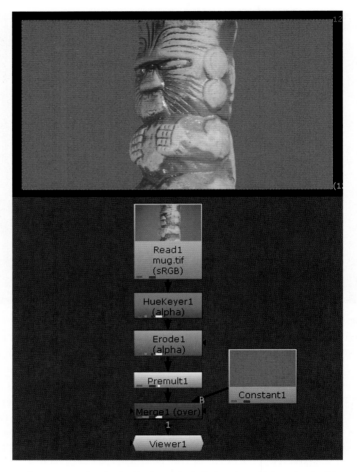

FIGURE 5.7 A greenscreen is keyed with a HueKeyer node. An Erode node is added to soften the alpha matte edge. A sample script is included as `huekeyer.nk` in the `Chapters/Chapter5/Scripts/` directory on the DVD.

Advanced Keyers

Nuke's advanced keyers were developed outside the program and are offered as plug-ins. Because the advanced keyers have enjoyed a long development cycle and heavy use within the visual effects industry, they provide a great deal of power and flexibility. Keylight, Ultimate, and Primatte fall into this category. Note that Ultimatte and Primatte are not available in the PLE version of Nuke.

Keylight uses a color difference methodology whereby all the colors within an input are compared to a single target color. The target color is defined by the Screen Colour parameter. When using the Keylight node, you can follow these basic steps:

1. Connect the Keylight node's Source pipe to the output you wish to key. Connect the output of the Keylight node to a Viewer.
2. Select the color you wish to key by clicking the color swatch button beside the Screen Colour parameter so that the eyedropper icon appears. Sample pixels in the Viewer by Cmd/Ctrl-clicking or Cmd/Ctrl+Shift-dragging a selection marquee. Once a color is established, a key is created.
3. To examine the alpha matte, change the View parameter menu from Final to Screen Matte (Figure 5.8). To refine the matte, adjust the Screen Gain and Screen Balance parameters. Screen Gain determines the aggressiveness with which the screen color is removed to create the matte. Higher values cause a wider range of color values to be

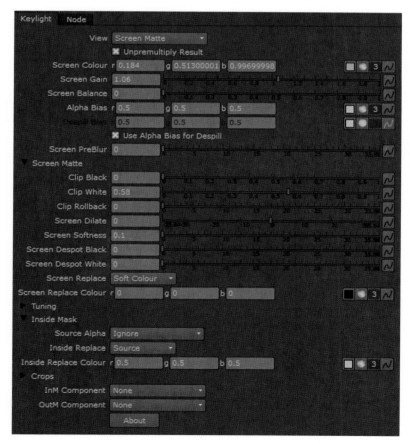

FIGURE 5.8 The Keylight node properties panel.

targeted. Screen Balance compares the intensity of the most intense color component of the screen color to the weighted average of the other two color components. For example, if you are removing a greenscreen, the green component is compared to the red and blue components; this process is applied to determine the relative saturation of the screen color of any given pixel. A Screen Balance of 0 forces the node to compare the primary component to the remaining component with the higher intensity. A Screen Balance of 1 forces the node to compare the primary component to the remaining component with the lower intensity. A Screen Balance of 0.5 compares the primary component to the two other components equally. Ultimately, different Screen Balance values create variations in the matte edge. Different screen colors require different Screen Balance values for optimum quality. (When the screen color is selected, the Screen Balance value is set automatically; however, you are free to change the value at any time.)

4. To make areas of the matte blacker or whiter, raise the Clip Black value or lower the Clip White value (in the Screen Matte section). Alpha matte values below the Clip Black value are clipped to 0 black. Values above the Clip White value are clipped to 1 white. To soften the matte edge, raise the Screen Softness value. To grow or shrink the 0-black area of the matte, adjust the Screen Dilate value. To restore lost edge detail, adjust the Clip Rollback parameter (this has no effect unless Clip Black and/or Clip White are set to non-default values).

5. If noise within the input is preventing the creation of a clean matte, you can raise the Screen Preblur parameter above 0. This preblurs the input and thus removes noisy pixels from the opaque portion of matte. However, high Screen Preblur values will create rounded matte edges.

6. To check the matte quality more carefully, switch the View menu to Status. Status presents an exaggerated view of the matte. Light green pixels represent problem areas where the screen color has been removed as spill and the corresponding matte is semi-transparent (Figure 5.9). If the adjustment of the aforementioned parameters fail to remove the green pixels, you can adjust the Screen Replace menu. By default, Screen Replace attempts to restore areas where screen color spill was present by using a color value defined by the Screen Replace Color parameter (which is black by default). If the Screen Replace menu is switched from Soft Colour to Hard Colour, the transitions at the edges of the replaced areas become rapid. If the Screen Replace menu is set to Source, the original colors of the unaffected input are utilized. Note that gray pixels within the Status view represent semi-transparency; however, they are not necessarily detrimental to the final alpha matte. Hence, it's not necessary to create a Status view that's composed of purely black and white pixels.

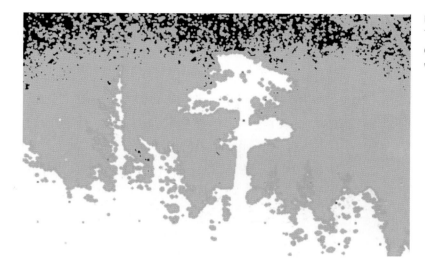

FIGURE 5.9 Close-up of a Status view. The light green pixels along the edge of a tree line represent problem areas where spill color is removed.

By default, the output of the Keylight node is premultiplied. However, you can create an unpremultiplied output by selecting the Unpremultiply Result parameter. The Keylight node carries three additional input pipes: Bg, InM (Inside Mask), and OutM (Outside Mask). To combine the keyed result with a new background, connect the Bg pipe to a suitable image and set the View menu to Composite. The InM input is designed to accept a holdout mask. A *holdout mask* restores a foreground element (a part of the image that should be 100% opaque). Holdout masks are useful when a foreground element is the same color as the screen color (e.g., green eyes match a greenscreen). The OutM input is designed to accept a garbage mask. A *garbage mask* quickly removes unwanted background objects, such as lights, camera rigs, greenscreen edges, and so on. The connected masks can take the form of a bitmap, bezier shape, or procedural texture. The InM Component and OutM Component menus (in the Crops section) determine whether the alpha matte information is derived from the mask's alpha channel or the luminance information from the mask's RGB channels.

A Keylight script is demonstrated in Figure 5.10. In this example, a sky is keyed from a bitmap featuring an off-season ski slope. Screen Colour is sampled from the bitmap and is set to cyan. Screen Gain is 1.05, Screen Balance is 0, Clip White is 0.58, Screen Softness is 0.1, and Screen Replace is set to Soft Colour.

Ultimatte uses color difference methodology, whereby all the colors within an input are compared to a single target color. However, Ultimatte offers a custom Viewer toolbar as well as a wide range of matte and spill

For additional information on the Keylight node, see the "Keylight" PDF available at The Foundry's website (*www.thefoundry.co.uk*).

FIGURE 5.10 A sky is keyed out with Keylight. A sample script is included as `keylight.nk` in the `Chapters/Chapter5/Scripts/` directory on the DVD.

adjustment parameters. When using the Ultimatte node, you can follow these basic steps:

1. Connect the Ultimatte node's Fg pipe to the output you wish to key. Optionally, connect the Bg pipe to an output that you wish to appear as a background. Connect the output of the Ultimatte node to a Viewer node.
2. Click the Screen Color eyedropper button and Cmd/Ctrl-click or Cmd/ Ctrl p Shift-dragging a selection marquee in the Viewer to sample the color you wish to key. The alpha matte is created and the Bg input appears. The Ultimatte node adds a toolbar to the top of the Viewer tab. You can use these controls to refine the matte (Figure 5.11).

FIGURE 5.11 The Ultimatte Viewer toolbar.

3. In the properties panel, switch the Overlay menu from Off to Screen. Semi-transparent red is overlaid in the Viewer. The red indicates the pixels that carry the screen color. Switch the Overlay menu to Subject. The red indicates the foreground pixels—that is, the pixels that do not carry the screen color (Figure 5.12). Note that semi-transparency of the alpha matte is not indicated by the overlay. You can add pixels to the Screen or Subject overlay by clicking the Overlay + button in the

FIGURE 5.12 The Overlay menu, when set to Subject, tints pixels that do not carry the screen color. This display does not indicate any semi-transparency within the alpha matte. With this example, the blue of a sky is selected as the Screen Color.

Primatte toolbar and Cmd/Ctrl-clicking or Cmd/Ctrl-dragging in the Viewer. You can also Cmd/Ctrl+Shift-drag a selection marquee. You can remove pixels from an overlay by clicking the Overlay − button. You can erode or expand the edge of the screen overlay by switching to the Screen Correct tab and adjusting the Shrink value. This may be useful for closing small holes that appear in the foreground section of the matte.

4. To examine the alpha matte directly, press the A key while the mouse is in the Viewer. Gray pixels indicate semi-transparency. Switch to the Density tab (Figure 5.13). Adjust the Brights and Darks parameters. Brights adjusts the intensity of the most intense foreground pixels. Darks adjusts the intensity of the least intense foreground pixels. Interactively set the Brights and Darks parameters by clicking the Matte + or Matte − button in the Primatte toolbar and Cmd/Ctrl-clicking, Cmd/Ctrl-dragging, or Cmd/Ctrl+Shift-dragging. The + button adds additional pixels to the foreground matte (pixels

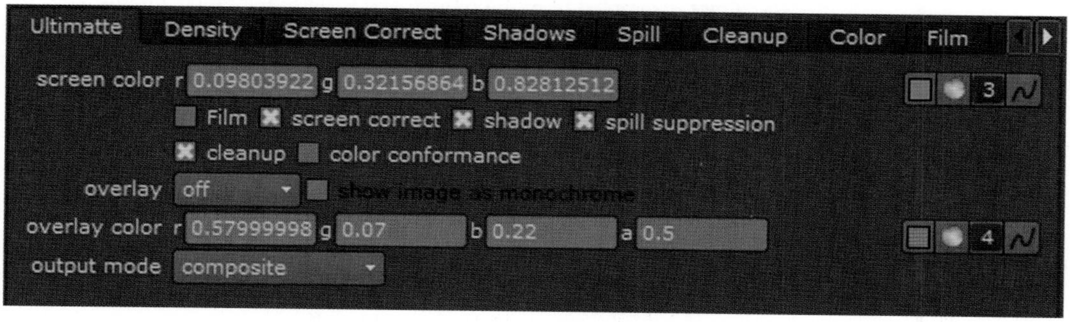

FIGURE 5.13 Ultimatte properties panel.

with a value of 1). The − button removes pixels from the foreground matte (and thereby assigns a value of 0).

5. If the foreground suffers from the excessive presence of the screen color (having arrived as spill) or is unduly altered by the automatic removal of the screen color, switch to the Spill tab. Adjust the Cool and Warm parameters, which control the amount of the screen color present in the foreground in cool-color areas and warm-color areas. You can also adjust the parameters to aesthetically alter the foreground color balance. To make this adjustment easier, return the Viewer to an RGB view and switch the Overlay menu back to Off.

6. If you use the Matte + or Matte − button in the Ultimatte toolbar, the Enable parameter of the Cleanup tab is automatically selected. You can also activate the parameter manually. The Cleanup parameter removes noise contained within the screen color (background) area of the matte. The higher the value, the more aggressive the removal of noise. You can blur the matte edge by raising the Blur parameter.

7. To output a premultiplied or unpremultiplied result, switch back to the Ultimatte tab and change the Output Mode to the appropriate option.

The Ultimatte node includes two additional input pipes: Gm (Garbage Mask) and Cp (Clean Plate). The Gm input accepts its namesake mask (see the Keylight section for a description). The Cp input is designed to accept a clean plate. A clean plate is used by the Screen Correction process of the node to remove inconsistencies that appear in the screen color area. Such inconsistencies may be caused by wrinkles in the chroma key fabric, shadows, film grain, video compression noise, smoke, or similar elements. If the Cp input remains unused, the node synthesizes a clean plate by examining the Fg input. The synthesized clean plate is significantly less accurate than an actual clean plate but can be useful for reducing anomalies caused by film grain or video compression artifacts. (A *plate* is a specific piece of film or video footage that is captured as a single shot and is intended for visual effects work.)

An example Ultimatte script is demonstrated in Figure 5.14. In this example, a sky is keyed from a bitmap featuring a mountain range and field. Screen Color is sampled from the bitmap and is set to light blue. Brights is set to 0.45, Darks is set to 126, and Blur is set to 4.7.

Primatte creates a key by generating a polyhedron shape within a 3D representation of the current color space. Pixels with values that fall within or on the shape are assigned transparency through the output alpha channel. The shape is established and altered by sampling pixels within the Viewer panel. To use Primatte, follow these basic steps:

1. Connect the Primatte node's Fg pipe to the output you wish to key. Optionally, connect the Bg pipe to an output that you wish to appear as a background. Connect the output of the Primatte node to a Viewer node.

FIGURE 5.14 A sky is keyed out with Ultimatte. A sample script is included as `ultimatte.nk` in the `Chapters/Chapter5/Scripts/` directory on the DVD.

2. Open the Primatte node's properties panel. Click the Current Color button (below the Operation menu) so that the eyedropper icon appears. In the Viewer, Cmd/Ctrl-click or Cmd/Ctrl+Shift-drag to sample the screen color. A matte is created and some of the pixels in the screen area become transparent, revealing the Bg input.

3. To fine-tune the resulting matte, step through the Operation menu. Each menu option allows you to make additional pixels transparent or return opaqueness to pixels previously sampled. Regardless of the Operation menu setting, select pixels in the Viewer with the Current Color button and the Cmd/Ctrl-click or Cmd/Ctrl+Shift-drag mouse operations.

4. By default, the Output Mode menu of the Primatte node is set to Composite. This allows the Bg input to appear. However, once the matte is created and you would like to use the Primatte's

output in conjunction with another part of the network, you must change the Output Mode menu to Premultiplied or Unpremultiplied. Once one of these two settings is chosen, the Bg input is disabled.

For a more detailed step-by-step guide, see "Tutorial 3: Removing an Imperfect Greenscreen" at the end of this chapter.

The Cover Composite

The cover illustration for this book, featuring a dancer in front of a mirror that reflects the grand hallway of an ornate building, was created in Nuke (Figure 5.15). The source footage features the dancer against a partial greenscreen (Figure 5.16).

FIGURE 5.15 The composited cover image.

FIGURE 5.16 The unaltered greenscreen plate.

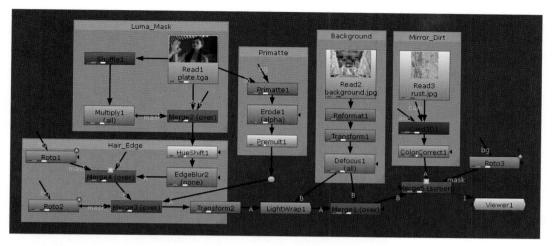

FIGURE 5.17 The node network used to create the composite. The backdrops indicate different sections of the network.

The node network is organized into several sections indicated by backdrop shapes (Figure 5.17). Following are brief descriptions of each network section.

Primatte. The greenscreen is removed using the Primatte plug-in. The resulting matte edge is softened with an Erode node. The result is premultiplied.

Luma_Mask. Because the Primatte node aggressively removes the fine hair detail of the dancer, a separate luma mask is created by copying the plate's red channel to the alpha with a Shuffle node, increasing the contrast of the alpha with a Multiply node, and recutting the plate with a Merge node that lacks an input B.

Hair_Edge. The luma mask result is fine-tuned with a EdgeBlur node and a HueShift node. The HueShift node removes the green spill trapped in the fine hairs. The luma mask result is then combined with the Primatte result through an additional Merge node. Parts of the set that are not covered by the greenscreen are cut away with two Roto nodes.

Background. The background image, which is a static bitmap, is thrown out of focus with a Defocus node and is rescaled, rotated, and repositioned with Reformat and Transform nodes.

Mirror_Dirt. Semi-transparent dirt is placed in the foreground by converting a texture bitmap into a 3D card, rotating the card, and color correcting it.

Ultimately, the dancer, the background, and the dirt are combined through two additional Merge nodes. The area the dirt appears is limited by masks drawn with an extra Roto node; the dirt is kept semi-transparent by using a Screen merge operation. The final result is color graded with a Color Correct node. A sample Nuke script is included as cover.nk in the

Chapters/Chapter5/Scripts/ directory on the DVD. (Please note that the background image and dirt texture are not included on the DVD due to copyright issues; however, you can replace the missing bitmaps with your own bitmaps through the empty Read nodes.)

Tutorial 3: Removing an Imperfect Greenscreen
Part 1: Keying with Primatte and Rotoscoping
Tutorial 3 takes you through the steps needed to remove a greenscreen (Figure 5.18).

FIGURE 5.18 A greenscreen setup that suffers from inconsistent color, shadows, and incomplete coverage.

The greenscreen suffers from the following problems:

- Inconsistent green color created by two different greenscreen fabrics.
- Wrinkles in the greenscreen, plus uneven lighting.
- Incomplete greenscreen coverage.
- Shadows from dancers on the greenscreen.

Nevertheless, using the Primatte keyer node, in addition to rotoscoping and using several additional filter nodes, provides a solution. (Note that Primatte is not available in the PLE version of Nuke; however, other keyers, such as Keyer or HueKeyer, are available.)

1. Create a new Nuke script. Choose Edit > Project Settings from the menu bar. In the Project Settings properties panel, set Full Size Format to 1280 × 720. If 1280 × 720 is not present in the menu list, choose New and enter the proper resolution in the New Format window.

2. Create a Read node. Browse for the `Tutorials/Tutorial3/ Plates/greenscreen/` directory and select the `greenscreen.##.tga 1 30` image sequence. Connect Viewer1 to the Read1 node. The sequence features two dancers crossing in front of a greenscreen.

3. In the Node Graph, RMB-click and choose Image > Constant. Select the Read1 node, RMB-click, and choose Keyer > Primatte. Connect the Bg input pipe of the Primatte1 node to the output of the Constant1 node. Open the Constant1 node's properties panel and change the Color to a hue that's easily seen, such as red. The Bg pipe of the Primatte node allows you to add a background, which will show in the area where the greenscreen has been removed. This offers a convenient means to test the effectiveness of the greenscreen removal.

4. The Primatte node works in its default state. However, it will remove the area of the input that is black. Open the Primatte1 node's properties panel (Figure 5.19). Click the Current Color

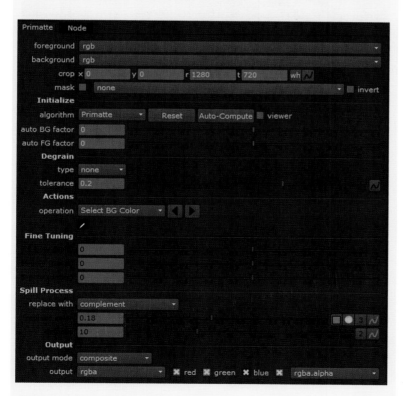

FIGURE 5.19 A Primatte properties panel in its default state.

button so that its eyedrop icon appears (the button is below the Operation menu). Place the mouse in the Viewer and Cmd/ Ctrl-click over the greenscreen to sample the greenscreen color. You can also Cmd/Ctrl+Shift-drag to draw a selection marquee and thereby select a group of pixels to average. For this tutorial, it's best to sample an area of the shadow to the left of the dancers as they pass. This ensures that the shadow is removed along with the more intensely bright areas of the greenscreen. As the green is removed, the green areas become semi-transparent or transparent. This allows the color of the Constant1 node to show through. Note that the green carried by the dancers' skin tone and the background walls is partially removed at this point (Figure 5.20).

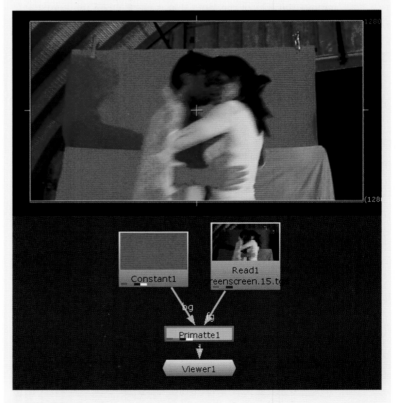

FIGURE 5.20 The initial key.

5. In the Primatte node's properties panel, change the Operation menu to Clean BG Noise. Cmd/Ctrl+Shift-drag selection marquees over areas of the greenscreen that are not fully transparent. For example, sample the lower right of the greenscreen, which contains brighter greens.

6. Change the Operation menu to Clean FG Noise. Cmd/Ctrl+Shift-drag selection boxes over areas of the dancers that have become transparent. This restores opaqueness to the dancers. You can restore all clothing and skin of the dancers without unduly altering the greenscreen area. Alter between Clean BG Noise and Clean FG Noise to produce the best result (Figure 5.21). You can reset the node at any time

FIGURE 5.21 The key is improved by utilizing the Clean BG Noise and Clean FG Noise operations.

by clicking the Reset button beside the Algorithm parameter; however, you will have to reselect a color through the Current Color button. While adjusting the Primatte node, save the script on a regular basis. It can be difficult to back up to an optimal step in the process by simply using Edit > Undo or Cmd/Ctrl+Z. As you adjust the node, move the time marker to different frames of the timeline to properly judge the results.

7. At this stage, green spill is trapped in the dancers' clothing and skin tone. You can reduce this by switching the Operation menu to Spill(−) and sampling the greenish area along the dancer's white clothing. While you are adjusting the various parameters of the Primatte1 node, feel free to examine the alpha channel of the

output. To do so, place the mouse in the Viewer panel and press the A key. Examining the alpha channel allows you to spot areas that remain semi-transparent (with values that are gray instead of black). You can return to the RGB view by pressing the A key again.

8. Once the greenscreen is removed, examine the edge quality of the resulting alpha matte. Due to the motion blur present in the video, along with native compression artifacts, the edge of the dancers appears rough and stairstepped. You can reduce this by adding an additional filter node. Select the Primatte1 node, RMB-click, and choose Filter > Erode (Blur). Open the Erode1 node's properties panel. Note that the Channels menu is set to None and the right Additional Channels menu is set to Rgba.alpha. Thus, the RBG channels are unaffected by the node. With the Erode1 node selected, RMB-click and choose Merge > Premult. To use the Erode1 node successfully, its output must be premultiplied. Open the Primatte1 node's properties panel. Note that the Output Mode menu, near the bottom of the panel, is set to Composite by default. This allows the Constant1 node to appear behind the image sequence. Switch the menu to Unpremultiplied. The constant color disappears. This step is also necessary to accurately gauge the Erode1 node's influence. Open the Erode1 node's properties panel. Adjust the Size and Blur parameters. Blur controls the size of a triangle convolution filter that averages the pixel values along the alpha edge and thus softens it (Figure 5.22). Higher values result in a wider, softer edge. Size shrinks the matte created by the Blur parameter, thus eroding it. For example, if Size is set to 5, the matte is eroded by five pixels. If Blur is a nonzero value, the taper from 100% transparency to 0% transparency remains soft. If you are unable to see the effect of a large Blur value, slowly raise the Size value.

9. The Erode1 node may erode the bottom edge of the matte. Thus, a gap opens up between the dancers and the frame edge. To quickly solve this problem, select the Premult1 node, RMB-click, choose Transform > Transform, and interactively move the dancers downward so that the gap disappears.

10. At this point, you can add a background image to make the composite more interesting. To do so, create a new Read node and import a bitmap or image sequence. A sample bitmap is

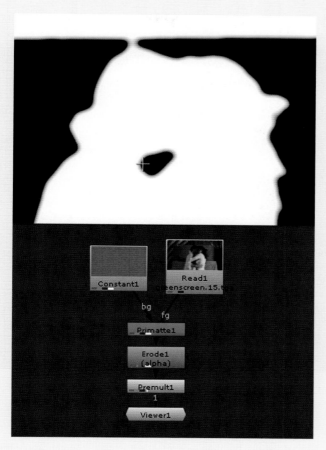

FIGURE 5.22 Close-up of the alpha channel. The matte edge is softened with the addition of Erode and Premult nodes.

included as `cave.tif` in the `Tutorials/Tutorial3/Bitmaps/` directory on the DVD. With no nodes selected, create a Merge node. Connect the input A pipe to the output of the Transform1 node. Connect the input B pipe to the output of the Read2 node. The dancers appear over the new background image (Figure 5.23).

11. At this stage, a portion of the set that was not covered by the greenscreen material remains visible. To remove the various

FIGURE 5.23 The output of the Premult1 node is moved down in Y with the Transform1 node. This prevents the appearance of a gap along the bottom of the dancers. A background is added through the Merge1 node.

parts of the building, you must rotoscope. You can apply the rotoscoping in two steps: a garbage mask to cut away the building and a second mask to restore the parts of the dancers that extend over the edge of the greenscreen. To create a garbage mask create a new Roto node (Draw > Roto), connect the output of the Read1 node to the Bg input of the Roto1 node, and connect a new Viewer to the output of the Roto1 node. After switching to the new Viewer tab, move the time marker to frame 1 and draw a closed shape that encompasses the building (Figure 5.24). Note that you can place points outside the bounding box. For more information on the Roto node and rotoscoping techniques, see Chapter 4. Move the time marker to frame 30. Adjust the shape. Because there is a slight left-to-right camera movement, two keyframe positions are necessary for the garbage mask.

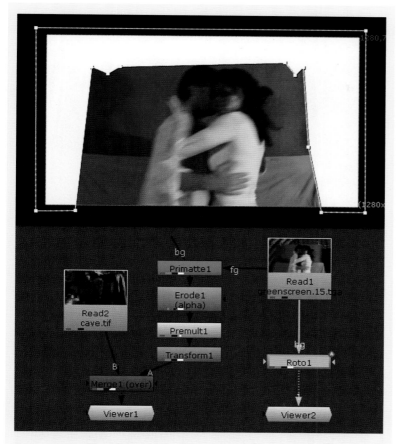

FIGURE 5.24 A bezier shape is drawn with a Roto node.

12. To convert the new shape into a functioning alpha matte, connect the output of the Roto1 node to the Mask input of the Merge1 node. Switch back to the Viewer1 tab. The dancers are cut out but the building remains. Open the Roto1 node's properties panel. Select the Inverted button beside the Bezier1 curve in the Curves section. The button features a small box with a diagonal line. Once the Inverted button is selected, the matte is inverted and the building is cut away (Figure 5.25).

13. Play back the timeline. The dancers are cut by the garbage matte as they move past the edge of the greenscreen. To restore the dancers, you can apply additional rotoscoping. To do so, create a new Roto node, connect the output of Read1 to the Bg of Roto2, and connect the output of Roto2 to Viewer2. Switch to the

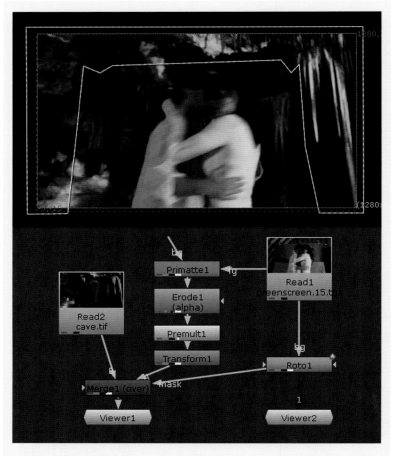

FIGURE 5.25 The shape is converted into a matte by connecting the output of the Roto1 node to the Mask input of the Merge1 node. The Inverted button for the shape is activated in the Curves section of the Roto1 properties panel.

Viewer2 tab. Move the time marker to frame 1. Draw a shape in the Viewer that covers the left side of the dancers. Once the shape is closed, it's filled with solid white. If you'd like to see through the fill to the image sequence, temporarily set the Roto2 node's Opacity parameter to 0. Alternatively, you can deselect the node's Visible button (Figure 5.26). Adjust the point smoothness and point feather to match the contours of the dancers and the softness of the inherent motion blur. Move to a different frame, such as frame 5. Adjust the shape to match the dancers' contours. The new point positions are automatically stored in a new keyframe. Continue to refine the shape over the course of the timeline.

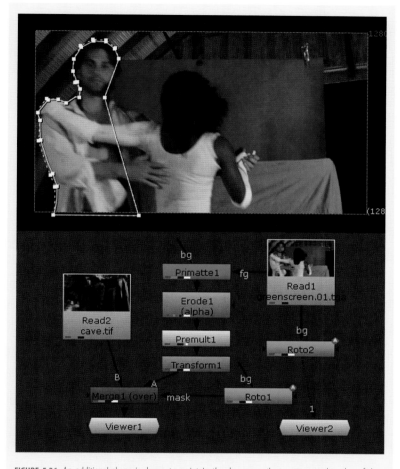

FIGURE 5.26 An additional shape is drawn to maintain the dancers as they move past the edge of the greenscreen. The Visible parameter for the shape is temporarily deselected so that the fill color does not obscure the image.

14. To utilize the alpha matte created by the Roto2 node, connect the output of Roto2 to the Bg input of Roto1. Such a connection adds the two alpha mattes together through an Over operation before sending the result to the Mask input of the Merge1 node. (The Opacity parameter of Roto1 and Roto2 must be set to 1 and the Visibility button of both shapes must be reactivated.) Switch to the Viewer1 tab to view the result (Figure 5.27). You can continue to refine the Roto2 shape. To make the bezier shape visible in the Viewer, open the Roto2 node's properties panel.

FIGURE 5.27 The alpha mattes of Roto1 and Roto2 are combined by connecting the output of Roto2 to the Bg input of Roto1. As seen on frame 1, the dancers are no longer cut off by the Roto1 shape.

This concludes Part 1 of Tutorial 3. A sample Nuke script is included as `Tutorial3.1.nk` in the `Tutorials/Tutorial3/Scripts/` directory on the DVD. In Chapter 6, we'll adjust the keyed greenscreen and the background bitmap with various filters to create better integration.

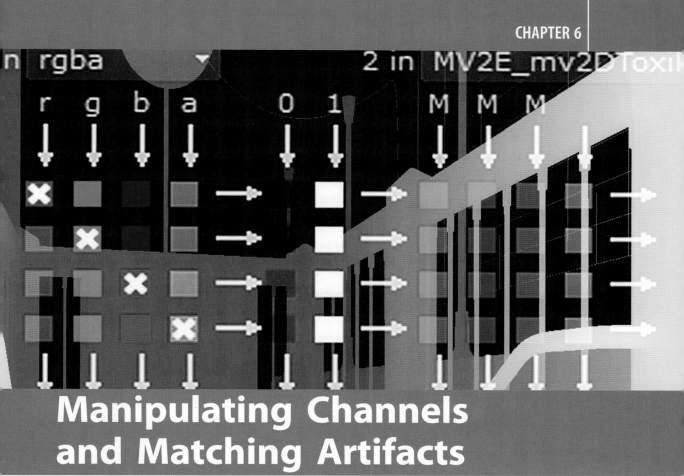

Manipulating Channels and Matching Artifacts

Any given node within Nuke affects specific channels. You do not have to limit yourself to the channels carried by an imported bitmap or image sequence. You can add, delete, copy, merge, and shuffle channels. You can work with common channels, such as RGB and alpha, or work with more esoteric ones like Depth and Motion. When manipulating specific channels, you can apply various Nuke filter nodes. While filter nodes designed for color manipulation are discussed in Chapter 3, ones specific to artifact matching or artifact removal are discussed in this chapter. (Various artifacts, such as blur and grain, are naturally produced by motion picture and video cameras.) In addition, Nuke offers various nodes that create stylistic results, apply custom filter effects through convolution math, and affect the quality to alpha matte edges.

This chapter includes the following critical information:

- Adding, shuffling, merging, deleting, and copying channels
- Adjusting alpha matte edges

- Applying convolution filters, including blurs, sharpens, and light effects
- Adding and removing noise and grain

Adding, Shuffling, and Combining Channels

As discussed in previous chapters, you can determine what channels a node affects by setting the node's Channels menu (Figure 6.1). The node indicates the affected channels by drawing long channel lines along the bottom left of the node icon in the Node Graph. If a channel is unaffected by the node (whereby the channel values remain unchanged), a short channel line is drawn.

FIGURE 6.1 The Channels menu set to the Rgba channel set.

Note that the Channels menu actually determines which channel set is used. A *channel set*, also referred to as a *layer*, is simply a group of channels. For example, if the Channels menu is changed to Rgba, the channel set includes red, green, blue, and alpha channels.

You can add one or more new channels to a node by utilizing one of Nuke's channel manipulation nodes. Additionally, you can delete, copy, merge, and shift channels. The channels may be RGB color channels, alpha channels, or specialty channels, which are described in this section.

Depth. The Depth channel, often called a Z-buffer or Z-depth channel, encodes the distance that objects are from the camera through grayscale values. (Technically, the values are scalar, in that any given pixel holds a single intensity value.) Objects close to the camera receive higher values. Objects far from the camera receive lower values (see Figure 6.11 later in this chapter). Depth channels allow the compositing program to place effects in virtual depth. For example, a blur may be placed in the background but not the foreground. Depth channels are demonstrated in the section "Working with Depth Channels" later in this chapter. A limited number of image formats, such as OpenEXR, can carry a depth channel in addition to RGB and alpha channels.

Motion. When a Channels menu is set to the Motion channel set, four separate motion vector channels are included: forward.u, forward.v, backward.u, and backward.v. In general, motion vectors encode the movement of every pixel within a frame from the current frame to the next frame or from the prior frame to the current frame. The movement is stored as color values, whereby any left/right X axis movement is stored in the u channel and any down/up Y axis movement is stored in the v channel. Forward channels encode movement from the current frame to the next frame, while backward channels encode movement from the prior frame to the current frame. You may find it necessary to add Motion channels when importing motion vector renders generated by an external 3D program. Additionally, Nuke provides several nodes that can generate motion vectors or convert the vectors into motion blur; hence, the presence of Motion channels allows the passing of motion vector information between nodes. Motion channels are demonstrated in the section "Motion Blurring" later in this chapter.

Forward and **Backward.** When a Channels menu is set to the Forward channel set, the forward.u and forward.v channels are provided. When a Channels menu is set to the Backward channel set, the backward.u and backward.v channels are provided.

Mask. A Mask channel is designed to carry alpha matte information.

RotoPaint_Mask. A RotoPaint_Mask channel is specifically designed for its namesake. You have the option to output the spline shapes or paint strokes generated by a RotoPaint node as an alpha matte by selecting the RotoPaint node's Output Mask parameter and setting the Output Mask menu to Rotopaint_mask.a. For more information on the RotoPaint node, see Chapter 4.

Adding and Removing Channels

You can add a channel to an output by connecting an AddChannels node (Channel > Add). The channel is set by the AddChannels node's Channels menu. The value given to the new channel is determined by the Color parameter, as shown in Figure 6.2. For example, the output of a Read node may lack an alpha channel. (If a bitmap or image sequence imported through the Read node lacks alpha, the Read node will not add the alpha information.) Hence, you can connect an AddChannels node to the Read node's output and change the AddChannels node's Channels menu to Alpha. If Color is set to 0-black, the alpha channel is 100% transparent. If Color is set to 1-white, the alpha channel is 100% opaque.

FIGURE 6.2 The AddChannels properties panel. The node is set to add an alpha channel to the input. The Color parameter determines the alpha value.

You can add multiple channels with the AddChannels node by setting the Channels2, Channels3, or Channels4 menu to a nonempty value (each menu

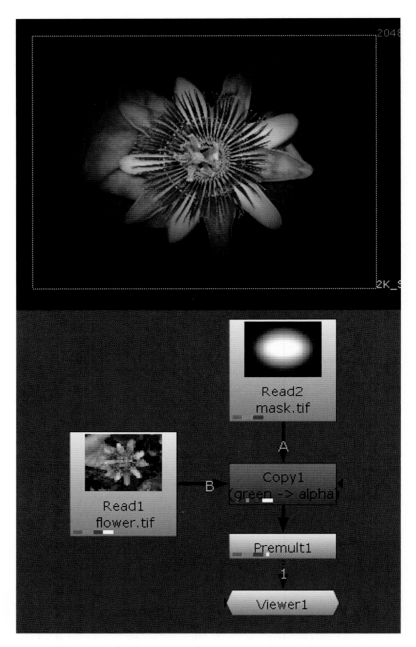

FIGURE 6.3 The alpha channel of a bitmap is replaced by the green channel of a second bitmap through the use of a Copy node. The output is thereby masked. A sample script is included as `copychannel.nk` in the `Chapters/Chapter6/Scripts/` directory on the DVD.

sits to the right of a word *and*). However, each new channel receives its value from the Color parameter.

The Remove node (Channel > Remove) lets you delete a channel by selecting the channel name from the Channels menu. You can delete additional channels through the Channels2, Channels3, and Channels4 menus.

Copying Channels

You can copy a channel from one node to another node by using the Copy node. To do so, follow these steps:

1. Choose Channel > Copy. Connect the input A of the new Copy node to the node that will provide the copied channels. Connect the input B of the Copy node to the node that will accept the copied channels.
2. Open the Copy node's properties panel. Select one or more channels to be copied by setting the Copy Channel From column menus. Select the channels that will be overwritten through the copy by setting the To column menus.

As an example, in Figure 6.3, the opaque alpha channel of a bitmap featuring a flower is overwritten by the green channel of a mask bitmap. The output is therefore masked by an oval shape.

Shuffling Channels

The ShuffleCopy node (Channel > ShuffleCopy) lets you copy the channels of two input nodes to create a synthesized output. The node's properties panel carries three columns of checkboxes (Figure 6.4). The left column represents the channels brought in by the input 1 pipe. The center column features an optional series of 0 and 1 checkboxes that allow you to set an output channel value to exactly 0 or 1. The right column represents the channels brought in by the input 2 pipe. The output channels are indicated by the left-to-right arrows that run along the rows. By default, only the output 1 pipe is activated, as is indicated by the Rgba setting of the Out1 menu to the far right of the panel. The Out2 menu, below the Out1 menu, is set to None.

You can decide which input channel will become the red, green, blue, and alpha channels for output 1 by selecting the column checkboxes. For example, if you wanted the output alpha to be taken from input 1, select the checkbox that lines up with the input 1 alpha column (labeled *a*) and select the output alpha row. If you want the output alpha channel to carry a value of 1, select the 1 checkbox that lines up with the central column and the output alpha row. You can mix and match the channel selections. For example, in Figures 6.4 and 6.5, input 1 has its red and blue channels swapped while the green and alpha channels are left intact. In this case, input 2 is ignored (no channels are selected in the input 2 column).

FIGURE 6.4 The red and blue channels of a landscape are swapped with a ShuffleCopy node.

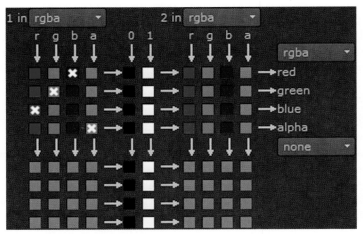

FIGURE 6.5 The ShuffleCopy node's properties panel, as set up for Figure 6.4. A sample script is included as shufflecopy1.nk in the Chapters/Chapter6/Scripts/ directory on the DVD.

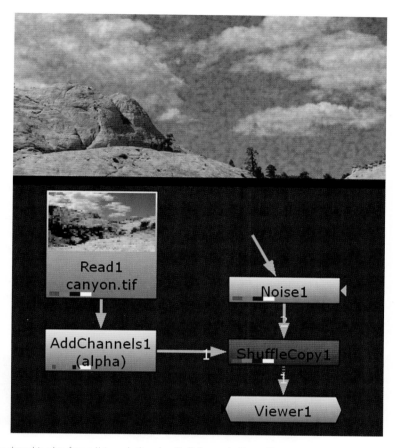

FIGURE 6.6 The blue channel is taken from a Noise node through a ShuffleCopy node. Thus, a blue noisy pattern appears over the landscape.

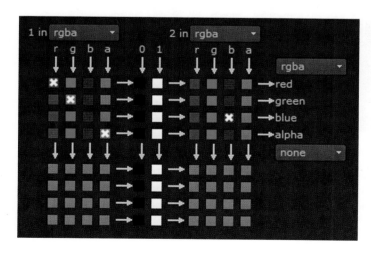

FIGURE 6.7 The ShuffleCopy node's properties panel, as set for Figure 6.6. A sample script is included as `shufflecopy2.nk` in the `Chapters/Chapter6/Scripts/` directory on the DVD.

As a second example, in Figures 6.6 and 6.7, the red, green, and alpha channels are taken from input 1 while the blue channel is taken from input 2. Because input 2 is connected to a Noise node, a noisy, grainlike pattern appears over the landscape.

When choosing input channels for inputs 1 and 2, you are not limited to RGBA. You can change the In1 and In2 menus, at the top of the columns, to any standard channel set or channel. The checkbox labels update to reflect the menu changes. You are equally free to change the Out1 and Out2 menus to channel sets or channels of your choice.

When you change the Out2 menu from None to a channel set or channel, the bottom block of checkboxes becomes unghosted. However, the node retains a single output. The Out2 menu allows you to add four additional channels to the output. For example, Out1 can output the Rgba channel set while Out2 outputs the Motion channel set, which includes forward.u, forward.v, backward.u, and backward.v channels. For example, in Figure 6.8, input 1 provides the Rgba channel set and input 2 provides the Motion channel set. In this case, the In2 menu and the Out2 menu must both be set to Motion to read and output the Motion channels. The column 2 checkboxes automatically change to u, v, u, v.

FIGURE 6.8 The ShuffleCopy node combines the RGBA channels of input 1 and the Motion uvuv channels of input 2 into a single eight-channel output.

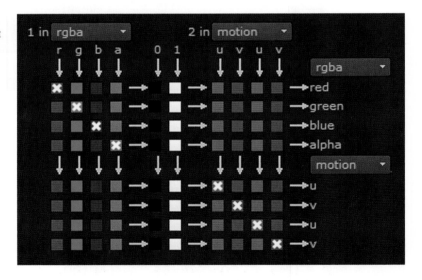

In addition, Nuke provides the Shuffle node. The Shuffle node carries the same functionality as the ShuffleCopy node, but only accepts one input. Hence, Shuffle is suitable for shifting channels within a single source.

Merging Channels

You can merge channels from one or two inputs with the ChannelMerge node (Channel > ChannelMerge). The merge is achieved by applying a mathematical merge operation as determined by the Operation menu. The node merges a single channel from input A and input B as defined by the A Channel and B Channel menus. The result is fed to the channel defined by the Output menu. If input A remains unconnected, both input channels are taken from input B. Any channel that is not chosen by the Output menu is taken from input B and is unaltered. As an example, in Figure 6.9, two alpha channels are combined with a ChannelMerge node. The Operation menu is set to Max, which outputs the brightest pixel value when comparing pixels between the two inputs. In this example, the RGB values of the original bitmaps are passed to alpha channels via Shuffle nodes.

Working with Depth Channels

Nuke provides two nodes, through the Filter menu, that are specifically designed for working with Depth channels: ZBlur and ZSlice. ZBlur creates a synthetic depth-of-field effect by reading a Depth channel (Figure 6.10). The strength of the resulting blur is set by the Size parameter, while the maximum amount of blur carried by distant objects is set by the Maximum parameter. The value within the Depth channel that is considered the center of the depth of field (the area in focus) is determined by the Focus Plane (C) parameter. To read the Depth channel appropriately, you must set the Math menu to a specific interpolation. For example, if the Depth channel was generated by Maya, set Math to Far$=-0$. Maya encodes Z values as -1 / `distance from camera` (Figure 6.11). For hints on which Math setting to use, hold your mouse over the Math menu to see the help dialog. The size of the depth of field is set by the Depth-Of-Field parameter; smaller values create a narrower focal range. If adjusting the node's parameters becomes difficult, temporarily select the Focal-Plane Setup parameter. This displays a false-color map where green represents the area within the focal range, red represents areas past the focal range, and blue represents areas in front of the focal range and areas with no geometry.

The ZSlice node, on the other hand, creates an alpha matte based on values contained within a depth file. A range of depth values are converted to opaque alpha, while depth values outside the range are converted to transparent alpha. The center of the range is established by the Center Of Slice parameter, while the size of the range is controlled by the Field Width parameter.

Note that Nuke automatically detects Depth channels. If a Depth channel exists, it's represented as a purple line to the right of the alpha line on the node icon. To view the Depth channel in the Viewer, change the Viewer's

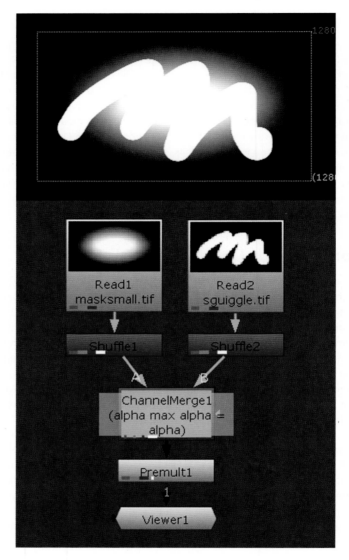

FIGURE 6.9 The alpha channels of two inputs are merged with a ChannelMerge node. A sample script is included as `channelmerge.nk` in the `Chapters/Chapter6/Scripts/` directory on the DVD.

center Channels menu from Rgba.alpha to Depth.Z and change the Display Style menu from RGB to A (Figure 6.12). (The center Channels menu allows you to replace the alpha channel with a different channel for viewing.) Despite these settings, the Depth channel may appear pure black. For example, a Depth channel created in Maya produces negative values. You can see the values if you place your mouse over the Depth channel and

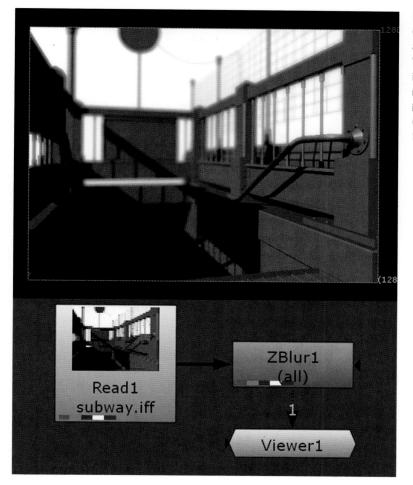

FIGURE 6.10 A synthetic depth-of-field effect added to a 3D render through a Depth channel and a ZBlur node. While the back of the subway entrance is out of focus, the foreground railing remains in focus. A sample script is included as `zblur.nk` in the `Chapters/Chapter6/ Scripts/` directory on the DVD.

watch the alpha value readout at the bottom of the Viewer panel. Also note that Nuke can read Maya IFF files, as illustrated by Figures 6.10 and 6.11, but cannot write Maya IFF files back out.

Alternatively, you can employ a Depth channel as a mask with a Merge node. For example, in Figure 6.13, a Depth channel creates an alpha matte that determines where the output of a Noise node appears over a blue field created by a Constant node. In this case, the Merge node's Channel Mask menu is set to Depth.Z and the Invert parameter is selected. Because the Depth channel is generated by Maya, it's necessary to multiply the depth values by a large negative number (which creates positive depth values) through a Multiply node. (For more information on Math nodes, see Chapter 10.)

The ZMerge node (Merge > ZMerge) allows you to combine two depth channels. Depth channel pixels considered "closest" to the camera are output by the node.

FIGURE 6.11 The Depth channel (as seen in Maya).

FIGURE 6.12 The two Channels menus (left and center) and Display Style menu (right) set to display a Depth channel.

Adjusting Alpha Mattes

When you generate an alpha matte, either through keying, rotoscoping, or creating a luma matte, it is often necessary to adjust the matte edges. The edges may suffer from stairstepping, where there is harsh transition from 0-alpha to 1-alpha, or the matte may be an incorrect size, causing the matte to fit the foreground element in an ill fashion. Nuke offers the following nodes in the Filter menu that target matte edges.

EdgeBlur softens the matte edge by adding a blurred copy of the edge to the RGB and alpha channels (Figure 6.14). The strength of the blur is set by the Size parameter, while the Edge Mult parameter erodes or expands the blurred area. For example, if Edge Mult is set to a low value, the blurred area is narrow; if Edge Mult is set to a high value, the blurred area is wide. You can adjust the color and brightness of the blurred area by adjusting the Tint and Brightness parameters.

Dilate, which is listed as Erode (Fast) in the Filter menu, provides a simple means to erode or expand the alpha matte. Negative Size values erode the matte, while positive values expand the matte. To avoid disturbing the

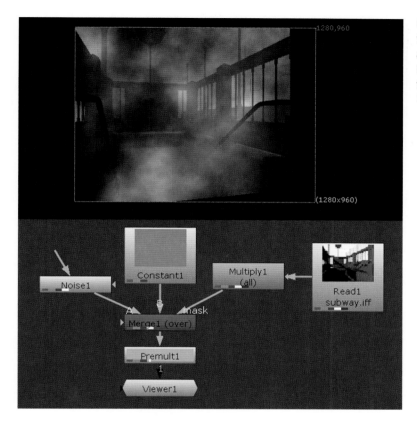

FIGURE 6.13 A Depth channel is used to mask a Noise node output through a Merge node. A sample script is included as zdepthmask.nk in the Chapters/Chapter6/Scripts/ directory on the DVD.

FIGURE 6.14 (Left) Close-up of an alpha matte edge. (Right) The edge after application of an EdgeBlur node with default settings. A sample script is included as edgeblur.nk in the Chapters/Chapter6/Scripts/ directory on the DVD.

173

RGB channels, set the Channels menu to Alpha. Connect a Premult node to the Dilate node's output to properly employ the resulting alpha matte. **FilterErode**, which is listed as Erode (Filter), works in the same manner as the Dilate node. However the FilterErode node adds a Filter parameter, which allows you to choose the exact style of convolution filter that erodes or expands the matte edge. For example, if Filter is set to the default Box, the node creates a result identical to Dilate, where the expanded matte edge features oversized, square pixels. If Filter is set to Gaussian, the resulting pattern along the edge is much smoother. Note that the FilterErode node's Channels menu is set to None and the Additional Channels menu is set to Rgba.alpha by default. Much like the Dilate node, you must connect a Premult node to the FilterErode node's output to properly employ the resulting alpha matte.

Erode, which is listed as Erode (Blur), offers a high-quality means to erode or expand the matte edge. This is achieved by blurring the edge and clamping the resulting values to maintain a relatively quick transition from 0-alpha to 1-alpha. The Size parameter sets the number of pixels by which the matte is shrunk or grown. Blur adds additional softening to the resulting matte edge; higher Blur values create a softer edge. The Quality parameter determines the quality of the initial edge blur: low Quality values create a stairstepped matte edge but will render more quickly; high Quality settings create a smoother matte edge. For a working example of the Erode node, see the Chapter 5 tutorial "Removing an Imperfect Greenscreen."

Matching Film and Video Artifacts

When motion picture film or digital video is shot, it creates distinct artifacts. The artifacts include depth-of-field blur, motion blur, noise, grain, and patterns created by the lens optics. Compositors are often required to recreate such artifacts so that various elements within the composite match or remain stylistically consistent.

Blurring and Convolution Filters

In the real world, a camera may produce an image that is partially blurred. The blur results from objects falling within an area outside the camera's depth of field. A *depth of field* is a range that a camera is able to sharply focus. Areas outside the depth of field are unfocused and thus appear blurry. Real-world camera lenses are able to focus at a specific distance. Depth of fields may be wide or narrow, depending on the lens length, the camera's aperture setting (f-stop), and the amount of available light (e.g., daytime versus nighttime).

Because depth of fields are an inherent part of photography, cinematography, and videography, the ability to blur elements is an important part of compositing. Aside from recreating depth of field, blurs are stylistically useful for softening elements. Nuke provides several blur filters. The filters are dependent on convolutions. A *convolution filter* slides a kernel over the image matrix to create averaged pixel color values. A *matrix* is a rectangular array of numbers arranged into columns and rows. Each pixel of a digital image provides a color value to each image matrix cell. A *kernel* is also a matrix, but is usually smaller than the image matrix and includes values derived from a specific filter function, such as a blur or sharpen.

The following are descriptions of Nuke's various blur filters, all of which are available through the Filter menu.

Blur employs a two-pass convolution filter. The size of the filter kernel matrix is set by the Size parameter. The larger the Size value, the more intense the blur. The style of convolution filter is set by the Filter parameter. The Box filter provides a simple and efficient kernel matrix but tends to produce horizontal and vertical edge streaking. The Triangle filter improves the blur by using a matrix that is sensitive to pixel distance. Quadratic and Gaussian filters provide two matrix variations that combine high-quality averaging with a maintenance of object edge detail. Each filter name refers to the shape of the filter function curve that ultimately creates the values used by the corresponding kernel matrix. (Box and Triangle filters use curves in their namesake shapes, while Quadratic and Gaussian filters use bell-shaped curves.) The Blur node's Quality parameter determines the overall quality of the blur. In effect, low Quality values cause the node to temporarily downscale in input, which causes the output to become blocky and pixelated.

Soften creates a namesake effect by adding a blurred copy of the input to the input (Figure 6.15). This creates a foggy, glowlike look. The blurred copy is created by applying Laplacian and blur convolution filters. Laplacian filters are designed to detect and separate high-contrast edges. The node's Size and Filter parameters control the blur and function in the same manner as the Blur node. The Minimum and Maximum parameters control the value range targeted by the Laplacian filter. If the value difference between Minimum and Maximum is small, fewer edges are separated. The Amount parameter controls the degree to which the blurred edges are added back to the original input.

Defocus creates a bokeh-based blur. A *bokeh* is a specific shape created by a lens when a point of light is out of focus. A bokeh corresponds to the shape of the camera aperture opening and generally takes on a circular or polygonal form. The Defocus node creates a circular bokeh (Figure 6.16). The intensity of the blur is set by the Defocus parameter. The height-to-width ratio of the circular bokeh is determined by the Aspect Ratio parameter. Values larger than 1 create an oval-shaped bokeh. The overall scale of the bokeh is set by the Scaling parameter. Large Scaling values create a large kernel matrix, which significantly slows the calculation.

FIGURE 6.15 A Soften node adds a foggy, glowlike blur to an image. A sample script is included as `soften.nk` in the `Chapters/Chapter6/Scripts/` directory on the DVD.

FIGURE 6.16 Close-up of background detail blurred with a Defocus node. Small, bright areas take on a circular shape. A sample script is included as `defocus.nk` in the `Chapters/Chapter6/Scripts/` directory on the DVD.

Convolve allows you to create a custom bokeh blur by converting an input to a kernal matrix and applying a convolution (Figure 6.17). The node converts input A into the matrix and applies the matrix to input B. You can connect a bitmap to input A through a Read node or use the output of another filter node. Because a convolution matrix can be computationally expensive, it is best to keep the resolution of input A small (e.g., 32 × 32). If necessary, you can insert a Crop node (Transform > Crop) between the input node and the Convolve node. With a Crop node, you can crop an input by defining the position of the left (X), bottom (Y), right (W), and top (H) edges.

DirBlur streaks an input along a vector defined by two handles (Figure 6.18). The BlurType parameter determines whether the node forms a linear motion blur, a zoom blur (the input is streaked toward the frame edge), or a radial blur. The BlurCenter handle defines the center of the zoom and radial blurs. The Target handle defines the direction of the linear blur, but is only active if the UseTarget parameter is selected;

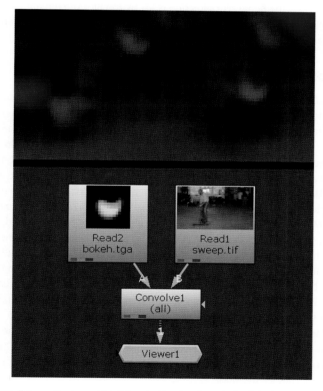

FIGURE 6.17 Close-up of background detail blurred with a Convolve node. Small, bright areas take on a U shape, as defined by a bitmap connected to the Convolve node's input A. A sample script is included as convolve.nk in the Chapters/Chapter6/Scripts/ directory on the DVD.

FIGURE 6.18 A zoom blur is created with the DirBlur node. A sample script is included as `dirblur.nk` in the `Chapters/Chapter6/Scripts/` directory on the DVD.

otherwise, the linear blur direction is set by the BlurAngle parameter. You can interactively LMB-drag both handles in the Viewer. The BlurLength parameter sets its namesake.

Motion Blurring

As discussed in previous chapters, you can activate motion blur through a Transform node's Motionblur parameter. If the transform properties of the node are animated over time, a motion blur steak appears. You can also create motion blur with MotionBlur2D and VectorBlur nodes (found in the Filter menu). For example, in Figure 6.19, a motion blur is added to a bitmap with an animated Transform node. The MotionBlur2D node carries two input pipes. The 2DTransf pipe accepts motion vector channels. When 2DTransf is connected to a Transform node, forward.u and forward.v channels are passed to the MotionBlur2D node. The second input pipe, which is unlabeled, accepts the input that is to be blurred. In Figure 6.19, the unlabeled input is connected through a dot so that the pipe remains visible. The MotionBlur2D node carries Shutter and Shutter Offset properties that are identical to those carried by the Transform node. Shutter determines how long the virtual shutter is open. If shutter is set to 0.5, the shutter is open for a half frame. Shutter Offset determines when the shutter opens. If Shutter Offset is set to Start, the shutter opens on the current frame, which is identical to the way a real-world camera functions. By default, the MotionBlur2D node's Output UV parameter is set to Motion; nevertheless, forward.u and forward.v chan-nels are output by the node.

To convert the MotionBlur2D node's output to an actual blur, the output is connected to a VectorBlur node. The VectorBlur node's UV Channels parameter is set to Motion. Multiply scales the motion vector channel values.

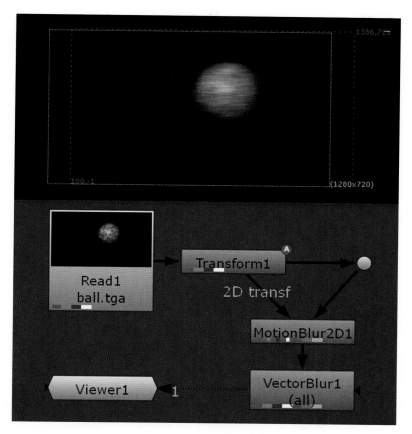

FIGURE 6.19 Motion blur is added to an input with MotionBlur2D and VectorBlur nodes. A sample script is included as `motionblur2d.nk` in the `Chapters/Chapter6/Scripts/` directory on the DVD.

The larger the Multiply value, the longer the blur streak becomes. If the VectorBlur node is connected to a MotionBlur2D node, Multiply scales the shutter duration set by the MotionBlur2D node's Shutter parameter. Offset further offsets when the shutter opens. The MotionBlur2D node uses two forms of blur calculation, as set by the Method parameter: Backward and Forward. The Method names refer to algorithms and do not refer to the specific motion vector channels passed to the node. The Backward method is efficient while producing a good result. The Forward method is more accurate but is extremely slow.

Alternatively, the VectorBlur node can accept motion vector channels from imported sources. For example, in Figure 6.20, a Maya-rendered OpenEXR image sequence that carries RGBA as well as custom motion vector channels is imported through the Read1 node. To transfer the custom motion vector channels to forward UV channels in Nuke, the output of the Read1 node is

The FurnanceCore plug-in set includes the F_MotionBlur node (The plug-ins appear in the Furnace or the FurnanceCore menu, depending on which version of Nuke you are running.) F_Motion-Blur uses motion estimation (tracking pixel value movement across multiple frames) to produce motion vectors. As such, the node is able to add additional motion blur to objects that are moving within an image sequence or movie. It requires a single input through the Src pipe. The Shutter Time param-eter sets the virtual shutter duration in frames while the Shutter Samples parameter sets the number of in-between images the node used to produce the motion blur streaks. The node provides optional input pipes for per-calculated motion estimation vectors and an alpha matte used to separate foreground and background objects.

For more information on the F_MotionBlur node, see the "User Guide for Furnace" PDF available at The Foundry's website (*www. thefoundry.co.uk*).

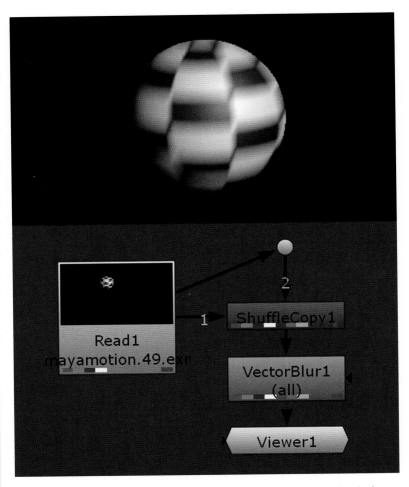

FIGURE 6.20 A VectorBlur node creates motion blur by reading the custom motion vector channels of an OpenEXR image sequence rendered in Maya. Note that the presence of custom channels is indicated by the dark green line at the far right of the node icons. A sample script is included as `motionimport.nk` in the `Chapters/Chapter6/Scripts/` directory on the DVD.

connected to a ShuffleCopy node (Figure 6.21). The resulting motion blur is created solely within Nuke. For a comparison of Backward and Forward method algorithms, as well as an additional working example of the VectorBlur node, see Tutorial 5, "Adding Motion Blur to a CG Render" in Chapter 7.

The MotionBlur3D node can produce similar motion blur for 3D objects animated within Nuke's 3D environment. This node is discussed in Chapter 9.

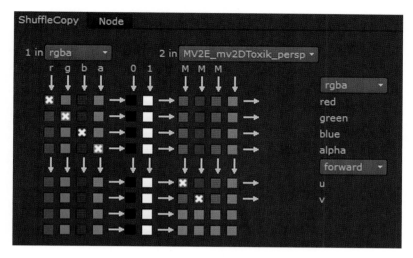

FIGURE 6.21 Custom motion vectors channels, stored under the MV2E_mv2DToxic_persp channel layer name, are transferred to the forward.u and forward.v channels with a ShuffleCopy node.

Sharpening

Nuke's Sharpen filter, in the Filter menu, makes an input less blurry. The node achieves this by applying a Laplacian edge detection and separation filter, blurring the result, and subtracting it from the original input. (This method is often referred to as an *unsharp mask*.) This results in higher contrast along edges and other small details. The Size and Filter parameters control the intensity and style of blur. The Amount parameter controls the intensity with which the blurred copy is subtracted from the original values. High Amount values create a sharper, higher-contrast result. The Minimum and Maximum parameters control the value range targeted by the Laplacian filter. If the value difference between Minimum and Maximum is small, fewer edges are separated. Note that the Sharpen node only varies from the Soften node in that it subtracts the blurred edges instead of adding them.

Light Effects

In general, camera lenses are complex structures composed of multiple glass elements. When bright light sources are placed in front of a camera, glints, flares, and glows may appear due to the optical nature of the lens. A *glint* is an intense specular highlight that briefly appears as a surface moves relative to the camera. For example, sunlight glints off a rolling ocean. A glint will take on a shape specific to the lens setup. For example, a glint may appear star-shaped. In contrast, a *lens flare* occurs when an intense light source strikes the lens in such a way as to partially obscure the subject. The shape of the flare is dependent on the construction of the lens. In the realm of photography, a *glow* refers to a radiant light that surrounds a brightly lit object. The glow occurs when light bounces off the object and in turn reflects off smoke, fog, or dust particles suspended in the air (the particles are referred to as *participating media*). A similar effect occurs when light scatters within the camera optics or through the various layers found within motion picture or still photography film stock (although this is referred to as *halation*). Nuke provides several nodes through the Draw and Filter menus to create glints, flares, and glows. These are described in this section.

Glint, found through the Draw menu, places star-shaped highlights over bright pixels within an input (Figure 6.22). Each highlight will remain fixed unless the input changes with each frame. If there is significant change in the input, the highlights appear to sparkle. The No. Of Rays, Length, Aspect Ratio, Odd Ray Length, and Rotation parameters determine the appearance of each highlight. You can control where the highlights appear by preprocessing the input with the Tolerance and Gamma parameters. Lower Tolerance values create a greater number of highlights. You can mask the input and thereby choose the areas in which the highlights appear by connecting an alpha matte to the node's Mask input. To use the mask, you must select the W parameter checkbox and choose the appropriate alpha matte channel through the corresponding menu. You can tint the input, and thereby change the highlight color, by changing the From Color value.

Flare, found through the Draw menu, creates a polygonal shape that represents a lens flare created by a single lens element (as opposed to an After Effects or Photoshop flare, which contains a string of polygonal shapes that represent multiple lens elements). Although the flare is round be default, you can flatten and adjust the edges through the node's Shape section. You can interactively place the flare by LMB-dragging the Position handle. The Size is set by the Radius parameter, which is broken into inner, middle, and outer ring cells. The area between the inner and middle rings is filled with the color set by the Inner Color parameter. The area between the middle and outer rings is filled with the color set by the Ring Color parameter.

Glow, found in the Filter menu, isolates bright areas of an input, blurs and color corrects the isolated areas, and adds the result back to the original input (Figure 6.23). The Tolerance parameter sets a threshold for the isolation of bright areas. Higher Tolerance values reduce the areas to only the brightest sections of the input. The Brightness parameter sets the intensity with which the blurred areas are added to the original input. The Tint and Saturation parameters allow you to adjust the color of the blurred areas.

Sparkles, found in the Draw menu, creates a single star-shaped glare. You can interactively position the glare by LMB-dragging the Position handle. The glare is not affected by the input image. Instead, its qualities are controlled solely by the properties in the node's Shape and Color sections. The glare will not change shape unless you manually animate the various properties.

FIGURE 6.22 Close-up of star-shaped glints created with a Glint node. A sample script is included as `glint.nk` in the `Chapters/Chapter6/Scripts/` directory on the DVD.

FIGURE 6.23 The Glow node is applied to a backlit image. Note that the glow effect removes detail from the brightest areas of the frame. A sample script is included as `glow.nk` in the `Chapters/Chapter6/Scripts/` directory on the DVD.

Other real-world light effects are created when light strikes participating media. For example, when the reflected light rays are shadowed by such objects as clouds or tree branches, they create visible light beams or "god rays." Nuke's GodRays and VolumeRays nodes allow you to create such beams. Both are found in the Filter menu.

GodRays averages together multiple copies of the input with each copy offset by values set by the Translate, Rotate, Scale, and Skew parameters. The offset occurs from the center point, which you can set by interactively moving the Center handle in the Viewer. The Translate handle determines the general direction of the copies and the resulting streaking. Used as is, the GodRays node creates a motion blur effect. However, if the node is combined with merges, masking, transformations, and/or color correction, you can emulate god rays produced when the sun or other bright light is shadowed within a participating media, such as water vapor (Figure 6.24). **VolumeRays** creates traditional god rays by sampling an input. The center of the effect is set by the Vol_Pos handle. The number and length of the rays is set by the Volume Options section. By default, the rays flicker.

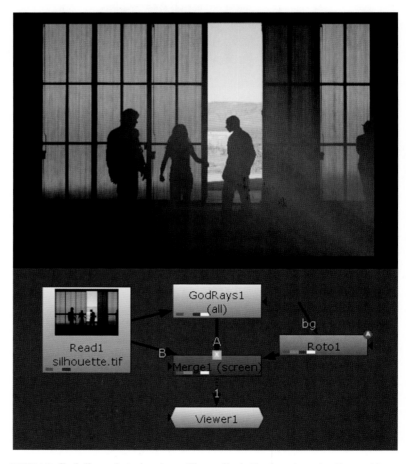

FIGURE 6.24 The GodRays node streaks an image. When combined with other nodes, such as Merge and Roto, a god rays effect is achieved. A sample script is included as godrays.nk in the Chapters/ Chapter6/Scripts/ directory on the DVD.

However, you can control the flicker speed and flicker granularity through the Use Flickering section. The node destroys the input image; however, you can combine it with the original input through an additional Merge node.

Light Wrap

When an object is placed in front of a bright background, bounced ambient light "wraps" around the object edges. You can recreate this wrap with Nuke's LightWrap node (Figure 6.25). The node operates by detecting the alpha matte edge of a foreground element, blurs the separated edge, uses the result to sample the background, and places the result over the foreground. The node's input B accepts the background and input A accepts the foreground. The Diffuse parameter sets the softness of the blur and Intensity controls the intensity with which the blurred edge is added to the original foreground. The color and intensity of the background affect the color and intensity of the blurred edge. To create a consistently bright light wrap, you can select the Disable The Luminance Based Wrap parameters. You can force the blurred edge to extend past the alpha matte edge by selecting the Enable Glow parameter. You can adjust the Saturation parameter to alter the namesake quality of the edge blur. The FGBlur parameter further softens the blurred edge, while BGBlur blurs the background input before readding the edge to the foreground. If you prefer to add a solid-colored light wrap, select the Use Constant Highlight checkbox and set the color through the Constant slider. By default, the node adds the blurred edge to the foreground, but you can select a different mathematical merge operation through the Highlight Merge operation. If you're curious what the light wrap looks like on its own, select the Generate Wrap Only checkbox.

Adding Noise and Grain

Motion picture film stock is dependent on silver halide grains embedded within the film emulsion. The grain is visible when the film is projected and is thus an inherent part of the medium. Video, whether it's analog or digital, is subject to shot noise (1-pixel fluctuations in color). In addition, digital video suffers from compression artifacts (irregular noise patterns caused by the lossy nature of compression schemes). Hence, compositors often find a need to add grain and noise to elements within a composite to keep the output consistent with film or video. Nuke provides the following nodes through the Draw menu to fulfill this need.

> **Grain** adds a synthetic film grain to the input. The node requires that the input carry an alpha channel. You can choose a specific motion picture film stock through the Presets parameter menu. You can adjust the size, color, and regularity of the grains through the namesake sections for each color channel.

FIGURE 6.25 A LightWrap node recreates light bounce along the upper edges of a CG render of a sphere. A sample script is included as lightwrap.nk in the Chapters/Chapter6/Scripts/ directory on the DVD.

ScannedGrain applies grain to an input by referencing an image sequence. The sequence is loaded through the node's Grain parameter. The intensity of the added grain per channel is set by the Amount R, G, and B cells. The node provides an interactive graph to fine-tune the contribution of the grain based on the intensity of the input pixel's red, green, and blue values. Although the ScannedGrain node is designed to add motion picture film grain, you can use it to add video compression artifacts or shot noise to an input (Figure 6.26). You can prepare a grain/ noise image sequence with the following steps:

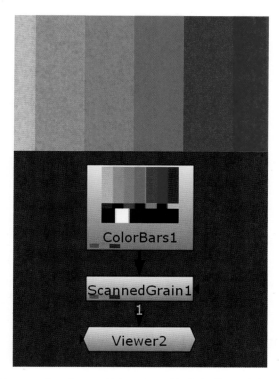

FIGURE 6.26 Video compression artifacts are added to an input with a ScannedGrain node. A sample script is included as scannedgrain.nk in the Chapters/Chapter6/Scripts/ directory on the DVD.

The Nuke FurnaceCore plug-in set includes the F_ReGrain node, which allows you to add grain to an input. You can use one of the Preset Stock options to create a synthetic grain based on a specific motion picture film stock. You can also connect a grain source to the node's Grain input pipe. If the Grain input is connected and the Preset Stock is set to Sample Grain, a sample box is drawn in the Viewer and represents the area in which grain is sampled. You can interactively move the box; for optimal quality, position the box over an area that contains a minimal amount of color and luminance variation as well as object detail. (To avoid unwanted color and luminance variation, prepare a grain source following the steps laid out in the section for the ScannedGrain node.) The Advanced section allows you to adjust the intensity of scale of the added grain per color channel.

For more information on the F_ReGrain node, see the "User Guide for Furnace" PDF available at The Foundry's website (*www.thefoundry. co.uk*).

1. Film or videotape a median gray card. Scan or convert the result into an image sequence. Two to three seconds is required to create random change in the grain pattern over time.
2. In Nuke, blur the image sequence and subtract the result from the original sequence. Add 0.5 to the resulting RGB. Write the final output as an Exr sequence (Figure 6.27).

Noise creates a procedural fractal noise pattern. You can use the output as a mask. For example, a Noise node is used as part of Part 3 of Tutorial 2 as featured in Chapter 4. Alternatively, you can create shot noise by reducing the X/Y Size value. The noise pattern is three dimensional. Thus, you can "move through" the noise by changing the Z parameter value. The Octaves parameter determines the number of noise functions that are added together to create a more complex pattern; for example, setting Octaves to 2 will layer two noise functions, each with a different scale. The Lacunarity parameter controls the gap between various noise frequencies; higher values create a smaller noise pattern.

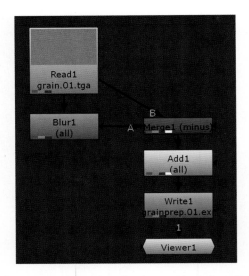

FIGURE 6.27 Video footage capturing compression artifacts is prepped for the ScannedGrain node with a specialized network. The network writes out as an Exr sequence. A sample script is included as `grainprep.nk` in the `Chapters/Chapter6/Scripts/` directory on the DVD.

Removing Grain and Dust

Occasionally, film grain, film dust, video compression artifacts, and video shot noise become undesirable. Hence, Nuke provides DegrainSimple, DegrainBlue, TemporalMedian, and DustBust nodes, as described here.

> **DegrainSimple** (in the Filter menu) averages the red, green, and blue channels through separate convolution blurs and thus softens small detail such as noise. The blur intensity is set by the R Blur, B Blur, and G Blur sliders.
>
> **DegrainBlue** (in the Filter menu) operates in the same manner as DegrainSimple, but only targets the blue channel, which generally holds heavier grain for motion picture film. The intensity of the blur is set by the Size parameter.
>
> **TemporalMedian** (in the Time menu) is designed to remove grain and noise by replacing the current value of each pixel with the median pixel value of the current, previous, and next frame. You can also use the node to reduce buzzing, stairstepping, and similar aliasing artifacts present in CG renders.
>
> **DustBust** (in the Draw menu) allows you to clone small areas of a frame to cover bits of dust or other small imperfections created during the cinematography or videography. To use the node, follow these steps:
>
> 1. Connect the output you want to touch up to the input of the DustBust node.
> 2. Cmd/Ctrl+Opt/Alt-click a dust spot in the Viewer. A small white "dust bust" box appears. Cmd/Ctrl-drag the box's center dot and release the

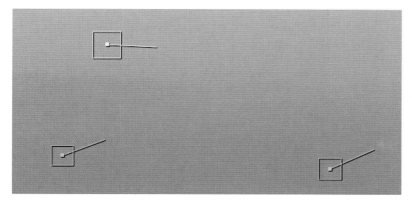

FIGURE 6.28 The boxes of a DustBust node cover dust spots with cloned areas of the frame. A sample script is included as `dustbust.nk` in the `Chapters/Chapter6/Scripts/` directory on the DVD.

mouse over a part of the screen you want to clone. For example, if you are removing a dust spot that occurs over the sky, Cmd/Ctrl-drag the dot to a clean part of the sky. When you release the mouse, a cloned spot covers the dust (Figure 6.28). You can scale the box up or down by LMB-dragging a box corner.

3. You can soften the edge of the cloned area by reducing the node's Edge Hardness value. If you are working with an image sequence from a movie, you can clone a different frame by changing the Frame Offset. If the Frame Offset is set to 0, the current frame is cloned.

4. You can add additional "dust bust" boxes by continuing to Cmd/Ctrl+Opt/Alt-click in the Viewer. Note that each box lasts one frame on the timeline.

NukeX provides the Denoise node through the Filter menu. Denoise averages pixels within each frame to reduce grain and noise. To use the node, follow these basic steps:

1. Connect the output you want to degrain to the node's Src pipe. Set the node's Source menu to Film or Digital to match the source type.

2. Interactively move the analysis region selection box in the Viewer. For optimal quality, position the box over an area that contains a minimal amount of color variation and object detail (e.g., a solid-colored wall, a sky, or a greenscreen).

3. The grain/noise is reduced. The aggressiveness of the removal is controlled by the DeNoise Amount parameter. You can fine-tune the removal of small, medium, and large grains through the Tune Frequencies section or target grain based on luminance through

the Tune Channels section. To reintroduce sharpening to edges, raise the Sharpen value.

4. Optionally, you can connect a noise source to the Noise pipe. For example, a similar piece of footage might contain areas where the noise is less obstructed by object detail; therefore, the Noise pipe provides the Denoise node with a pattern that is more easily identified.

In addition, the Nuke FurnaceCore plug-in set includes F_DeGrain and F_DeNoise nodes. F_DeGrain is specifically designed to remove grain from a still image. The basic steps for its use are as follows:

1. Connect the output you want to degrain to the node's Src pipe.
2. Change the Original Colour Space menu to match the color space of the original footage. For example, digital video footage is captured as sRGB and motion picture film is scanned as Cineon.
3. Interactively move the green analysis region selection box in the Viewer. For optimal quality, position the box over an area that contains a minimal amount of color variation and object detail (e.g., a solid-colored wall, a sky, or a greenscreen).
4. The grain/noise is reduced. The aggressiveness of the removal is controlled by the DeGrain Amount parameter. You can fine-tune the removal of small, medium, and large grains through the Frequencies section or target grain in a specific color channel through the Channels section.

F_DeNoise also tackles noise and grain, but combines temporal averaging (averaging pixels across multiple frames) with motion estimation. F_DeNoise carries many of the same parameters as F_DeGrain and requires the same basic steps to employ it. However, F_DeNoise adds the Plate Size parameter, which must be set to the resolution of the original footage (prior to any cropping or scaling). In addition, the F_DeNoise node provides Vec and Noise inputs. The Vec input accepts motion estimation vectors created from the footage in a step external to the F_DeNoise node; such a connection will speed up the node's calculation. The Noise input works in the same fashion as it does for the Denoise node.

The FurnaceCore plug-in set also includes F_DeFlicker2. The node attempts to remove luminance flickering, such as that created by a flickering light bulb. The Deflicker Amount parameter controls the aggressiveness of the removal while the Analysis Range determines how many surrounding frames are examined to identify the flicker.

For more information on the F_DeGrain, F_DeNoise, and F_DeFlicker2 nodes, see the "User Guide for Furnace" PDF available at The Foundry's website (*www.thefoundry.co.uk*).

Stylistic and Test Filters

Nuke provides several filters, in the Filter menu, that create stylistic effects. These include Laplacian, Emboss, BumpBoss, and Median.

Laplacian applies its namesake. As discussed in the section "Blurring and Convolution Filters" earlier in this chapter, a Laplacian filter separates high-contrast edges. The node achieves this by blurring the input and subtracting the original from the result. The Size parameter sets the size of the blur filter. The smaller the Size value, the smaller and thinner the separated edges are. Note that the node does not affect the alpha channel. The nonedge areas are left black.

Emboss creates the illusion of 3D bumpiness by offsetting high-contrast edges isolated within the input. By default, the node places the emboss effect over a gray background. However, you can add the emboss effect to the original input by switching the Emboss Type parameter to Effect. The direction of the virtual light is controlled by the Angle parameter. (The 3D quality is emulated by offsetting a bright and dark copy of the isolated edges; hence, there is a virtual highlight and virtual shadow for each "bump.")

BumpBoss creates an embossed effect but uses input A to distort input B. The size of the bump detail is set by its namesake parameter. The intensity of the bump is set by the Line Height. You can interactively direct the virtual light by moving the Center and Light Position handles in the Viewer.

Median applies a form of convolution filter that replaces the input pixel value with a value that represents a median of surrounding pixels. That is, the pixel values in the kernel area are sorted and the middle value is selected. This blurs low-contrast areas while maintaining sharp edges along high-contrast transitions. The Size parameter sets the filter size. Small Size values allow small detail to survive, while large Size values simplify the input, creating a painterly result (Figure 6.29).

In addition, Nuke provides several filters that create specific 2D art suitable for testing various networks (these are found in the Draw menu). The Constant node produces a solid color and can serve as a temporary sky or a backdrop to test the success of a keying filter. You can employ the CheckerBoard node to see the results of a particular filter more clearly. The ColorBars and ColorWheel nodes create patterns that are ideal for testing monitor calibration.

Creating Custom Convolutions

Nuke's Matrix node allows you to create your own custom convolution filter. When you choose Filter > Matrix, the Enter Desired Matrix Size dialog opens. Once you enter Width and Height values, the node is created. At that point, you are free to enter values into the matrix cells, which represent the values

FIGURE 6.29 A painterly effect is created with a Median node with the Size parameter set to 15. A sample script is included as median.nk in the Chapters/Chapter6/Scripts/ directory on the DVD.

of the convolution kernel matrix that is slid over the input image. When working with positive matrix cell values, it's often desirable to select the Normalize checkbox. Normalize divides the matrix result by the sum of the matrix values; this allows the output to retain the same brightness as the input. Figure 6.30 illustrates a 5 × 5 matrix with values that emulate a Gaussian blur. For additional matrix examples, see Tutorial 4, "Creating Custom Convolution Filters," at the end of this chapter. Note that the size of the matrix relative to the resolution of the input affects the intensity of the filter. In other words, a small matrix has little impact on a large-resolution input.

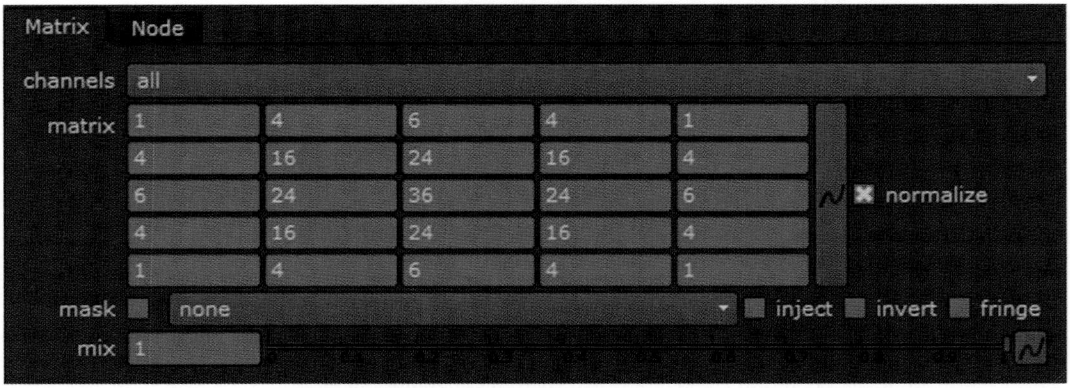

FIGURE 6.30 A 5 × 5 convolution matrix created with a Matrix node. The values emulate a Gaussian blur. A sample script is included as matrix.nk in the Chapters/Chapter6/Scripts/ directory on the DVD.

Tutorial 3: Removing an Imperfect Greenscreen
Part 2: Applying Filters for Better Integration

In Part 1 of this tutorial, we keyed the greenscreen and rotoscoped the nongreenscreen areas to place the dancers with a new background. In Part 2, we'll add filters to create a more believable and aesthetic integration.

1. Open the Nuke script you saved after completing Part 1 of this tutorial. A sample Nuke script is included as `Tutorial3.1.nk` in the `Tutorials/Tutorial3/Scripts/` directory on the DVD.

2. Select the Transform1 node and choose Color > ColorCorrect. Refer to Figure 6.31 for the final node network. Open the new ColorCorrect1 node's properties panel. Click the 4 button beside Master Gain. Enter 0.6 into the G cell and enter 0.4 into the B cell. This reduces the green and blue intensity of the plate and thus gives the dancers a yellowish cast that better matches the new background.

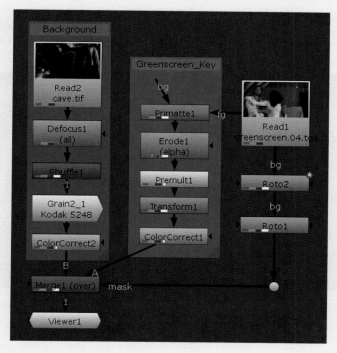

FIGURE 6.31 The final node network for Tutorial 3.

3. Select the Read2 node and choose Filter > Defocus. In the Defocus1 node's properties panel, set the Defocus parameter to 8. This blurs the background. Small detail takes on a circular shape, which matches an out-of-focus real-world lens. A blurred

background also matches a real-world, low-light-level shoot where a narrow depth of field is necessary to expose the film or video.

4. Select the Defocus1 node and choose Channel > Shuffle. Select the Shuffle1 node and choose Draw > Grain. Note that an error message appears in the Viewer. The Grain1 node requires an alpha channel to function. Open the properties panel for the Shuffle1 node. Select the box in the 1 column and the alpha row. This adds an opaque alpha channel to the output. The Grain1 node now functions. Open the Grain1 node's properties panel. Reduce the Red, Green, and Blue values in the Intensity section until the added grain is very subtle. Because the background is a static bitmap, an added grain will better match the greenscreen plate. Although the plate was shot with a video camera, the video contains subtle, shifting shot noise and compression artifacts.

5. Select the Grain1 node and choose Color > ColorCorrect. Open the ColorCorrect2 node's properties panel. In the Master section, increase the Contrast and reduce the Gain until the black areas of the background better match the black area of the female dancer's hair. Matching the "blacks" within the various elements helps to make the composite more convincing (Figure 6.32).

FIGURE 6.32 The final composite. Blur and grain is added to the background, while both the background and foreground are color balanced to better match.

6. Choose the Merge1 node and create a test render by choosing Render > Flipbook Selected from the menu bar. Continue to adjust the various filter nodes, including those used to key the greenscreen and adjust the matte edge, until no more improvement can be made.

This concludes Tutorial 3. As a bonus step, arrange the nodes, apply Backdrops, and add Dots to create a neat and organized

node network. A sample Nuke script is included as
`Tutorial3.final.nk` in the `Tutorials/Tutorial2/Scripts/`
directory on the DVD.

Tutorial 4: Creating Custom Convolution Filters

Tutorial 4 takes you through the steps needed to create several custom
convolution filters with the Matrix node.

1. Create a new Nuke script. Create a new Read node and import
    a bitmap or image sequence that will serve as a test bed for
    custom convolution filters. You can use any of the bitmaps
    included on the DVD. Note that it will be easier to see the result of
    a matrix with a smaller resolution image.
2. Choose Filter > Matrix. In the Enter Desired Matrix Size dialog box,
    enter 3 for the Width and Height. Connect the new Matrix node to
    the output of the Read node. Connect the output of the Matrix
    node to a Viewer.
3. In the Matrix node's properties panel, enter the following values
    into the matrix cells:

$$\begin{array}{rrr} -1 & -1 & -1 \\ -1 & 8 & -1 \\ -1 & -1 & -1 \end{array}$$

    This creates a Laplacian edge detection filter (Figure 6.33). In this
    case, the Normalize checkbox is left unselected.
4. Update the matrix cells with the following values:

FIGURE 6.33 The result of a Laplacian matrix.

$$\begin{array}{ccc} 1 & 2 & 1 \\ 2 & 4 & 2 \\ 1 & 2 & 1 \end{array}$$

Select the Normalize checkbox. This creates a "tent" blur filter (Figure 6.34).

FIGURE 6.34 The result of a tent blur filter matrix.

5. Update the matrix cells with the following values:

$$\begin{array}{ccc} 0 & -2 & 0 \\ -2 & 11 & -2 \\ 0 & -2 & 0 \end{array}$$

Leave the Normalize checkbox selected. This creates a sharpen filter (Figure 6.35).

FIGURE 6.35 The result of a sharpen filter matrix.

This concludes Tutorial 4. A sample Nuke script is included as `Tutorial4.final.nk` in the `Tutorials/Tutorial4/Scripts/` directory on the DVD. The sample script includes all three matrix variations.

CHAPTER 7

Time Warping and Image Distortion

When you shoot motion picture film or video footage, it's captured at a specific frame rate. When an image sequence or movie is imported into Nuke, it's read at a frame rate determined by the project settings. Nevertheless, you can slow down or speed up the sequence or movie by changing the frame rate with Nuke nodes designed to warp time. However, warps are not limited to time. Nuke provides a number of filters that distort or warp the colors of an input.

This chapter includes the following critical information:

- Understanding Nuke time management
- Time warping to speed up or slow down an image sequence
- Applying time-based blurs and simple editing functions
- Distorting inputs and morphing distortions

Working with Time

The frame rate of a Nuke project is determined by the Fps parameter of the Project Settings panel. However, the frame rate achieved by the timeline playback is set by the Desired Playback Rate cell (labeled Fps and to the right of the playback buttons). For example, if Fps is set to 30 and an image sequence is imported through a Read node, the sequence is read by the project at 30 frames per second (fps). If the Desired Playback Rate is set to 30, Nuke attempts to play back the timeline at 30 fps to achieve real time. If the image sequence is 30 frames long, the timeline plays it back over 1 second. However, if the Desired Playback Rate is set to 10, Nuke displays 10 fps without altering the length of the timeline; in other words, the 30-frame sequence plays back over 3 seconds. If the Desired Playback Rate is set to 60, the 30-frame sequence plays back over ½ second. To achieve the real-time playback, Nuke skips or repeats frames in a nondestructive fashion. Note that the Desired Playback Rate cell displays the actual frames per second achieved during the playback (which is dependent on the complexity of the composite and the speed of the PC or Mac). Here are a few additional tips to keep in mind:

- When you render a flipbook (Render > Flipbook Selected through the menu bar), the playback speed is set by the frame rate at the bottom left of the FrameCycler window.

If a node network includes one or more Write nodes, you can launch a render by choosing Render > Render All (to render all Write nodes) or Render > Render Selected (to render a selected Write node) from the menu bar.

- If you import a QuickTime or AVI movie through a Read node, the file's inherent frame rate is ignored in favor of the project frame rate.
- Changing the Desired Playback Rate does not alter the way in which frames are written out. For example, if the timeline is 30 frames long, the Flipbook or Write node will write out all 30 frames. Although you can choose a different frame range, Nuke will not repeat or skip over frames during the write process.
- To alter the duration of an imported image sequence or movie without changing the project's Fps setting, apply some form of time warping. *Time warping* is a generic name for retiming, where an image sequence or movie is made to play back faster (with fewer frames) or slower (with additional frames).

While several nodes are designed to time warp, other time-based nodes create specialized blurs or provide a means to undertake simple editing in the program.

Simple Time Warping Nodes

Nuke provides two nodes for simple time warping: Retime and TimeWarp. Both are found in the Time menu and are described in this section.

Retime speeds up or slows down in input by discarding or repeating frames. The Speed parameter controls the retiming. Values below 1 slow the footage. Values above 1 speed up the footage. The Output Range Output Last cell indicates the new length in frames. If the input is slowed and the Filter and Shutter parameters are left at their default settings, frames are repeated as is; however, if Filter is set to Box and Shutter is set to a value above 1, in-between frames are synthesized by blending together surrounding frames. For example, if Speed is set to 0.5 and Shutter is set to 1.5, new in-between frames are 50% blends of the current and next frame.

TimeWarp offers similar functionality to the Retime node with the Filter parameter operating in an identical manner. However, TimeWarp includes an Input Frame parameter, which is automatically keyframed to form a linear curve (Figure 7.1). Reshaping this curve in the Curve Editor allows for fine control over the time warping. For example, altering the curve slope through the manipulation of tangent handles causes the speed of the retime to change over the duration of the timeline (Figure 7.2). You can access the Curve Editor directly by clicking the node's Curve Editor button. To synthesize new frames, the TimeWarp node relies on the Input

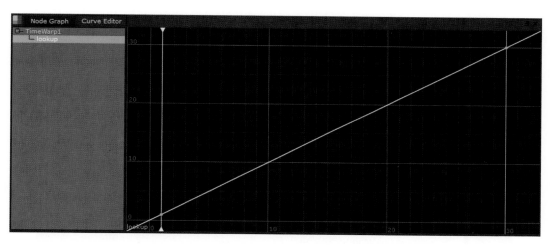

FIGURE 7.1 Default linear curve (labeled Lookup) created for the Input Frame parameter of a TimeWarp node. With such a curve, no time warping occurs as the appropriate frames are retrieved for each frame of the timeline.

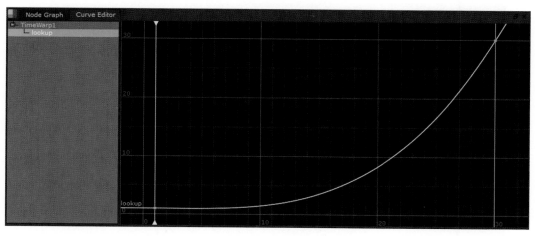

FIGURE 7.2 Reshaped Lookup curve. With this curve, the output is initially slowed (the shallow slope of the curve) before it is sped up (the steep slope of the curve). The flat portion of the curve, at the curve start, creates a temporary freeze-frame. A sample script is included as `timewarp.nk` in the `Chapters/Chapter7/Scripts/` directory on the DVD.

Length parameter. To automatically enter the correct value based on the applied time warp, click the Set To DF/DT button.

Motion Estimation and Optical Flow

Motion estimation is a process in which motion vectors are generated to track elements within an image sequence or movie over time. *Optical flow*, on the other hand, is the apparent motion of elements, objects, or edges within an image sequence or movie relative to the viewer. Hence, nodes that employ motion estimation are using optical flow theory. For example, motion estimation might track a red dot on the screen as it moves left to right over time. As such, a 2D motion vector is generated that represents that motion. However, the reality is that pixels with specific X and Y coordinates are changing color with each frame. In other words, the pixels aren't moving; the viewer only perceives motion because the red dot is in a different location with each frame.

Nuke's OFlow node (Time > OFlow) employs motion estimation and optical flow techniques to generate time warping. To apply the node, follow these basic steps:

1. Connect the input you wish to retime to the Src pipe of the OFlow node. Open the OFlow node's properties panel and set the Timing parameter menu to Speed (Figure 7.3). Set the Speed parameter cell. Speed values below 1 slow the input and values above 1 speed up the input. For example, if Speed is set to 2, the input runs twice as fast.

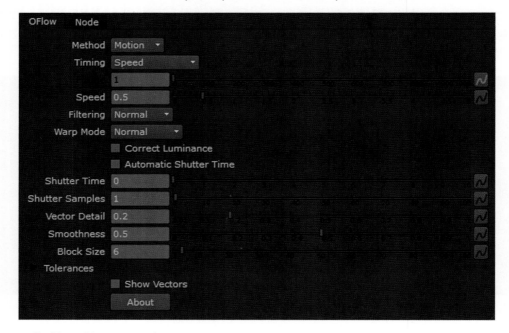

FIGURE 7.3 The OFlow node's properties panel.

2. Set the Method menu to an interpolation. The Motion method creates optical flow motion vectors and is able to accurately synthesize in-between frames. The Blend interpolation blends together existing frames to create new ones. The Frame interpolation repeats existing frames without alteration.

3. If Method is set to Motion, adjust the Vector Detail value. Vector Detail determines the resolution of the motion vector field. A Vector Detail of 1 creates a motion vector for every pixel within an input. Lower Vector Detail values are less accurate but are more efficient. If you'd like to view the motion vectors, select the Show Vectors checkbox (Figure 7.4).

FIGURE 7.4 Close-up of motion vectors created by the OFlow node for a sequence featuring rapidly moving dancers.

4. To introduce motion blur trails to moving elements within synthesized frames, set the Shutter parameter to a nonzero value. A Shutter value of 0.5 is equivalent to a half frame-long blur. To refine the resulting blur, raise the Shutter Samples value (Figure 7.5). If the synthesized frames are creating artifacts, such as "edge drag" where moving objects are distorting the static background, try setting the Warp Mode menu to Occlusions.

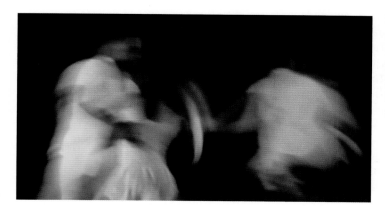

FIGURE 7.5 Exaggerated motion blur trails created for a synthesized frame. The Shutter is set to an usually high value of 10. Shutter Samples is set to 100. A sample script is included as oflow.nk in the Chapters/Chapter7/Scripts/ directory on the DVD.

You can vary the speed of an input over time by setting the Timing menu to Source Frame. You can then keyframe the Frame parameter to determine which frame of the input you want to appear on a particular frame of the timeline. You can adjust the resulting animation curve in the Curve Editor.

Note that time warping does not change the duration of the timeline. If you speed up an input with Retime, TimeWarp, or OFlow, the last frame of the input is held to fill any empty space at the end of the timeline. If you slow down an input, the end of the input may exceed the last frame of the timeline. Therefore, you may need to reset the Frame Range values in the Project Settings properties panel.

The Furnace plug-in set includes F_Kronos, a motion estimation/ optical flow time warping node. Many of the parameters of the F_Kronos node are identical to the OFlow node. Thus, the basic workflow for both nodes is the same. Nevertheless, the F_Kronos node provides additional input pipes, which include MoSrc (if connected, source used to generate motion estimation vectors), Matte (alpha matte used to isolate moving foreground elements), and FgVec/ BgVec (precalculated motion vectors for foreground and background).

For more information on the F_Kronos node, see the "User Guide for Furnace" PDF available at The Foundry's website (*www. thefoundry.co.uk*).

Time-Based Blurs

Nuke includes several nodes that go backward or forward in time to average pixel values and thus create stylistic blurs. The nodes, found in the Time menu, include FrameBlend, TimeBlur, and TimeEcho and are described here.

FrameBlend creates motion blur trails by blending together the current frame with a number of subsequent frames as set by the Number Of Frames parameter.

TimeBlur creates a motion blur trail by averaging the current frame with a number of fractional frames as set by the Divisions parameter over a duration set by the Shutter parameter. You can offset the blur trail by adjusting the Shutter Offset value. TimeBlur is designed to motion blur animated masks or inputs animated through a Transform node. Because TimeBlur examines fractional frames (e.g., 5.1, 5.2, 5.3, and so on), it can be expensive to process all the upstream nodes (all the nodes flowing into the node's input). Hence, Nuke provides a NoTimeBlur node, which you can place above the node that you want TimeBlur to affect. Any node upstream of NoTimeBlur does not provide fractional frame information. For a working example of the TimeBlur node, see Tutorial 5, "Adding Motion Blur to a CG Render," at the end of this chapter.

TimeEcho creates a stylistic blur by merging multiple frames together. The Frames To Look At parameter sets the numbers of frames that are merged together (the node always uses previous frames). The Frames To Fade Out determines the number of frames that are given reduced weight during the merge (the frames furthest back in time are given the lowest weight). The node provides three mathematical blending modes through the TimeEcho Method menu: Plus (pixel values added without clamping to 1), Max (the highest pixel value between the merged frames is used), and Average (the average pixel value between merged frames is used).

FIGURE 7.6 Stylistic motion blur is created with the TimeEcho node. A sample script is included as `timeecho.nk` in the Chapters/ Chapter7/Scripts/ directory on the DVD.

Simple Editing in Nuke

Nuke provides a set of nodes you can use for simple editing tasks within the program. For example, you can offset or reverse an input sequence, "freeze" a frame, or create fade-ins, fade-outs, and dissolves. Found in the Time menu, TimeOffset, FrameHold, AppendClip, and FrameRange are described here.

TimeOffset holds the first frame of an input sequence for a number of frames as determined by the Time Offset parameter. You can quickly reverse the frame order by selecting the node's Reverse Input checkbox and leaving First Frame set to 0.

FrameHold creates a freeze-frame by repeating frame *n* as defined by the First Frame parameter. If the Increment parameter is a nonzero value, the node will jump across the frames incrementally. For example, if First Frame is 1 and Increment is 2, the node jumps from 1 to 3 to 5; in this case, frame 1 is repeated for frame 2, frame 3 is repeated for frame 4, and so on.

AppendClip offers a means to fade into a sequence from black, fade out of a sequence to black, and/or dissolve between two inputs. The Fade In and Fade Out parameters determine the frame duration of the namesake events. The Dissolve parameter sets the duration of the dissolve, which occurs at the end of the input 1 sequence. For example, if you connect a 20-frame sequence to input 1, a second 20-frame sequence to input 2, and set the Dissolve value to 5, the dissolve occurs between frames 15 and 20 on the timeline. (The dissolve is carried out by changing the opacity of the inputs.) In this case, frame 1 through 5 of input 2 is placed between frame 15 and 20 on the timeline. Thus, to play back input 1 and input 2 at their full length, the project's Frame Range Last_Frame (in the Project Settings properties panel) must be set to 35. If Dissolve is set to 0, a "hard cut" occurs between all the inputs. You can connect more than two inputs and thus emulate a simple editing program where you order clips on the timeline.

FrameRange allows you to "cut" an input to a shorter duration by entering start and end frame values in the Frame Range parameter cells. You can combine this node with the AppendClip node to give you greater control over the edit (see Figure 7.7).

FIGURE 7.7 A dissolve between two inputs is carried out by an AppendClip node. Two FrameRange nodes shorten each input to a 20-frame duration. A sample script is included as `appendclip.nk` in the `Chapters/Chapter7/Scripts/` directory on the DVD.

Image Distortion

Image distortion alters the color values of an input so it appears as if specific elements or features are "pushed" around the frame. The distortion may be as simple as a horizontal flip or may be complex enough to make the input virtually unrecognizable. Nuke includes distortion nodes in the Transform menu.

Simple Distortion Nodes

Simple distortion nodes include Mirror, Tile, and IDistort, discussed here.

Mirror offers a quick way to flip an input vertically and/or horizontally with Vertical and Horizontal checkboxes.

Tile repeats the input vertically and/or horizontally through the Columns and Rows parameters. You can use the node to create texture bitmaps useful for a 3D program such as Maya. Note that the bounding box resolution is not affected; the input is simply shrunk.

IDistort uses the UV channels of the input to distort the RGB values of the same input. For example, in Figure 7.8, the image of a dancer is heavily altered. Forward UV channels are added to the input through a ShuffleCopy node (Figure 7.9). The red and green channels of a Noise node provide the Forward UV values. Where the UV values are high, the RGB pixels are "pushed" down and to the left. Where the UV values are low, the push is minimal. The overall intensity of the distortion is

The STMap node (Transform > STMap) is a truly unqiue UV distortion filter. The node is able to re-texture a CG render *after* the render is imported into Nuke. This requires the creation of a separate floating-bit UV render that colors the 3D model based on the UV values of any given surface point. For more information on the STMap node, see the "Nuke User Guide" and "Nuke Reference Guide" PDFs available at The Foundry's website (*www.thefoundry.co.uk*).

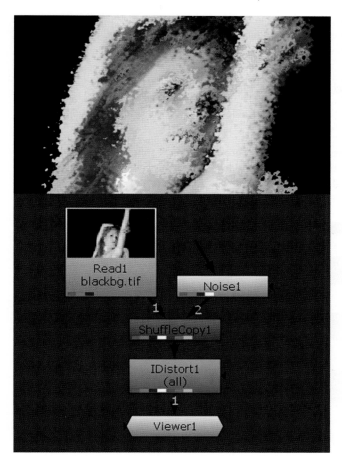

FIGURE 7.8 An input is heavily distorted with an IDistort node. The red and green channels of a Noise node are transferred to Forward UV channels through a ShuffleCopy node. A sample script is included as idistort.nk in the Chapters/Chapter7/Scripts/ directory on the DVD.

FIGURE 7.9 The ShuffleCopy node settings.

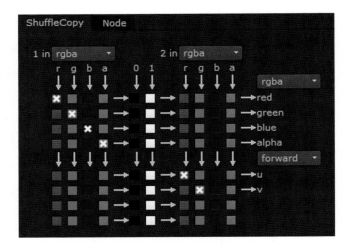

controlled by the IDistort node's UV Scale parameter. You can push the resulting pixels up and to the right by raising the UV Offset value. The IDistort node does not function unless the incoming UV channels are set by the node's UV Channels menu.

Advanced Distortion Nodes

Advanced distortion nodes include LensDistortion, GridWarp, and Spline-Warp, discussed here.

LensDistortion applies a concave or convex spherical distortion to an input to emulate a real-world lens. To add a concave distortion, raise the Radial Distortion 1 and/or Radial Distortion 2 parameter sliders above 0 (Figure 7.10). To add a convex distortion, lower the Radial

If you're running NukeX, you can use the LensDistortion node to remove preexisting distortion from an input. There are three options for detecting the distortion: image analysis, grid analysis, and line analysis, each of which receive their own tab in the node's properties panel. Image analysis tracks features within an image sequence or movie to identify distortion. Grid analysis detects distortion present by examining a grid or checker-board shot on film or video; this requires the creation of a special test shot. Line analysis provides an interactive means to draw lines in the Viewer to identify edges that are straight in real life.

For more information on the LensDistortion node and its distortion analysis, see the Nuke "User Guide" and "Reference Guide" PDFs available at The Foundry's website (*www.thefoundry.co.uk*).

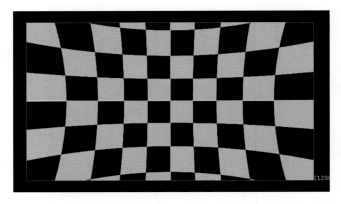

FIGURE 7.10 An output of a Checkerboard node is given a concave spherical distortion with a LensDistortion node. A sample script is included as `lensdistortion.nk` in the `Chapters/Chapter7/Scripts/` directory on the DVD.

Distortion 1 and/or Radial Distortion 2 parameter sliders below 0. Radial Distortion 1 creates a more aggressive distortion than Radial Distortion 2. You can offset the distortion center by entering values between −1 and 1 in the Distortion Center X and Y cells.

GridWarp lets you "push" pixels around the screen by interactively altering the points of two grids. The GridWarp node has changed significantly between Nuke v6.2 and v6.3. With v6.2, choosing Transform > GridWarp creates a GridWarp node, while choosing Transform > GridWarp in v6.3 creates a GridWarp3 node. Hence, parallel sets of instructions are included in this section. To apply the GridWarp/GridWarp3 node, follow these steps:

1. Connect the Src pipe of the GridWarp/GridWarp3 node to the input you wish to warp. Open the GridWarp node's properties panel. Two grids appear in the Viewer. The pink grid is the Source Grid, which establishes the area to be warped. The light blue grid is the Destination Grid, which defines how the warp occurs. Click the Image Size buttons (v6.2) or the Resize Image buttons (v6.3) in the Source Grid and Destination Grid sections (Figure 7.11 and 7.12). This snaps the grids to the input resolution.

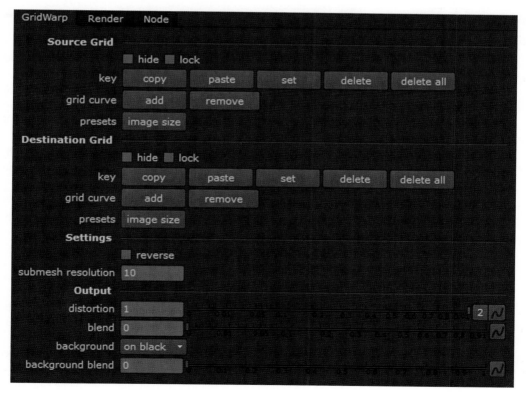

FIGURE 7.11 The GridWarp node's properties panel, as seen in Nuke v6.2.

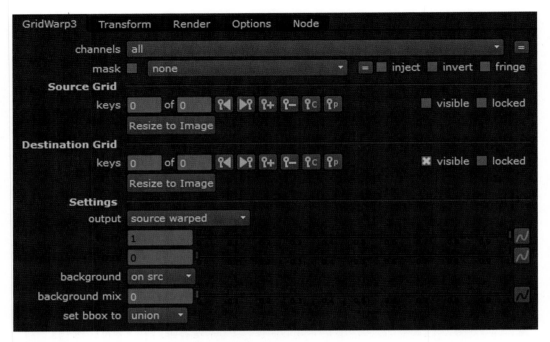

FIGURE 7.12 The GridWarp3 node's properties panel, as seen in Nuke v6.3.

2. If you are using v6.2, select the Hide checkbox in the Destination Grid section. If you are using v6.3, deselect the Visible checkbox in the Destination Grid section and select the Visible checkbox in the Source Grid section. This allows the Source Grid to be seen by itself. If you are using v6.2, set the Distortion parameter, in the Output section, to 0. If you are using v6.3, set the Output menu to Source. This prevents distortion from occurring while you manipulate the Source Grid. LMB-drag the Source Grid's points so that the grid curves encompass the feature to be warped. For example, you can reshape the grid to fit a face or specific features of a face, such as the mouth, nose, and eyes (Figure 7.13). When you click a point in the Viewer, its tangent handle becomes visible. You can LMB-drag the handle to alter the grid's curve segments. To create a sharp corner, LMB-drag the tangent handles of a point so that they become shorter.

3. If the grid density is too low to encompass a feature, add an additional vertical or horizontal grid curve in v6.2 by clicking the Add button beside the Grid Curve parameter in the Source Grid section and LMB-click a preexisting curve in the Viewer. If you LMB-click a horizontal curve, a vertical curve is added. If you LMB-click a vertical curve, a horizontal curve is added. If you are using v6.3, Cmd/Ctrl+Opt/Alt-click an existing horizontal or vertical line.

4. When the Source Grid is suitably shaped, hide the Source Grid and show the Destination Grid by using the Hide (v6.2) or Visible (v6.3)

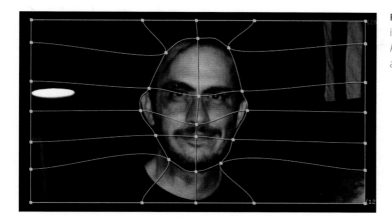

FIGURE 7.13 The Source Grid, as seen in v6.2, is shaped to follow the features of a face. Additional horizontal and vertical curves are added to more closely follow the face contours.

checkboxes. Note that the Destination Grid retains its original shape (with the exception of additional curves added as part of step 3). Click the Copy button (v6.2) or Copy Key Frame To Clipboard button (v6.3) in the Source Grid section and click the Paste button (v6.2) or Paste Key Frame From Clipboard button (v6.3) in the Destination Grid section. This copies the Source Grid shape to the Destination Grid.

5. If the input is an image sequence or movie, you can animate the grid changing over time by clicking the Key buttons in the Source Grid and Destination Grid sections. Once the Key buttons are activated, further changes to the grids are automatically keyframed. You can delete a keyframe on the current frame of the timeline by clicking the Delete button (v6.2) or Delete The Current Key button (v6.3).

6. Set the Distortion parameter back to 1 (v6.2) or set the Output menu to Source Warped (v6.3). LMB-drag the points of the Destination Grid to create the warp (Figure 7.14). When you've finished adjusting the grid, hide it once again by selecting the Hide checkbox in the Destination Grid section.

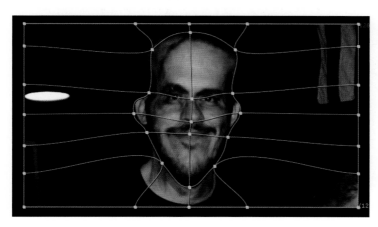

FIGURE 7.14 The warp is created by LMB-dragging the Destination Grid points. A sample v6.2 script is included as `gridwarp.nk` in the `Chapters/Chapter7/Scripts/` directory on the DVD. A v6.3 script is also included as `gridwarp63.nk`.

209

It's also possible to create an animated morph with the GridWarp node. This is discussed in the next section. In addition, you can use the older GridWarp node in v6.3 by creating the node via a TCL script line. To do so, press the X key in the Node Graph, select the TCL radio button in the Command dialog box, enter GridWarp into the Command field (note the capitalization), and click the OK button. (The TCL scripting language is discussed in Chapter 10.)

SplineWarp lets you "push" pixels around the screen by interactively drawing and adjusting Bezier splines. Much like the GridWarp node, the SplineWarp node went through a significant change with v6.3. Thus, parallel sets of instructions are included in this section. To apply the node, you can follow these steps:

1. Connect the Src pipe of the SplineWarp/SplineWarp3 node to the input you wish to warp. Open the node's properties panel (Figures 7.15 and 7.16). If you are using v6.2, select the First Bezier Masks Deform checkbox. In the Viewer, Cmd/Ctrl+Opt/Alt-click to add points to a Bezier curve that forms a mask. To end the curve, LMB-click off the curve. The mask determines what part of the input is affected by the warp. Areas outside the mask are unaffected by the node. You can close the Bezier curve by RMB-clicking a point and choosing Open/Close Curve from the shortcut menu. If you are using v6.3, select the Bezier tool from the SplineWarp3 toolbox, which appears along the left side of the Viewer tab (Figure 7.17), and LMB-click in the Viewer. To close the curve, press the Enter key. The new curve is listed in the Curves section of the v6.3 node's properties panel.

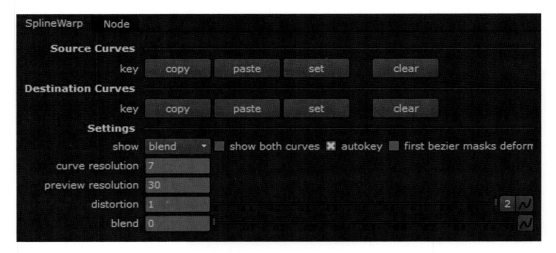

FIGURE 7.15 The SplineWarp node's properties panel, as seen in v6.2.

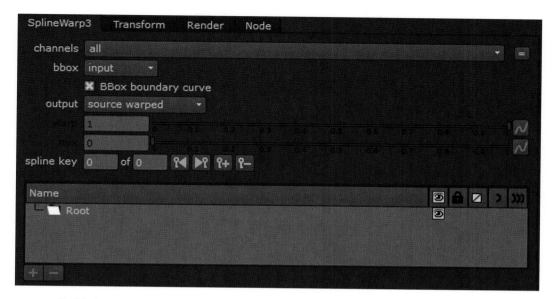

FIGURE 7.16 The SplineWarp3 node's properties panel, as seen in v6.3.

Click the Hard Boundary button beside the curve name in the Curves section. The button features a backward-C shape. With the Hard Boundary button activated, the curve serves as a boundary for the warp effect. Pixels outside the Hard Boundary curve are unaffected by the node.

2. If you are using v6.2, change the Show parameter menu to Src (Source). In the Viewer, Cmd/Ctrl+Opt/Alt-click to add points to a Bezier curve that defines the features or elements that will be warped. For greater precision, you can create multiple curves. To

FIGURE 7.17 The SplineWarp3 toolbox, as seen in v6.3; the Bezier curve tool is the center button.

211

start a new curve, LMB-click off the first curve and Cmd/Ctrl+Opt/ Alt-click where you want the new curve to start. You can move any point at any time by LMB-dragging it. If you are using v6.3, select the Bezier tool from the SplineWarp toolbox and LMB-click to define the features or elements that will be warped. To end a curve in v6.3 without closing it, switch to a different tool, such as the Select All tool.

3. If the input is an image sequence or movie, animate the curves changing shape over time. With v6.2, the Autokey checkbox is selected so that changes are automatically keyframed. Although v6.3 doesn't have an autokey button, the curves are keyframed nonetheless.

4. If you are using v6.2, change the Show menu to Blend. For each Source curve, there is a matching blue Destination curve (Figure 7.18). LMB-drag the points of the Destination curve(s) to define how the input will be warped. If the Distortion parameter is set to 1, the warp occurs as you move the Destination curve points (Figure 7.19). To see Source and Destination curves in the Viewer at the same time, select the Show Both Curves checkbox. Source curves are pink while Destination curves are light blue. If you are using v6.3, change the

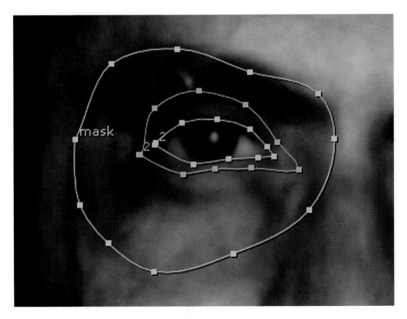

FIGURE 7.18 Mask curve (green), Source curve (pink), and Destination curve (light blue) displayed as the Show menu is set to Blend in v6.2. Distortion is set to 0, and the View Both Curves checkbox is selected. A sample script is included as splinewarp.nk in the Chapters/Chapter7/Scripts/ directory on the DVD.

FIGURE 7.19 Resulting warp with the curves hidden by toggling Overlay Off (press the O key or RMB-click in the Viewer and choose Overlay).

Output menu to Source Warped. For each Source curve, there is a matching blue Destination curve. LMB-drag the points of the Destination curve(s) to define how the input will be warped. To see Source and Destination curves in the Viewer at the same time, set the Output menu to Morph. To reduce the warp intensity, lower the Warp parameter value. If you'd like to move curve points without seeing the distortion in v6.3, set the Output menu to Source.

It's also possible to create an animated morph with the SplineWarp node. This is demonstrated in Tutorial 6, "Adding Damage to a Plate," at the end of this chapter.

Morphing

The technique of morphing takes the process of image distortion one step further by altering the distortion over time. In addition, morphing combines the distortion with animated opacity so that two inputs take on each other's form over time.

The GridWarp/GridWarp3 and SplineWarp/SplineWarp3 nodes both contain parameters you can animate to create a morph. To use GridWarp/GridWarp3 in this fashion, follow these steps:

1. A morph requires two inputs. Connect the first input to the GridWarp node's Src pipe and the second input to the Dst input pipe. Open the GridWarp node's properties panel.
2. If you are using v6.2, select the Hide checkbox in the Destination Grid section. If you are using v6.3, deselect the Visible checkbox in the Destination Grid section and select the Visible checkbox in the Source Grid section. This allows the Source Grid to be seen by itself. If you are using v6.2, set the Distortion parameter, in the Output section, to 0.

If you are using v6.3, set the Output menu to Source. This prevents distortion from occurring while you manipulate the Source Grid. LMB-drag the Source Grid's points so that the grid curves encompass the feature to be warped. For example, you can reshape the grid to fit features of a landscape, such as the horizon line, peaks of distant mountains, lines of foliage, and so on (Figure 7.20). When you click a point in the Viewer, its tangent handle becomes visible. You can LMB-drag the handle to alter the grid's curve segments. To create a sharp corner, LMB-drag the tangent handles of a point so that they become shorter.

FIGURE 7.20 Source Grid adjusted to match features of the Src input landscape.

3. If the grid density is too low to encompass a feature, add an additional vertical or horizontal grid curve in v6.2 by clicking the Add button beside the Grid Curve parameter in the Source Grid section and LMB-click a preexisting curve in the Viewer. If you LMB-click a horizontal curve, a vertical curve is added. If you LMB-click a vertical curve, a horizontal curve is added. If you are using v6.3, Cmd/Ctrl+Opt/Alt-click an existing horizontal or vertical line.

4. When the Source Grid is suitably shaped, hide the Source Grid and show the Destination Grid by using the Hide (v6.2) or Visible (v6.3)

checkboxes. If you are using v6.2, change the Blend menu to 1; if you are using v6.3, change the Output menu to Destination. This reveals the Dst input. Note that the Destination Grid retains its original shape (with the exception of additional curves added as part of step 3). LMB-drag points to shape the Destination Grid. When creating a morph, match the Dst features to the Src features. For example, in Figure 7.21, the grid curve that defined the top of the mountain range within the landscape is matched to the top edge of the graffiti within the alleyway. Additionally, the grid curve that defined the horizon line within the landscape is matched to the edge of the asphalt road within the alleyway.

FIGURE 7.21 The Destination grid is shaped to line up features of the Dst input (graffiti) with the features of the Src input (landscape).

5. With the timeline on frame 1, set Distortion and Blend to 0 (v6.2) or Warp and Mix to 0 (v6.3) and keyframe each parameter. Move to the last frame of the timeline and set Distortion and Blend to 1 (v6.2) or Warp and Mix to 1 (v6.3). If you are using v6.3, set Output to Morph. Play back the timeline or create a Flipbook. The output incrementally dissolves between the Src input and the Dst input (Figure 7.22). At the same time, the Src input is incrementally warped to fit the shape of the Dst input, while the Dst input changes from the Src shape to an unwarped state. To reverse the morph, swap the keyframe values for the first and last frame.

FIGURE 7.22 Frames 1, 7, 15, 22, and 30 from the resulting 30-frame morph. Note the distortion of both the landscape and graffiti over time. A sample v6.2 script is included as `gridwarpmorph.nk` in the `Chapters/Chapter7/Scripts/` directory on the DVD. A v6.3 script is also included as `gridwarpmorph63.nk`.

Tutorial 5: Adding Motion Blur to a CG Render

Tutorial 5 takes you through the steps needed to apply motion blur to a nonblurred CG render. We'll apply the TimeBlur node to a single frame of an image sequence, then compare the result to the VectorBlur node, which uses a separate motion vector render.

1. Create a new Nuke script. Choose Edit > Project Settings from the menu bar. In the Project Settings properties panel, set Full Size Format to 1280 × 720. If 1280 × 720 is not present in the menu list, choose New and enter the proper resolution in the New Format dialog box. Set the Fps parameter to 30. Set the Frame Range to 1,10.

2. Create a new Read node. Browse for the `Tutorials/Tutorial5/Renders/rocket/` directory and select the `rocket.##.exr 1 10` image sequence. Connect Viewer1 to the Read1 node. The sequence features a CG rocket moving right to left across the screen.

3. Select the Read1 node and choose Time > FrameHold. In the FrameHold1 node's properties panel, set the First Frame parameter to 6. This "freeze-frame" the image sequence at frame 6.

4. Select the FrameHold1 node and choose Transform > Transform. Move the timeline to frame 1. In the Transform1 node's properties panel, click the Animation Menu button beside Translate and choose Set Key from the menu. Interactively move the rocket render to the right of the frame, past the right edge of the bounding box. Move the timeline to frame 10. Interactively move the rocket render to the left of the frame, past the left edge of the bounding box. Position the render so that its motion path makes a slight right-to-left down slope (Figure 7.23). This recreates the animation that was originally contained within the image sequence.

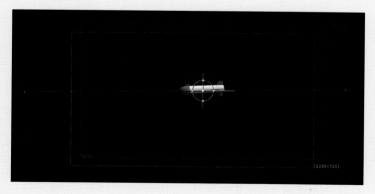

FIGURE 7.23 A single frame of the rocket render is given a motion path by animating the Translate parameter of a Transform node.

5. Move the timeline to frame 5. Select the Transform1 node and choose Time > TimeBlur. The output is instantly given a motion blur streak. Open the TimeBlur1 node's properties panel, and set Shutter to 0.5. This shortens the blur trail, making it the appropriate length for a ½-frame shutter. Change the Divisions parameter to 50. This forces the node to use 50 fractional-frame iterations when generating the blur trail and creates a smooth result. Note how the motion blur trail goes forward in time. You can make the trail go ¼-frame backward in time and ¼-frame forward in time by setting the Shutter Offset menu to Centred (Figure 7.24).

FIGURE 7.24 The rocket is given motion blur with a TimeBlur node. Divisions is set to 50, Shutter is set to 0.5, and Shutter Offset is set to Centred.

6. With no node selected, choose Channel > ShuffleCopy. We'll use this node to create an offshoot network that creates motion blur through motion vector channels. Connect the input 1 pipe of the ShuffleCopy1 node to the Read1 node (thus creating a second output pipe for the Read1 node). With no node selected, choose Other > Dot. An unconnected dot carries an input and output pipe. Connect the dot's output pipe to input 2 of the ShuffleCopy1 node. Connect the dot's input pipe to the output of the Read1 node (thus creating a third output pipe for the Read1 node). See Figure 7.25 for the final node network. Create a new Viewer (Viewer > Create New Viewer through the menu bar) and connect it to the output of ShuffleCopy1. Switch to the Viewer 2 tab.

7. The OpenExr render of the rocket contains two custom channels as well as standard RGBA. To retrieve the motion vector channels, you must adjust the ShuffleCopy1 node. Open the ShuffleCopy1 node's properties panel. Set the In2 menu to

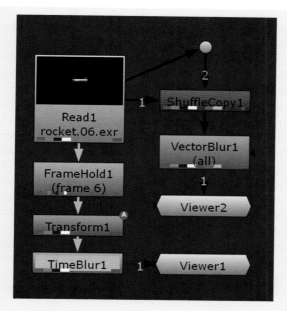

FIGURE 7.25 The final node network for Tutorial 5.

MV2E_mv2DToxik_persp. MV2E_mv2DToxik_persp is a custom motion vector channel created by the mental ray renderer in Maya. Set the Out2 menu to Forward. Below the In1 menu, select the R, G, B, and A checkboxes that line up with the red, green, blue, and alpha rows (see Figure 7.26). Below the In2 menu, select the first two M checkboxes that line up with the U and V rows. This

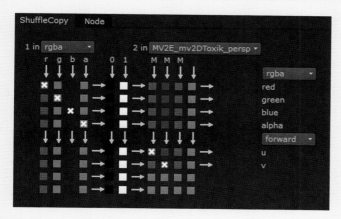

FIGURE 7.26 The ShuffleCopy1 node's settings.

group of settings forces the node to combine the RGBA channels of the rocket render with the motion vector MM channels of the same render. The motion vector MM channels are "shuffled" over to the UV channels so that they are recognizable by nodes downstream.

8. Select the ShuffleCopy1 node and choose Filter > VectorBlur. Open the VectorBlur1 node's properties panel. Set the UV Channels menu to Forward. A motion blur streak appears on the rocket. However, the streak is contained to the body of the rocket and does not proceed or follow it. Change the Method menu to Forward. The Forward method streaks the blur beyond the body of the rocket, which is more realistic. Change the Multiply parameter to 0.5. This is equivalent to setting a shutter to ½ frame. The streak becomes shorter. However, the streak is drawn from the current frame to a ½ frame in the future. To make the streak start ¼ frame in the past and go ¼ frame in the future, set the Offset parameter to −0.25 (Figure 7.27). Offset is equivalent to the TimeBlur node's Shutter Offset parameter.

FIGURE 7.27 Motion blur produced by a VectorBlur node and motion vector channels carried by the OpenEXR render.

9. Compare the motion blur created by the VectorBlur node to the motion blur created by the TimeBlur node. Experiment with different TimeBlur and VectorBlur shutter settings.

    This concludes Tutorial 5. A sample Nuke script is included as `Tutorial5.final.nk` in the `Tutorials/Tutorial5/Scripts/` directory on the DVD.

Tutorial 6: Adding Damage to a Plate

Part 1: Creating an Animated Warp with SplineWarp

Tutorial 6 applies damage to a car featured in a piece of film footage with an animated warp. We'll use a SplineWarp node.

1. Create a new Nuke script. Choose Edit > Project Settings from the menu bar. In the Project Settings properties panel, set Full Size Format to 640 × 480, which is the resolution of predigital standard-definition television. Set the Fps parameter to 30. Set the Frame Range to 1,80.

2. Create a new Read node. Browse for the `Tutorials/ Tutorial6/Plates/car/` directory and select the `car.###.tga 1 80` image sequence. The sequence features a piece of vintage film footage of a cross-country car race. Create a new Read node. Browse for the `Tutorials/Tutorial6/ Renders/debris/` directory and select the `debris.###.tga 70 80` image sequence. The sequence features a CG render of a piece of debris that flies through the air. Click the Frame Range Lock button (on the right side of the timeline) and enter 60-80 in the Frame Range cell. With this setting, the timeline only plays back frames 60 to 80. Because the debris only appears at the end of the sequence, it's not necessary to play back the first 60 frames when testing the morph.

3. Create a new Merge node. Connect input B to Read1 and input A to Read2. Connect a Viewer to the output of the Merge1 node. Move the timeline to frame 73. The debris appears over the edge of the lead car's hood (Figure 7.28). This will serve as the starting point for a morph that creates virtual damage to the car. Note that Nuke places the debris footage at the correct place on the timeline even though the sequence is only 10 frames long.

4. If you are using Nuke v6.2 or earlier, select the Read1 node and choose Transform > SplineWarp. If you are using Nuke v6.3 or later, select the Read1 node, press the X key in the Node Graph, select the TCL radio button in the Command dialog box, enter SplineWarp into the Command field (note the capitalization), and click the OK button. Using the Command dialog box is necessary in v6.3 to create the older SplineWarp node (as opposed to the newer SplineWarp3 node). The Src input pipe is connected automatically to the output of Read1. Open the SplineWarp1 node's properties panel. Select the First Bezier Masks Deform checkbox. In the Viewer, Cmd/Ctrl+Opt/Alt-click to add points to a Bezier curve that forms a mask. To end the curve, LMB-click off the curve. The mask determines what part

FIGURE 7.28 On frame 73, CG debris appears at the edge of the car's hood. Note that the Frame Range cell of the timeline is set to 60-80.

of the input is affected by the warp. Areas outside the mask are unaffected by the node. You can close the Bezier curve by RMB-clicking a point and choosing Open/Close Curve from the shortcut menu. For more information on manipulating the SplineWarp curves, see the "Advanced Distortion Nodes" section earlier in this chapter.

5. Because the camera and the car are in motion, the Mask curve must be animated to follow the car hood. To animate the Mask curve position, move to a different frame on the timeline, LMB-drag a selection marquee around the curve, and move all the selected points by LMB-dragging the transform handle. Note that you must LMB-drag the handle by its central point. Because the motion of the camera and car are somewhat erratic, reposition the Mask curve at frames 74, 75, 76, 77, 78, 79, and 80.

6. Change the Show parameter menu to Src (Source). In the Viewer, Cmd/Ctrl+Opt/Alt-click to add points to a Bezier curve that defines the features or elements that will be warped. For greater precision, you can create multiple curves. To start a new curve, LMB-click off the first curve and Cmd/Ctrl+Opt/Alt-click where you want the new curve to start. Because the camera and the car are in motion, the Source curves must be animated to follow specific features. For example, in Figure 7.29, five Source curves are drawn to follow the chrome bumper components and hood contour where the debris appears to strike. To animate the position of the curves, move to a different frame on the timeline, LMB-drag a selection marquee around the curves, and move all the selected points by LMB-dragging the transform handle.

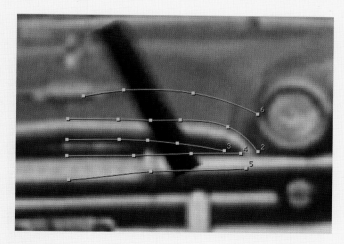

FIGURE 7.29 Source curves, as seen on frame 73.

Because the motion of the camera and car are somewhat erratic, reposition the Source curves at frames 74, 75, 76, 77, 78, 79, and 80.

7. Change the Show parameter menu to Blend. For each Source curve, there is a light blue Destination curve. However, the animation applied to the Source curves is not applied to the Destination curves unless you make a copy. To copy the animation, move the timeline to frame 73, click the Copy button in the Source Curves section, and click the Paste button in the Destination Curves section. Repeat this process for frames 74, 75, 76, 77, 78, 79, and 80.

8. Return to frame 73. LMB-drag points on the Destination curves to create a warp. The pixels distort as you move the points (Figure 7.30). Move the timeline to frame 74. LMB-drag to points to make the warp consistent over time. Alternatively, you can copy and paste Destination curve keyframes across time. For example, move to frame 73, click the Copy button in the Destination Curves section, move to frame 74, and click the Paste button in the Destination Curves section; with these steps, the point positions for frames 73 and 74 are identical. You can also cause the damage to "grow" over time, in which case each Destination curve can carry a slightly different shape for each frame.

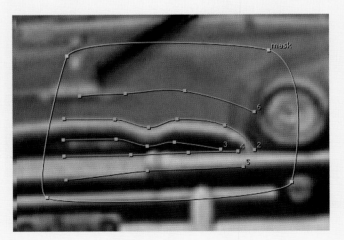

FIGURE 7.30 Mask curve (green) and Destination curves (blue), as seen on frame 76. The warp creates a dent in the chrome of the grill.

9. Move to frame 73. RMB-click the Animation Button beside Distortion and choose Set Key. Move to frame 72, and set Distortion to 0. This creates an off/on switch for the warping so that no warp occurs before frame 73. Create a Flipbook to test the warp animation.

This concludes Part 1 of Tutorial 6. A sample Nuke v6.2 script is included as `Tutorial6.1.nk` in the `Tutorials/Tutorial6/Scripts/` directory on the DVD. In Chapter 8, we'll add additional damage to the car hood through motion tracking.

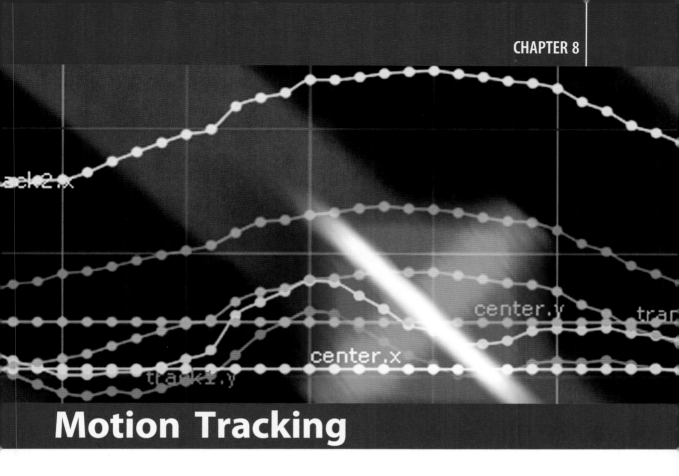

Motion Tracking

Visual effects compositing requires the integration of CG elements, matte paintings, and similar artwork with live-action film or video. Because camera motion is often present, as well as the motion of characters and props, it's necessary to create corresponding motion paths. In Nuke, you can apply these paths to static elements and thus give them matching movement.

This chapter includes the following critical information:

- Motion tracking and matchmoving
- Corner pin tracking
- Plate stabilization and jitter addition

Motion Tracking Overview

Motion tracking is the process by which the motion of a pattern in a piece of film or video footage is identified. The identified motion may be utilized in one of the following ways:

- The motion is applied to a secondary element, such as bitmap artwork or a CG render of a prop, so that the element appears to follow the pattern. For example, a CG prop may be placed in the hand of an actor. This is referred to as *transform tracking*. In this situation, the camera may be static.

- The motion is applied to a secondary element so that the element appears to be shot with the same camera that created the original motion. For example, if a video featuring a left-to-right pan is motion tracked, the left-to-right movement can be applied to the secondary element. This form of tracking is known as *matchmoving*.
- The detected camera motion is removed from the film or video. Thus, the film or video is stabilized.
- The detected camera motion is applied to a secondary source, such as a static image sequence. Thus, the real-world camera movement is grafted onto the secondary source.

Nuke provides the Tracker, CornerPin, and Stabilize nodes in the Transform menu to carry out the various motion tracking tasks.

Transform Tracking and Matchmoving

Nuke's Tracker node offers an efficient means to transform track and matchmove. You can create one of more motion paths for identified patterns. To create a motion path with a Tracker node, follow these steps:

1. Select the node you wish to transform track and choose Transform > Tracker. A sample image sequence is included as `motion.##.tga` in the `Chapters/Chapter8/Plates/motion/` directory on the DVD. Open the Tracker1 node's properties panel. When the panel opens, a track anchor appears in the Viewer. The anchor is composed of an inner box (the pattern area), an outer box (the search area), and a center point (Figure 8.1). The anchor is named Track1.
2. LMB-drag the anchor's center point to place the anchor over a pattern you wish to track. A pattern may be a small feature that remains visible throughout the duration of the image sequence or movie. For example,

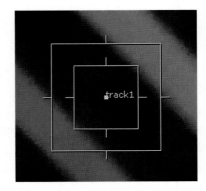

FIGURE 8.1 Track1 anchor in its default state.

a pattern might be the pupil of a character's eye, a small sign or label, or a window or other unique element of a building. Ideally, the pattern should contain high-contrast elements and should not suffer from excessive motion blur. Resize the pattern box to loosely fit the pattern. You can resize the box by LMB-clicking a box line or box corner and LMB-dragging the point that appears.

3. Click to the Track To The Last Frame button (Figure 8.2). The timeline play backs and the node constructs a motion path for the anchor (Figure 8.3). Manually play back the timeline by using the playback controls located below the Viewer. If the transform tracking is successful, the anchor will follow the chosen pattern closely. If the tracking is unsuccessful, you are free to reposition the anchor, adjust the pattern box, and use the Track To The Last Frame or Track To The First Frame buttons to update the motion path. (For additional problem-solving suggestions, see the "Troubleshooting Transform Tracking" section later in this chapter.) The anchor position is automatically keyframed; this is indicated by the blue cells beside the Track1 Transform X and Y properties.

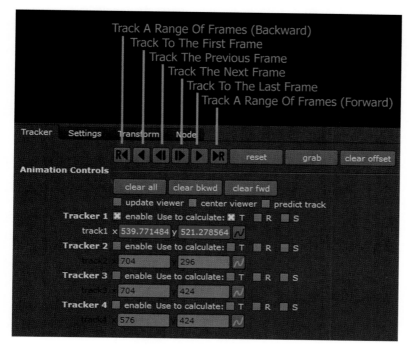

FIGURE 8.2 The Tracker tab of the Tracker node's properties panel. The Track buttons are located along the top. The Tracker 1 Track X and Y parameters are automatically animated as a motion path is generated by the Track buttons.

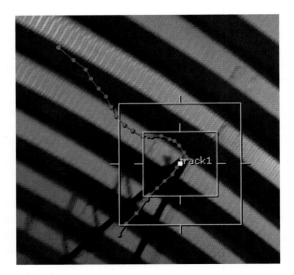

FIGURE 8.3 The anchor is positioned and scaled to surround the triangular end of a ceiling bracket. The Track To The Last Frame button successfully creates a motion path for the chosen pattern. A sample script is included as tracker.nk in the Chapters/Chapter8/Scripts/directory on the DVD.

Applying the Motion Path Data

To apply the motion path data to a secondary source, such as a separate Read node, select the Tracker node and choose Edit > Duplicate from the menu bar. Connect the secondary source to the input of the duplicated Tracker node. Open the duplicated Tracker node's properties panel and switch to the Transform tab (see Figure 8.6 later in this section). Change the Transform menu to Match-Move. Connect the output of the duplicated Tracker node to the Viewer. If you wish to merge the secondary source over the tracked image sequence or movie, follow these additional steps:

1. Create a Merge node. Connect the input A of the Merge node to the output of the duplicated Tracker node. See Figure 8.4.
2. Connect the ouput of the Read node that carries an image sequence or movie to the input B of the Merge node. Connect the Viewer to the output of the Merge node.
3. Play back the timeline. The secondary output receives its motion from the duplicated Tracker node.

Note that the secondary source may not appear over the motion path displayed by the duplicated Tracker node. This is particularly evident if the secondary source is a smaller resolution than the project resolution (Figure 8.5).

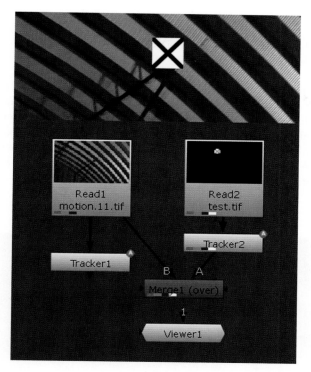

FIGURE 8.4 A duplicated Tracker node and a Merge node place the matchmoved artwork over the ceiling. (The artwork is a black-and-white X surrounded by alpha transparency.) A sample script is included as transformtrack.nk in the Chapters/Chapter8/Scripts/ directory on the DVD.

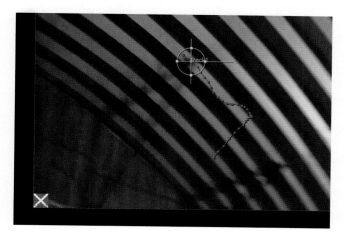

FIGURE 8.5 A 50 × 50 resolution bitmap, featuring a red-and-white X, is placed at the bottom-left corner by a duplicated Tracker node on frame 1.

231

This occurs for the following reasons:

- When the Transform menu is set to matchmove, the Translate X and Translate Y properties (also listed on the Transform tab as illustrated by Figure 8.6) are applied to the node's input.
- By default, the frame 1 position of the anchor is stored as 0,0 by Translate X and Y. In contrast, Nuke considers the bottom-left corner of the composite as 0,0. Hence, when Translate X and Y are 0,0, the secondary source is placed at the bottom-left corner of the composite. The frame 1 position is known as the identity transform. You can choose a different frame to serve as the identify transform by changing the Reference Frame value in the Transform tab.

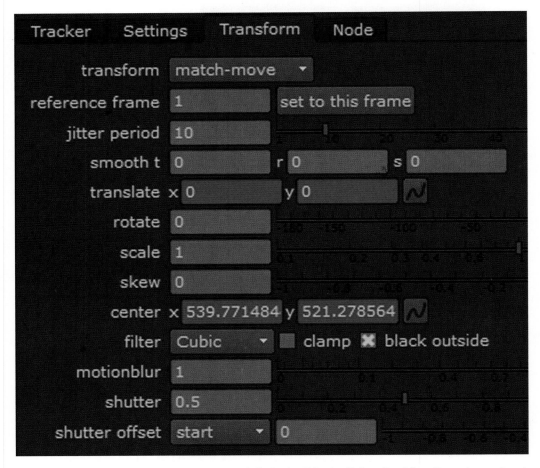

FIGURE 8.6 The Transform tab of the Tracker node's properties panel. The Translate X, Translate Y, Center X, and Center Y properties are animated automatically when a motion path is generated for a tracked pattern.

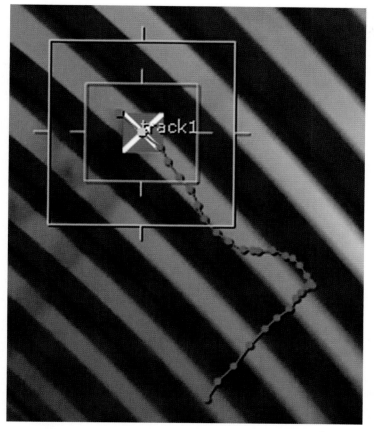

FIGURE 8.7 The artwork is positioned over the anchor through the addition of a Transform node. A sample script is included as transformoffset.nk in the Chapters/Chapter8/Scripts/ directory on the DVD.

To offset the secondary source so that it lines up with the motion path more closely, follow these extra steps:

1. Select the secondary source node and choose Transform > Transform.
2. While the Transform node and the duplicated Tracker node are open in the properties panel, interactively move the transform handle so that it lines up with the anchor or otherwise appears in the correct location.
3. Play back the timeline. The secondary source continues to follow the motion path, but is no longer offset (Figure 8.7).

Note that the pattern most suitable for transform tracking may not be in a location where you'd like to position the secondary source. Hence, offsetting the secondary source is a common task.

Activating Motion Blur

Once the transform tracking/matchmoving data is applied to an input, you can activate motion blur through the Tracker node. To do so, set the Motionblur parameter, in the Transform tab, to a nonzero value. This allows the input to take on the same blur that's carried by the moving pattern (e.g., a moving hand) or the moving camera (Figure 8.8).

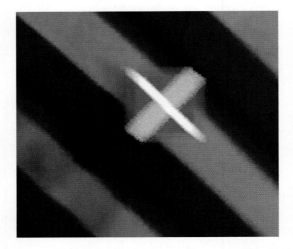

FIGURE 8.8 The Tracker node's Motionblur parameter is set to 1, allowing the matchmoved artwork to take on the same blur as the background.

Troubleshooting Transform Tracking

As you use the Track buttons to calculate the motion path of an anchor, you may run into the following problems:

- The calculation stops because the node is unable to locate the pattern.
- The anchor jumps to an incorrect pattern.
- The calculation doesn't fail; however, the resulting motion path is very jittery (full of small peaks and valleys).

You can restart the motion path calculation at any time, either in the forward or backward direction. You can restart the calculation on any frame of the timeline. You can track a single frame by using the Track The Previous Frame or Track The Next Frame buttons. You can track a specific frame range by clicking the forward or backward Track A Range Of Frames buttons; when you click, a Enter Backward/Forward Tracking Range dialog box opens. To improve the odds of success, you can also try the following techniques:

- Resize the pattern box of the anchor. If the pattern box is too large, nearby patterns may interfere with the node's ability to identify the pattern you have singled out.
- Resize the outer search box of the anchor. The larger the search box, the farther the node will go to find the pattern if it no longer falls into the pattern box. A large search box may be useful when a great deal of motion blur is present. However, a large search box will slow the calculation.
- Interactively move the anchor if it has slipped away from the pattern. For example, if the anchor is in the incorrect location for frame 10, move the timeline to the frame 10, and LMB-drag the anchor so that it correctly encompasses the pattern. Proceed to recalculate the motion path from frame 11 forward.
- To avoid recalculating large areas of the motion path, use the Track The Previous Frame or Track The Next Frame buttons.

If a Tracker parameter has X and Y animation, you can protect the animation from further changes by deselecting the corresponding Enable checkbox in the Tracker tab. To remove a motion path for all enabled trackers, click the Clear All button. You can also delete motion path keyframes in front of the current frame or behind the current frame by clicking the Clear Bkwd or Clear Fwd buttons.

To remove jitter from a motion path, switch to the Transform tab (see Figure 8.6) and enter nonzero values into the Smooth T (Translate), R (Rotate), and/or S (Scale) cells. The Value represents the number of frames that are averaged together to create the new motion path. The higher the values, the smoother the motion path becomes.

Tracking Rotation and Scaling

In its default state, the Tracker node only notes positional changes. However, you can force the node to detect rotation and scaling. Rotation may occur if an object is spinning or the camera tilts. Scaling may occur if an object moves toward or away from the camera or the camera lens changes focal length through a zoom. To track rotation and scaling, follow these steps:

1. Switch to the Settings tab of the Tracker node's properties panel. Change the Warp Type menu to the transformation combination that suits the input. You have the choice of Translate, Translate/Rotate, Translate/Scale, Translate/Rotate/Scale, or Affine. Affine represents a cumulative transformation that includes translate, rotate, scale, and shear.
(For example, if the top of a boxlike pattern moves to the right and the bottom of the same pattern moves to the left, the otherwise square pattern forms a trapezoid and is thus sheared.)
2. Switch to the Tracker tab. Select or deselect the T (Translate), R (Rotate), and/or S (Scale) checkboxes to match the Warp Type menu.

3. Proceed to position the anchor point and calculate the motion track using the steps outlined earlier in the "Transform Tracking and Matchmoving" section.

When you choose to calculate rotation or scale, the corresponding properties in the Transform tab are automatically animated. If you set the Transform menu to Affine and shear is detected, the Skew property is animated. Also note that the Center X and Y properties are animated for all transform tracking calculations. Center X and Y determine the location of the transform handle and thus where the center is for rotation and scaling transformations. If the transform tracking is relatively simple, the Center X and Y may not change throughout the duration of the timeline. In such a case, you can delete the animation by clicking the corresponding Animation Menu button and choosing No Animation. You can manually change the Center X and Y values or interactively move the transform handle by Cmd/Ctrl-LMB-dragging the handle center point; this moves the entire motion path.

Employing Multiple Anchors

The Tracker node allows you to use multiple anchors. Multiple anchors can increase the accuracy of the tracking when heavy motion blur or erratic camera movement is present. Multiple anchors are also better suited to detect changes in rotation and scale. Multiple anchors are equally useful when a single pattern does not last the entire duration of the timeline, whether the pattern is temporarily occluded or leaves the frame.

To activate additional anchors, select Tracker2, Tracker3, and/or Tracker4 checkboxes in the Tracker tab. Select the T, R, and/or S checkboxes beside each activated Tracker property to match the Warp Type menu (see the previous section). Move and scale the new anchors as you would for the default Tracker1 anchor. Each anchor receives a motion path when the Track buttons are activated. However, the motion path granted to the Translate X and Y properties of the Transform tab is an average of all the anchor motion paths. That is, the matchmove translation output by the node is an average of all the anchor point positions.

As an example, in Figures 8.9, 8.10, and 8.11 an input features a city at night. The camera rapidly tilts and zooms, creating heavy motion blur. To detect the rotate and scale change, Tracker1 and Tracker2 are activated, along with the corresponding T, R, and S checkboxes. The Warp Type menu, in the Settings tab, is set to Translate/Rotate/Scale. Due to the heavy blur, the anchors boxes are enlarged. The Track1 anchor surrounds an entire building. The Track2 anchor surrounds the bright lights on top of two neighboring buildings. To create a complete motion path for each pattern it was necessary to apply the techniques listed in the "Troubleshooting Transform Tracking" section earlier in this chapter.

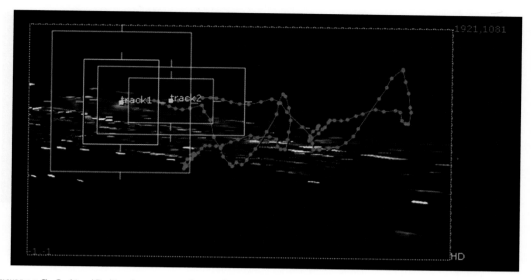

FIGURE 8.9 The Track1 and Track2 anchors, as seen on frame 1 of a blurry night shot of a city. A sample script is included as `rotatescale.nk` in the `Chapters/Chapter8/Scripts/` directory on the DVD.

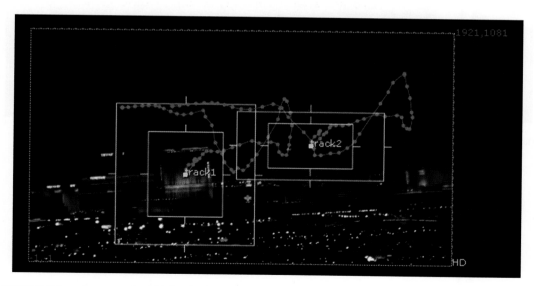

FIGURE 8.10 Same anchors, seen on frame 54. Note the change in rotation and scale of the selected patterns. Because frame 54 contained the least amount of motion blur, the anchors were initially positioned on this frame.

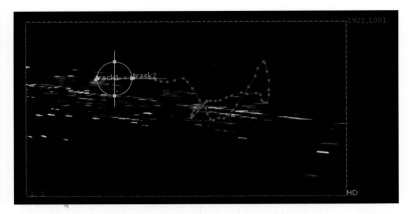

FIGURE 8.11 The averaged motion path created by the Translate X and Y parameters of the Transform tab.

Editing Motion Path Curves

When the Tracker node calculates a motion path, it automatically keyframes properties in the Tracker and Transform tabs and thus creates corresponding animation curves with a keyframe at every frame of the timeline (Figure 8.12).

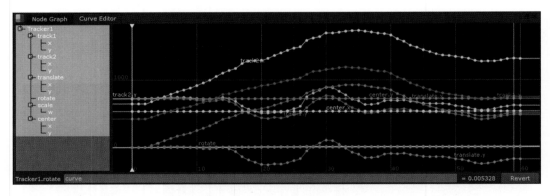

FIGURE 8.12 Animation curves created by a Tracker node.

You can edit the curves and keyframes as you would for any other animated property for any other node. Here is a review of the animation curves the node creates:

track*n* X and Y The location of the Track*n* anchor in screen space.
translate X and Y The output translation animation.
rotate The output rotation animation.
scale W and H The output scale animation.
skew The output shear animation; values above 0 move the top of the output to the right and the bottom of the output to the left. Values below 0 have the opposite result.

center X and Y The center point from which transformations are carried out; these curves are often static.

The translate, rotate, and scale curve values change when the Transform menu is switched from Matchmove to Stabilize, Add Jitter, or Remove Jitter. In fact, the Stabilize mode inverts the curve values present for the Match-Move mode. The Remove Jitter mode inverts the curve values present for the Add Jitter mode. Stabilize, Add Jitter, and Remove Jitter are discussed in the following two sections.

Stabilization

Stabilization employs transform tracking techniques to remove camera motion from an input. Stabilization is used to remove extraneous movement from handheld camera work or to remove the left/right weave suffered by damaged motion film stock. The Tracker node carries a Stabilize mode, which you can apply with the following steps:

1. Apply the Tracker node as you would when transform tracking. The techniques listed in the "Transform Tracking and MatchMoving" section earlier in this chapter are valid for stabilization.
2. Once you've created suitable motion paths for the anchors, switch to the Tracker node's Transform tab and change the Transform menu to Stabilize. The input is repositioned with each frame so that the transform handle, revealed by the Transform tab, stays fixed to the same location. The node achieves this by applying offset animation to the node's Translate X, Translate Y, Center X, and Center Y parameters.

When the input is offset, it moves past the edge of the output bounding box (Figure 8.13). Thus, one or more empty black edges are revealed. To avoid the

The FurnaceCore plug-in set includes the F_Steadiness node, which uses a form of corner pin tracking to stabilize a frame. The corner pin positions are determined by the node once the input is analyzed via the Analyse button. Analyzation occurs over a duration set by the Analysis Start and Analysis Stop parameters. To smooth the detected motion by averaging corner pin positions, set the Mode parameter to Smooth. To stabilize the input in reference to a chosen frame (where all other frames are translated so that they line up with the chosen frame), set Mode to Lock. You can pick a lock frame by changing the Lock Frame value in the Advanced section.

The F_Align node, also provided by FurnanceCore, is identical to the F_Steadiness node. However, F_Align lacks the Mode menu. Instead, F_Align provides a Ref (Reference) input pipe in addition to the Src (Source) input pipe. As such, F_Align translates the Src input to line up with the Ref input, which can be a single frame or a separate image sequence culled from the same footage used for the Src input. For more information on the F_Steadiness and F_Align nodes, see the "User Guide for Furnace" PDF available at The Foundry's website (*www.thefoundry.co.uk*).

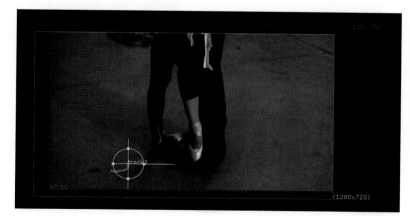

FIGURE 8.13 A Tracker node stabilizes an input. The chosen pattern (a tape mark on the floor) is pinned to its frame 1 position. This is achieved by translating the entire input, causing it to move past the edge of the output bounding box. A sample script is included as `stabilize.nk` in the Chapters/Chapter8/ Scripts/ directory on the DVD.

edges, you can add a Transform node to the output of the Tracker node and thereby scale the output so that the black areas are no longer visible.

Additionally, Nuke provides the Stabilize2D node for the application of stabilization data. However, the node requires expressions to function. Hence, the node is reviewed in Chapter 10.

Adding and Removing Jitter

The Add Jitter mode of the Tracker node is designed to add high-frequency camera movement to an otherwise static input. High-frequency movement includes shaking but does not include large camera movements, such as pans or tilts. The Add Jitter workflow is identical to the Match-Move mode as is outlined in the section "Transform Tracking and Matchmoving" earlier in this chapter. This includes the duplication of the Tracker node. However, the Transform menu must be set to Add Jitter. For example, in Figure 8.14, the camera motion carried by an image sequence imported through the Read1 node is stored by the Tracker1 node. Tracker2, which is a duplicate of

FIGURE 8.14 The high-frequency camera motion carried by the Read1 image sequence is passed to the static bitmap carried by the Read2 node through a Tracker node with its Transform menu set to Add Jitter. A sample script is included as `addjitter.nk` in the `Chapters/Chapter8/ Scripts/` directory on the DVD.

Tracker1, is connected to the output of the Read2 node, which carries a static bitmap. The Tracker2 node's Transform menu is set to Add Jitter, thus transferring the camera movement to the static bitmap. To avoid seeing the black edges created when Read2 is moved past the output bounding box, a Transform node is added with Scale set to 1.02.

In contrast, the Tracker node's Remove Jitter mode is designed to remove high-frequency camera motion. The workflow for Remove Jitter is identical to Stabilize (see the previous section). However, the Transform menu must be set to Remove Jitter. You can switch the Transform menu between Stabilize and Remove Jitter to see the difference in the modes' outputs.

Corner Pin Tracking

Corner pin tracking is a variant of transform tracking/matchmoving that uses four anchors to identify a rectangular pattern. For example, corner pin tracking is ideal for tracking a billboard, poster, window, or doorway. The Tracker node provides four anchors necessary for corner pin tracking. However, to apply the resulting motion paths to a secondary source, you must utilize the CornerPin2D node. To undertake corner pin tracking in Nuke, follow these steps:

1. Connect a Tracker node to the output you wish to motion track. Activate the Tracker2, Tracker3, and Tracker4 checkboxes in the node's properties panel. Place and scale the four anchors at the four corners of the rectangular pattern. Calculate the motion paths. Use the techniques listed in the "Transform Tracking and Matchmoving" section earlier in this chapter to create the motion paths. If there are rotational and/or scale changes to the chosen pattern, consider activating the Track*n* R and/or S checkboxes as well as changing the Warp Type menu to the matching transform set. If the pattern is rotating and diminishing in perspective, change the Warp Type menu to Affine so that shear is considered as part of the transformation.

2. Create a CornerPin2D node (Transform > CornerPin) and connect its input pipe to the output that will receive the tracking data. For example, the output may be a Read node that carries a bitmap of a movie poster. Connect a Viewer to the CornerPin2D node.

3. Open the Tracker and the CornerPin2D nodes' properties panel. Place the mouse pointer over the Animation Menu button beside Track1 X and Y in the Tracker node's Tracker tab. Cmd/Ctrl+LMB-drag away from the button. The mouse pointer changes to a + sign. Continue to drag to the Animation Menu button beside the To1 X and Y parameter of the CornerPin2D node (Figure 8.15). Release the mouse button. A link is created between the Track1 and To1 parameters. Thus, the motion tracking data is passed to the CornerPin2D node (the link is an automated expression). The link is indicated in the node graph as

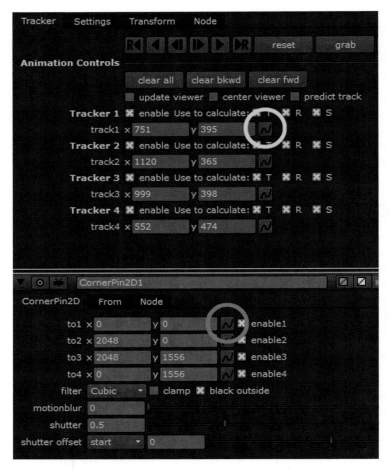

FIGURE 8.15 To transfer corner pin motion tracking data, Cmd/Ctrl+LMB-drag from the Tracker node's Track*n* Animation Menu button (yellow circle) to the CornerPin2D node's To*n* Animation Menu button (green circle).

a green arrow flowing from the Tracker to the CornerPin2D node. Once the link is established, the bottom-left corner of the CornerPin2D input is snapped to the location of the Track1 anchor.

4. Repeat step 3 to link Track2 to To2, Track3 to To3, and Track4 to To4. The CornerPin2D input is thus distorted to fit the pattern.

5. Connect the output of the CornerPin2D node to input A of a Merge node. Connect the output of the tracked image sequence or movie to input B of the Merge node. The CornerPin2D output is thus composited on top of the film or video that contained the original motion.

For additional information on linking, see Chapter 10. For an additional example of corner pin tracking, see Tutorial 8, "Replacing a Screen with Corner Pin Tracking," at the end of this chapter.

Tutorial 6: Adding Damage to a Plate
Part 2: Transform Tracking

In Part 1 of this tutorial, we added damage to the grill of a car with a SplineWarp node. In Part 2, we'll add to the damage by transform tracking a piece of static artwork to the car hood.

1. Open the Nuke script you saved after completing Part 1 of this tutorial. A sample Nuke script is included as `Tutorial6.1.nk` in the `Tutorials/Tutorial6/Scripts/` directory on the DVD. Click the Frame Range Lock button (on the right side of the timeline) and enter 60-80 in the Frame Range cell. With this setting, the timeline only plays back frames 60 to 80. Because the debris only appears at the end of the sequence, it's not necessary to play back the first 60 frames when testing the morph or motion tracking. Select the SplineWarp1 node and press the D key to temporarily disable it.

2. Create a new Read node. Browse for the `Tutorials/Tutorial6/Bitmaps/` directory and select `damage.tga`. The bitmap features a digital matte painting that features damage to the hood of the car. Create a new Merge node. Connect the output of Read3 to input A of Merge2. Connect the output of Read1 to input B of Merge2. Connect the output of Merge2 to the Src pipe of the SplineWarp1 node. See Figure 8.16 for the final node network.

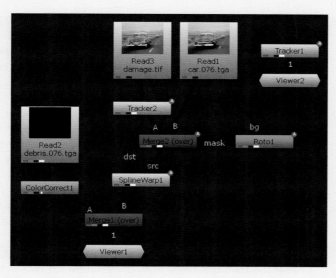

FIGURE 8.16 The final node network for Tutorial 6.

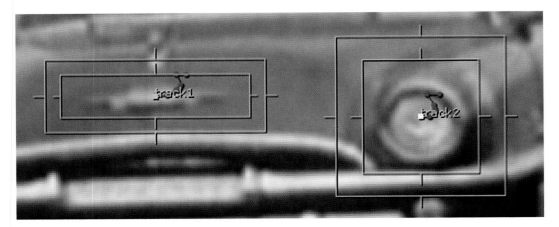

FIGURE 8.17 Track1 and Track2 anchors are positioned and scaled to surround two patterns on the car.

3. Select the Read1 node and choose Transform > Tracker. Create a new Viewer and connect it to the output of Tracker1. Switch to the new Viewer tab. Open the Tracker1 node's properties panel. Switch to the Settings tab. Change Warp Type to Translate/Rotate/ Scale. Switch back to the Tracker tab. Select the Enable checkbox beside Tracker2. Select the T, R, and S checkboxes beside Tracker1 and Tracker2.

4. Move the timeline to frame 73. Frame 73 is the frame on which the CG debris "contacts" the front of the car. Position and scale the Track1 and Track2 anchors to surround two patterns on the car. For example, surround the chrome hood emblem and the screen-right headlight. You can temporarily hide the CG debris by selecting the Read2 node and pressing the D key.

5. Click the Track To The Last Frame button. The Tracker1 node creates motion paths for the two anchors. Manually play back the timeline to ensure that the anchors follow the chosen patterns correctly. If necessary, recalculate the motion paths using the techniques listed in the section "Troubleshooting Transform Tracking" earlier in this chapter.

6. With the Tracker1 node selected, choose Edit > Duplicate from the menu bar. LMB-drag and drop the Tracker2 node on the pipe between the Read3 node and the Merge2 node. Open the Tracker2 node's properties panel. Switch to the Transform tab. Change the Transform menu to Match-Move. Switch back to the Viewer1 tab. Play back the timeline. The damage artwork is motion tracked to the Read1 image sequence. At this point, the damage appears too early. Move the timeline to frame 73. Open the

Merge2 node's properties panel. Set Mix to 0. RMB-click the Mix parameter's Animation Menu button and choose Set Key. Move the timeline to frame 75. Set Mix to 1. This fades the damage in over two frames.

7. At this stage, the entire damage artwork is merged over the image sequence. However, only the immediate area around the damage is needed. With no node selected, choose Draw > Roto. Open the Roto1 node's properties panel. In the Viewer1 tab, Cmd/Ctrl-click to draw a mask around the damage area. LMB-drag a selection marquee around the mask to select all the points. RMB-click over a point and choose Increase Feather several times (Figure 8.18). Connect the Merge2 node's Mask input pipe to the Roto1 node output.

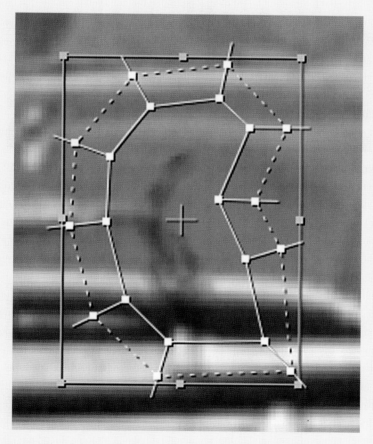

FIGURE 8.18 A mask, drawn with a Roto node, creates a matte for the damage artwork.

8. Enable any disabled node by selecting it and pressing the D key. Render a Flipbook to test the transform tracking and SplineWarp deformation (Figure 8.19).

This concludes Tutorial 6. As a bonus step, color grade the CG debris to better match the image sequence. For example, insert a ColorCorrect node between the Read2 node and the Merge1 node. A sample Nuke script is included as `Tutorial6.final.nk` in the `Tutorials/Tutorial6/Scripts/` directory on the DVD.

FIGURE 8.19 Detail of final composite with CG debris, SplineWarp deformation of grille and hood, and transform-tracked damage artwork.

Tutorial 7: Patching a Set with a Matchmove

Tutorial 7 fixes an unattractive portion of a set by matchmoving a static piece of artwork to the camera movement contained within an image sequence. We will carry out the matchmoving with the Tracker node.

1. Create a new Nuke script. Choose Edit > Project Settings from the menu bar. In the Project Settings properties panel, set Full Size Format to 1280 × 720. Set the Fps parameter to 30. Set the Frame Range to 0,29.

2. Create a new Read node. Browse for the `Tutorials/Tutorial7/Plates/jump/` directory and select the `jump.##.tga 0 29` image sequence. The sequence features dancers moving within a large airplane hanger (Figure 8.20).

FIGURE 8.20 The undoctored plate.

3. Create a new Read node. Browse for the `Tutorials/Tutorial7/ Bitmaps/` directory and select `fix.tga`. The bitmap features a digital matte painting intended to cover the upper portion of the hanger.

4. Select the Read1 node and choose Transform > Tracker. Connect a Viewer to the output of Tracker1. Open the Tracker1 node's properties panel. The Track1 anchor becomes visible in the Viewer. Position the anchor over a high-contrast pattern that remains visible throughout the duration of the timeline. For example, place the anchor over one of the window frame intersections (Figure 8.21). (The dancers cannot be used for tracking as they move independent of the camera.) Scale the anchor's pattern box to loosely encompass the pattern.

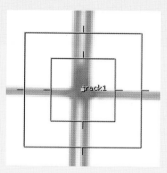

FIGURE 8.21 Anchor positioned and scaled over a window frame intersection.

5. Click the Track To The Last Frame button. The node plays the timeline and generates a motion path for the pattern. Manually play back the

timeline to check that the anchor follows the pattern correctly. If the motion path is incorrect, adjust the anchors and apply the Track buttons. For additional suggestions, see the "Troubleshooting Transform Tracking" section earlier in this chapter.

6. Once a motion path is suitably generated, select the Tracker1 node and choose Edit > Duplicate from the menu bar. Connect the Tracker2 node to the output of the Read2 node. Create a Merge node. Connect the Merge1 node's input B pipe to the output of Read1. Connect the Merge1 node's input A pipe to the output of Tracker2. Connect the output of the Merge1 node to a Viewer. See Figure 8.22 for the final node network.

7. Open the Tracker2 node's properties panel. Switch to the Transform tab. Change the Transform menu to Match-Move. The Tracker2 node's Translate X and Translate Y animation are transferred to the Read2 node.

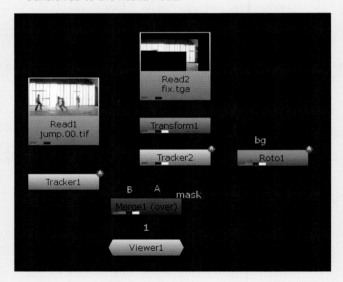

FIGURE 8.22 The final node network for Tutorial 7.

8. Play back the timeline. The Read2 bitmap follows the motion of the camera; however, it obscures the Read1 image sequence. With no nodes selected, choose Draw > Roto. Open the Roto1 node's properties panel. In the Viewer, Cmd/Crtl-click to draw a closed garbage mask and thus isolate the top of the matte painting while discarding the lower portion (Figure 8.23). Connect the Merge1 node's Mask input pipe to the output of the Roto1 node. Feather the mask edge by selecting mask points and LMB-dragging the feather handle away from the mask curve.

FIGURE 8.23 A mask, drawn with a Roto node, crops the matte painting. (The Read1 node is temporarily disabled.)

9. Play back the timeline. At this point, the matte painting provided by the Read2 node is not lined up with the image sequence. The painting was created from a single frame of the sequence; however, its resolution is slightly larger than the project resolution—1656 × 864. To offset the painting, select the Read2 node and choose Transform > Transform. Open the Transfrom1 node's properties panel and change the Translate X and Y values to −110,4. Play back the timeline. The painting sits in the correct position (Figure 8.24).

FIGURE 8.24 The final Tutorial 7 composite.

This concludes Tutorial 7. A sample Nuke script is included as `Tutorial7.final.nk` in the `Tutorials/Tutorial7/Scripts/` directory on the DVD.

Tutorial 8: Replacing a Screen with Corner Pin Tracking

Tutorial 8 replaces the screen of a smart phone with new artwork. We will achieve this by using Tracker and CornerPin2D nodes.

1. Create a new Nuke script. Choose Edit > Project Settings from the menu bar. In the Project Settings properties panel, set Full Size Format to 1920 × 1080. Set the Fps parameter to 30. Set the Frame Range to 1,40.

2. Create a new Read node. Browse for the `Tutorials/Tutorial8/ Plates/phone/` directory and select the `phone.##.tga 1 40` image sequence. The sequence features a moving shot of a handheld smart phone.

3. With the Read1 selected, choose Transform > Tracker. Connect a Viewer to Tracker1. Open the Tracker1 node's properties panel. Switch to the settings tab. Change the Warp Type menu to Translate/Rotate/Scale. Switch back to the Tracker tab. Select the Enable checkbox beside Track2, Track3, and Track4. Select the T, R, and S checkboxes beside Track1, Track2, Track3, and Track4.

4. Position the anchors so that their center points rest at the corners of the phone screen where it meets the back edge of the phone body (Figure 8.25). Enlarge the anchors boxes. Because there is heavy motion blur as the phone rotates, larger pattern and search boxes will help the Tracker become more successful at following the chosen patterns (the corners).

5. Click the Track To The Last Frame button. The Tracker1 node generates motion paths for the anchors. The tracking will most likely fail due to the rapid rotation of the phone between frames 13 and 25. If the tracking fails, manually play back the timeline. Determine the frame on which the anchors slip away from the corners. Back up one frame. Click the Clear Fwd button to remove keyframes forward of the current frame. Proceed to click the Track The Next Frame multiple times to manually create the motion path one frame at a time. With each frame, examine the anchor positions. If any anchor slips from its corner, interactively move it back into the correct place in the Viewer. Continue to step forward until the node can successfully place all four anchors. At that time, click the Track To The Last Frame button to finish creating the motion paths.

6. Manually play back the timeline. Examine the anchor positions. If any of the positions remain inaccurate, manually adjust the anchor positions in the Viewer. After adjusting an anchor position, use the Track The Next Frame and Track The Previous Frame to update, and thus make more accurate, nearby keyframes.

7. Once the motion paths have gained sufficient accuracy, choose Transform > CornerPin with no nodes selected. Open the Tracker1 and CornerPin2D1 nodes' properties panels. Create a link between

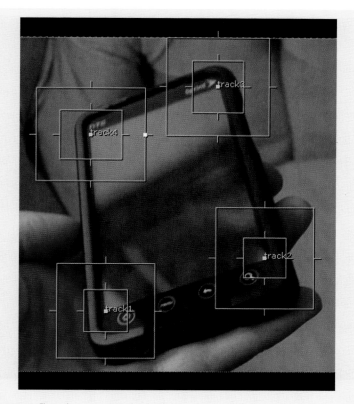

FIGURE 8.25 The anchors are positioned and scaled over the corners of the phone screen.

the Tracker1's Track1 Animation Menu button and the CornerPin2D1's To1 Animation Menu button by Cmd/Ctrl+LMB-dragging between the buttons. (See the section "Corner Pin Tracking" earlier in this chapter.) Repeat the linking process between Track2 and To2, Track3 and To3, and Track4 and To4.

8. With no nodes selected, choose Image > ColorBars. Connect the output of ColorBars1 to the input of CornerPin2D1. Create a Merge node. Connect the input A pipe to the output of CornerPin2D1. Connect the input B pipe to the output of Read1. Connect the Viewer to the Merge1 node. (See Figure 8.26 for the final node network.) The Colorbars1 output, which takes on the project resolution by default, is distorted to fit the phone screen.

9. Select the ColorBars1 node and choose Filter > Blur. Open the Blur1 node's properties panel and set Size to 10. This softens the otherwise hard-edged bars so they better match the slightly soft video. Open the Merge1 node's properties panel. Set Mix to 0.6. This gives semi-transparency to the bars and allows the reflections carried by the original phone screen to show through. Open the

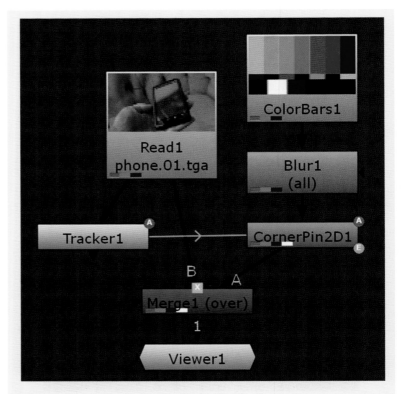

FIGURE 8.26 The final node network for Tutorial 8.

FIGURE 8.27 The final Tutorial 8 composite.

CornerPin2D1 node's properties panel. Set Motionblur to 1. This blurs the bars and allows them to match the rotational blur streaks of the phone (Figure 8.27).

This concludes Tutorial 8. A sample Nuke script is included as `Tutorial8.final.nk` in the `Tutorials/Tutorial8/Scripts/` directory on the DVD.

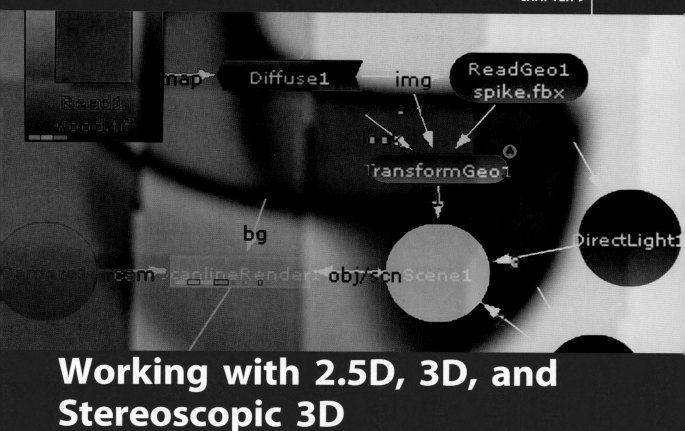

CHAPTER 9

Working with 2.5D, 3D, and Stereoscopic 3D

Compositing programs have entered the 3D arena by offering 3D environ-ments in which 2D elements can be translated, scaled, and rotated. Nuke adds to this functionality by supporting 3D cameras, lights, geometry, and geometry shaders. The 3D tools are not intended to replace traditional 3D programs, but give the compositor an additional tool set for solving prob-lems. Separately, stereoscopic 3D projects are available in Nuke, whereby left- and right-eye views of the same subject are combined to create the illusion of real-word depth.

This chapter includes the following critical information:

- Creating a 3D environment
- Manipulating cameras and lights
- Assigning geometry shaders
- Importing and exporting geometry
- Setting up a stereoscopic project

Working with 2.5D and 3D

Nuke offers a full 3D environment with cameras, lights, primitive geometry, and geometry shaders. In addition, several nodes provide a means to import geometry, lights, camera, and transforms from external 3D programs. 3D environments within compositing programs are often referred to as 2.5D or 2½-D for several reasons:

- Compositing programs must "flatten" the view of the 3D camera into 2D screen space for other nodes or filters to use the 3D information. Nuke carries this out by rendering the view with a specialized node.
- Many times, 3D geometry is restricted to cards—2D bitmaps, image sequences, or videos that are rotated in 3D space as if they are playing cards or postcards.

Setting Up a 3D Environment

To create a functioning 3D environment in Nuke, you must connect Scene, Camera, and Render nodes in a network. If you are using Nuke v6.1 or earlier, the ScanlineRender node is available. If you are using Nuke v6.2 or later, you have the option to use the PrmanRender node. You can follow these steps to set up a simple 3D environment:

1. In the Node Graph, RMB-click and choose 3D > Scene. With no nodes selected, choose 3D > Camera. With no nodes selected, choose 3D > ScanlineRender. (See the sidebar later in this chapter for information on the PrmanRender node.) Connect the Camera1 node to the ScanlineRender1 node's Cam input pipe. Connect the Scene1 node to the Obj/Scn input pipe. Connect a Viewer to the output of ScanlineRender1. See Figure 9.1 for the network layout.
2. Change the View Selection menu from 2D to 3D. The menu is to the right of the Zoom menu at the top of the Viewer panel (Figure 9.2). Initially, the

FIGURE 9.1 Network required to create a 3D environment.

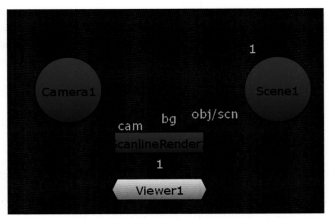

view of the 3D environment is empty. Alt-MMB-drag or use the MMB scroll wheel to dolly backward. A wireframe camera icon appears (Figure 9.3). This is the Camera1 icon. The view is presented through a default working camera. You can change to the Camera1 view by switching the Camera Or Light To Look Through menu from Default to Camera1 (see Figure 9.2).

FIGURE 9.2 From left to right: Zoom menu, View Selection menu, 3D View Mode button, and Camera Or Light To Look Through menu.

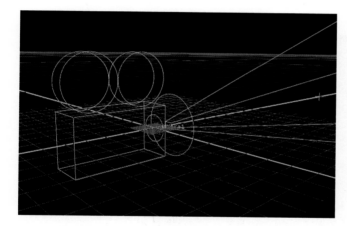

FIGURE 9.3 The Camera1 icon as seen in the 3D view through the default camera.

Nuke's 3D environment is similar to other 3D programs such as Maya or 3ds Max. A grid represents the XZ plane with positive Y as the up axis. You can interactively move the default camera view by Opt/Alt+LMB-dragging to scroll, Opt/Alt+MMB-dragging to dolly forward or backward, and/or Opt/Alt+RMB-dragging to orbit. You can interactively move Camera1 while looking through its lens by Ctrl-clicking the 3D View Mode button so that it turns green (see Figure 9.2) and using the Opt/Alt mouse key combinations. You can interactively position the Camera1 icon by switching the Camera Or Light To Look Through menu back to Default, clicking on the camera icon so that it turns green, and LMB-dragging the transform handle that appears at the icon center. You can interactively rotate the icon by Cmd/Ctrl+LMB-dragging the same axis handle. In addition, you can manually change the Camera1 node's Translate and Rotate parameters through the properties panel.

Creating Cards and Primitives

After you create a 3D environment, you can add geometry. The simplest form of geometry is a card, whereby a node output is mapped to a primitive plane.

257

To create a card, choose 3D > Geometry > Card. Connect the output you wish to map to the card to the Img input of the Card node. Connect the ouput of the Card node to the input of the Scene node. For example, in Figure 9.4, a Read node carrying an imported bitmap is connected. You can position and rotate the card within the 3D space by using the Opt/Alt and Cmd/Ctrl mouse button combinations outlined for the camera in the previous section. Alternatively, you can change the Translate, Rotate, Scale, and Skew values in the Card node's properties panel. By default, the transform pivot is in the center of the card; however, you can change this by altering the node's Pivot parameter values. Although the Card geometry is perfectly flat, you can deform it by switching to the node's Deform tab, changing the Type menu to Bilinear or Bicubic, and interactively LMB-dragging the deformation control points in the Viewer. If Type is set to Bicubic, you can LMB-drag the points' tangent handles.

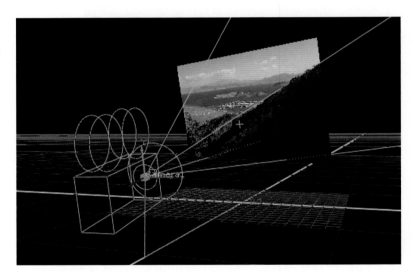

FIGURE 9.4 A landscape bitmap is converted to a card with the Card node. A sample Nuke script is included as card.nk in the Chapters/Chapter9/ Scripts/ directory on the DVD.

In addition to the Card node, Nuke provides a set of 3D primitives. These include a Cube, Cylinder, and Sphere, all of which are accessible through the 3D > Geometry menu. Aside from common transforms, the primitives carry properties specific to their construction. For example, the Sphere node includes Rows/Columns (subdivisions), Radius, U Extent, and V Extent.

If more than one geometry node exists in the Node Graph, all the geometry nodes must be connected to a Scene node to be rendered by a Scanline-Render node. A Scene node groups all the geometry inputs into a single output. Each input pipe is consecutively numbered.

Note that primitive geometry (not including the Card node) appears pure white in the 3D view and is not present in the 2D view until the geometry nodes are assigned shaders. Additionally, a surface assigned to a shader remains pure black until one or more lights are placed in the scene. The following two sections describe shader and light nodes.

Creating Lights

By default, no lights are present in Nuke's 3D environment. You can create light nodes, however, through the 3D > Lights menu. If more than one light node exists in the Node Graph, all the light nodes must be connected to a Scene node for their impact to be seen. You can transform light icons as you would camera icons and geometry. The strength of each light is controlled by an Intensity parameter. Descriptions of the five light types follow.

FIGURE 9.5 Left to right: Point, Direct, and Spot light icons.

Point produces a omnidirectional source emanating from the center of a spherical icon (Figure 9.5). A Point light is similar to a real-world light bulb. The light icon's position affects the light quality, but not its rotation. **Direct** creates parallel rays of light as if the light source is infinitely far away. The position of the icon is unimportant; however, the rotation of the icon affects the light quality. The icon features five lines extending from a sphere. The direction of the lines indicates the direction the light is flowing. **Spot** emulates a spot light used on stage or on a movie set. The light icon features four lines extending from a small sphere. The cone diameter is set by the node's Cone Angle parameter. The Cone Penumbra Angle parameter creates a soft falloff at the cone's edge. Negative values soften the edge inward while positive values soften the edge outward. In contrast, the Cone Falloff determines how rapidly the intensity of the light diminishes from the cone center to the cone edge; higher values create a more rapid falloff. Point and Spot nodes also carry the Falloff Type menu, which determines how much the light intensity diminishing over distance. If the menu is set to No Falloff, the light does not degrade. If the menu is set to Quadratic, the light intensity is inversely proportional to the square of the distance (similar to Earth's atmosphere). The Linear option creates a less aggressive falloff, while Cubic creates a more aggressive falloff.

Light acts like a Point, Direct, or Spot node when the node's Light Type menu is set to one of the light type names. The Light node also offers the ability to import lights through the FBX file format, which is demonstrated in the section "Importing Cameras and Lights" later in this chapter.

Environment uses a spherically mapped input to determine the light's specular color, which appears as a reflection on the geometry surface. This node is demonstrated in the next section.

Connecting Shaders

Geometry nodes must be connected to shader nodes before lights affect the surface brightness or specularity. In the general realm of 3D, a *shader* (sometimes called a *material*) is a small program that determines the shading qualities of a surface during a render. In Nuke, you can connect a shader node to the Img input of a geometry node. You can create a shader node through the 3D > Shader menu. The shaders are described here.

Diffuse includes the diffuse component of a surface, which determines how the surface scatters light and thus how bright or dark the surface appears. You can choose a specific surface color with the White parameter. You can add a texture map to the shader by connecting an input to the node's Map input pipe. The input may be a Read node that carries a bitmap or any another Nuke node that creates an interesting pattern.

Emission offers the ambient component of a surface. The ambient component represents the net sum of all reflected light reaching the surface and thus determines the color of the surface where no light directly touches it. Geometry assigned to an Emission shader appears flat and lacks any variation in shading. In fact, the shader is unaffected by the presence of lights. The node's sole slider, Emission, raises or lowers the surface brightness. The node also carries a Map input.

Specular provides the specular component of a surface. However, the shader does not include the diffuse component. A specular reflection is a mirrorlike reflection where the outgoing rays travel in a single direction. A specular reflection is often emulated by a 3D program by creating a specular highlight, which is rendered as a "hot spot." Nuke's Specular shader creates a specular highlight of which the color is determined by the node's White parameter. The size of the specular highlight is set by the Min Shininess and Max Shininess parameters (the average value of the two parameters is used by the node to determine the shininess). To create a large specular highlight, set Min Shininess and Max Shininess to low values. To create a small specular highlight, set Min Shininess and Max

Shininess to high values. To create an irregular specular highlight, connect the node's mapSH input pipe to another node that carries a pattern. Additionally, the Specular shader can create a mirrorlike reflection if it is lit by an Environment light. For example, in Figure 9.6, Min Shininess and Max Shininess are set to 2. The rotation of the Environment light icon affects the reflection; however, the position and scale (so long as Scale X, Y, and Z are equal) of the icon does not matter. To alter the color, intensity, and blur of the reflection, adjust the matching parameters in the Environment node's properties panel. Note that the Environment light is designed to accept spherically mapped high dynamic range image (HDRI)

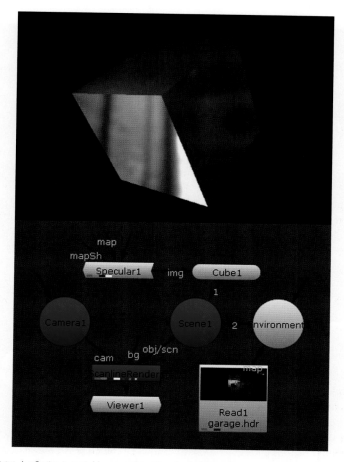

FIGURE 9.6 A reflection is created by connecting a Specular shader to a primitive Cube node and lighting the scene with an Environment light carrying a spherically mapped HDRI bitmap of a garage. A sample Nuke script is included as `reflection.nk` in the `Chapters/Chapter9/Scripts/` directory on the DVD. (Due to copyright reasons, the HDRI file is not included with the script; however, the file and similar spherical HDRI bitmaps are available for free download at *www.turbosquid.com*.)

bitmaps. For more information on HDRI, see the section "HDRI in Nuke" later in this chapter.

Phong combines the parameters of the Diffuse, Emission, and Specular shaders into a single node. The node carries mapD (diffuse), mapE (emission), mapS (specular), and mapSH (shininess) input pipes, each of which can accept a unique input. (The mapSH pipe appears as an arrow pipe stub at the left side of the node icon.) For example, in Figure 9.7, a Phong node is connected to a primitive sphere. Each of the map pipes are connected to a different input. A Noise node is connected to the mapS and mapSH inputs, thereby creating a splotchy specular highlight. The

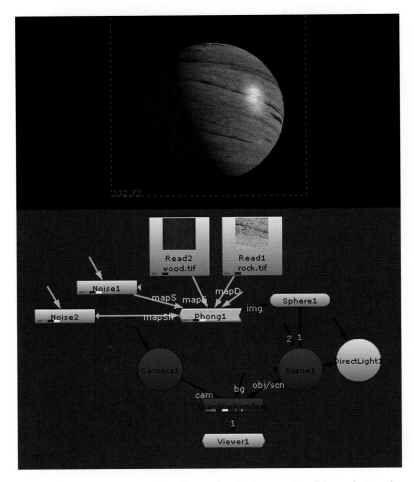

FIGURE 9.7 Multiple maps are connected to a Phong node, which is connected to a Sphere node. A sample Nuke script is included as phong.nk in the Chapters/Chapter9/Scripts/ directory on the DVD.

node reads the pixel values of the mapSH input contained in the channel set by the Shininess Channel parameter. Where low values are encountered, the Min Shininess value is applied; where high values are encountered, the Max Shininess value is applied.

Note that the BasicMaterial node offers the same parameters and inputs as the Phong node; with recent releases of Nuke, the two nodes create virtually identical renders.

FillMat assigns a solid color to the surface in the RGB and alpha channels. The shader is unaffected by lights and serves as a matte; hence, it "cuts holes" into any other surface that sits behind it.

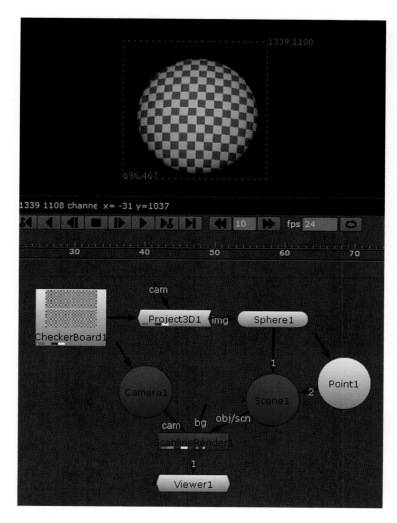

FIGURE 9.8 The pattern of a Checker node is projected onto a primitive Sphere node with a Project3D node. A sample Nuke script is included as `project3d.nk` in the `Chapters/Chapter9/Scripts/` directory on the DVD.

Project3D projects a texture onto a mesh from the view of the camera connected to a Scene node utilized by a geometry node. Optionally, you can connect an alternative camera to the node's Axis/Cam input pipe. The projected texture must be connected to the node's unlabeled input pipe (Figure 9.8). Connect the node's output pipe to the Img input of the Geometry node.

Each Shader node carries an unlabeled input pipe. With the pipe, you can merge two shaders together. For example, in Figure 9.9, a Specular node and a Diffuse node are chained together.

FIGURE 9.9 Two Shader nodes are chained together to create a texture that has Diffuse and Specular components. A sample Nuke script is included as shaders.nk in the Chapters/Chapter9/ Scripts/ directory on the DVD.

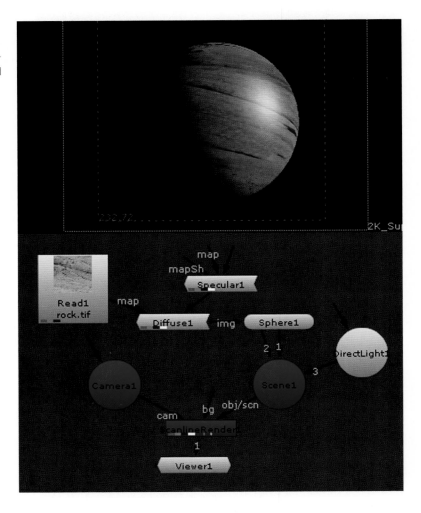

Importing Geometry

You can import polygon meshes into Nuke's 3D environment through an FBX or OBJ file. FBX is a platform-independent 3D data file format developed by Autodesk. OBJ is a widely used 3D file format developed by Wavefront. Popular 3D programs such as Maya and 3ds Max are able to export FBX and OBJ files. To import a mesh, follow these steps:

1. Choose 3D > Geometry > ReadGeo. Open the new node's properties panel. Click the File Browse button and retrieve an FBX or OBJ file. Two sample files—`cup.fbx` and `cup.obj`—are included in the `Chapters/Chapter9/Scripts/` directory on the DVD. Connect output of the ReadGeo node to a Scene node of a working 3D environment. The geometry appears in the Viewer (Figure 9.10).

FIGURE 9.10 Geometry imported through a ReadGeo node. A sample Nuke script is included as `readgeo.nk` in the `Chapters/Chapter9/Scripts/` directory on the DVD.

2. If you read an OBJ file, all the polygon meshes in the file are imported. If you read an FBX file, you must choose the mesh you want to import through the Node Name menu (Figure 9.11). For example, if you use the `cup.fbx` file, you can set the menu to Cup or Shaker to choose the cup mesh of the smaller salt shaker mesh.
3. The imported mesh appears pure white in the 3D view (and is missing from the 2D view) until you connect a shader node to the ReadGeo node's Img input. You must add one or more lights to see shading in the 3D view. Note that transform values are carried by the FBX files; in other words, imported FBX meshes are not necessarily at 0,0,0 with 0 rotation and a scale of 1.

The ReadGeo node's Display menu offers several different ways to display the mesh in the 3D view (wireframe, textured, and so on). In addition, you have

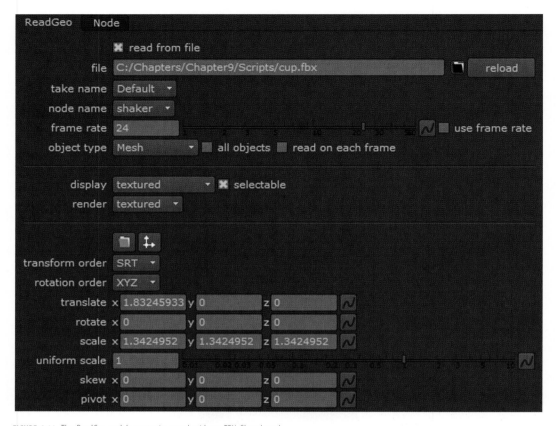

FIGURE 9.11 The ReadGeo node's properties panel with an FBX file selected.

the option to render a flat-shaded, untextured version in the 2D view at any time by switching the node's Render menu from Textured to Solid; this may be useful for creating a RGB matte.

Modifying Geometry

Once a polygon mesh is imported into Nuke or a primitive geometry node is added to the 3D environment, you can apply simple modeling modifications through the 3D > Modify menu. Modify nodes must be inserted between the geometry node and the associated Scene node. The Modify nodes are briefly describe here.

TransformGeo provides an easy means to interactively move a mesh by creating a large transform handle that is accessible in the 2D view. The node carries its own set of transform properties, which you can animate without affecting the transformations of the connected geometry node.

Normals offers the ability to edit surface normals. *Normals* are vectors that are perpendicular to a polygon face that are used to determine the brightness of any given surface point. Imported meshes are single sided in Nuke; therefore, a surface may appear flipped or "inside-out." You can reverse the normals and therefore flip a surface by selecting the Invert checkbox. You can also "soften" or "harden'" normals by changing the Action menu to Build and adjusting the Angle Threshold. Angle Threshold determines whether a smooth transition or hard transition between adjacent faces is rendered. If Angle Threshold is set to 0, hard transitions are drawn for all the faces and the surface is thus faceted (Figure 9.12). If Angle Threshold is set to 180, all the transitions are rendered smooth (Figure 9.13). If Angle Threshold is set to an in-between value, only adjacent faces that possess an angle between normals that is less than the value are left with a hard transition. Note that the Normals node works best with OBJ geometry; the node may fail to affect the smoothness of an FBX model.

FIGURE 9.12 Imported geometry is faceted with the Normals node. Angle Threshold set to 0. A sample Nuke script is included as normals.nk in the Chapters/Chapter9/Scripts/ directory on the DVD.

Trilinear allows you to warp a mesh by distorting a destination box. The location of the destination box corner points are determined by the P0 through P7's X, Y, and Z parameter values. The warp is carried out by fitting the mesh's bounding box to the destination box. (A 3D bounding box is a cube that represents the minimum volume necessary to enclose

FIGURE 9.13 The Angle Threshold is set to 180, which smoothes the surface.

all the mesh's vertices; bounding boxes are generally parallel and perpendicular to the 3D world axes.)

ProceduralNoise distorts the mesh by moving vertices based on values within a 3D noise field (Figure 9.14). The noise parameters are identical to the Noise node (Draw > Noise), although the ProceduralNoise node separates the X and Y scale of the noise pattern. See Chapter 6 for more information.

RadialDistort creates a convex or concave distortion around a central point. If the Distortion parameter is given a value above 0, the top and bottom of the mesh expands, while center vertices are pulled inward in a concave fashion. If Distortion is given a value below 0, the opposite happens, creating a convex effect. The Power Bias parameter controls the intensity of the distortion. You can set the location of the central point by changing the Rotation Center X, Y, and Z values.

LogGeo distorts the mesh by repositioning each vertex. This is achieved by multiplying the X/Y/Z positional vertex values through a power function. The intensity of the distortion is controlled by the Log X, Y, and Z parameters. For example, if you enter 2 into each axis field, each vertex positional value is raised to the power of 2 (e.g., 3^2). The Clamp Black checkbox forces the vertices to keep only positive X, Y, and Z axis values while the Swap checkbox inverts all the functions (e.g., 3^2 becomes 2^3).

LookupGeo allows you to distort a mesh by shaping curves in a graph editor. With the graph, the input vertex positional values are represented by the left/right X axis, while the output positional vertex positional values

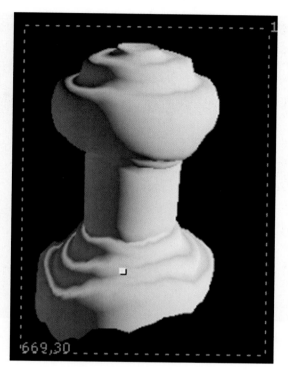

FIGURE 9.14 Imported geometry is distorted with a ProceduralNoise node. A sample Nuke script is included as `proceduralnoise.nk` in the `Chapters/Chapter9/Scripts/` directory on the DVD.

are represented by the up/down Y axis. For example, to push in one side of the mesh so that no vertex has an X value greater than 0.6, select the X axis in the left column and shape the curve (Figures 9.15 and 9.16). You can insert new curve points by Cmd/Ctrl+Opt/Alt-clicking a selected curve. You can move points and tangent handle by LMB-dragging.

CrosstalkGeo add to the functionality of the LookupGeo node by adding crossover curves. These are listed in the left column and are indicated by the → symbol. The crossover curves look up the value of the first axis and add it to the second axis value. By default, the crossover curves are flat and carry a 0 value along their entire duration. Altering these curves generally causes the model to be skewed/sheared along the second axis.

UVProject creates new UV values for each mesh vertex. UV values are used to relate points on a surface to pixels within a texture. By default, imported FBX or OBJ geometry provides an initial set of UV values. Nuke primitives, such as cards and spheres, also carry a default UV set. You can set the style of the UVProject node's projection through the Projection menu. If Projection is set to Perspective, the UVs are projected from the

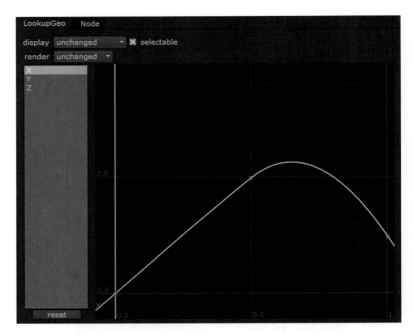

FIGURE 9.15 Reshaped X curve of a LookupGeo node.

FIGURE 9.16 Resulting deformation of cup geometry. A sample Nuke script is included as `lookupgeo.nk` in the `Chapters/Chapter9/Scripts/` directory on the DVD.

view of the camera connected to the associated Scene node. If the Projection menu is set to Plane, the UVs are projected from an axis plane as determined by the Plane menu (Figure 9.17). If the Projection menu is set to Spherical or Cylindrical, the UVs are projected from a virtual sphere or a cylinder. In contrast to 3D programs such as Maya, there is no interactive projection handle with which you can manipulate the projection. However, the node provides a U Scale and V Scale slider to adjust the UV coverage of the projection, as well as Invert U and Invert V checkboxes to flip the resulting texture in the U or V direction. The UVProject node also provides an Axis/Cam input pipe; you can connect an alternative camera node to this pipe and use it with the Perspective projection setting.

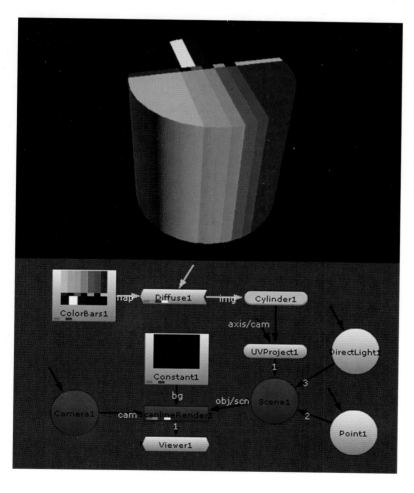

FIGURE 9.17 A ColorBars node is used as a texture on a primitive cylinder. A UVProject node is connected to the Cylinder node with its Projection set to Planar and the Plane menu set to ZX. As a result, the color bar pattern is legible on the top and bottom, but is streaked along the Y axis. A sample Nuke script is included as uvproject.nk in the Chapters/Chapter9/ Scripts/ directory on the DVD.

MergeGeo merges multiple geometry nodes into a single output. This is useful if you wish to apply a single modify node, such TransformGeo or UVProject, to multiple geometry nodes with a single step. You can apply a single shader to the MergeGeo node by using an ApplyMaterial node. To do so, connect the unlabeled input pipe of the ApplyMaterial node to the output of the MergeGeo node (Figure 9.18). Connect a shader node, such as Diffuse, to the Mat input pipe of the ApplyMaterial node. Connect the output of the ApplyMaterial node to the Scene node.

FIGURE 9.18 Two ReadGeo nodes (one carrying a snowman and the other a ground plane) are merged with a MergeGeo node. An Apply-Material node assigns a Noise texture to the merged geometry. A sample Nuke script is included as mergegeo.nk in the Chapters/Chapter9/ Scripts/ directory on the DVD.

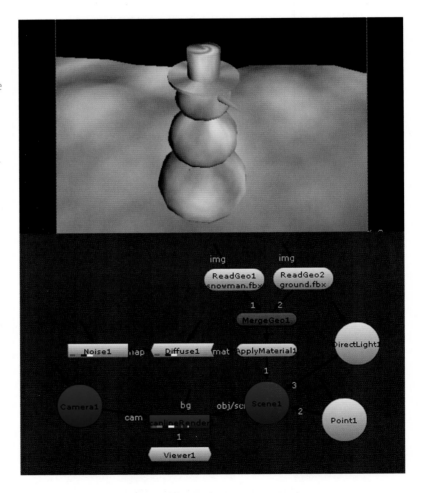

Importing Cameras and Lights

Nuke supports the ability to import cameras, lights, and transform channels through an FBX file. To import a camera, follow these steps:

1. Choose 3D > Camera. Open the new Camera node's properties panel. Select the Read From File checkbox. Switch to the File tab. Click the File browse button and retrieve the FBX file that contains a camera. A sample file is included as camera.fbx in the Chapters/Chapter9/scripts/ directory on the DVD; this file features a camera created in Maya. A dialog box opens, warning that the importation of a camera overwrites the current properties of the Camera node. Click the Yes button to close the dialog box.

2. In the File tab, change the Node Name menu to the camera you wish to import (Figure 9.19). With the camera.fbx file, the desired camera is named CameraA. Note that a number of orthographic cameras are listed with the Producer prefix. These cameras are provided automatically when an FBX file is exported. Change the Frame Rate menu to match the frame rate used by the program that created the FBX file. The camera.fbx file was created at 24 fps.

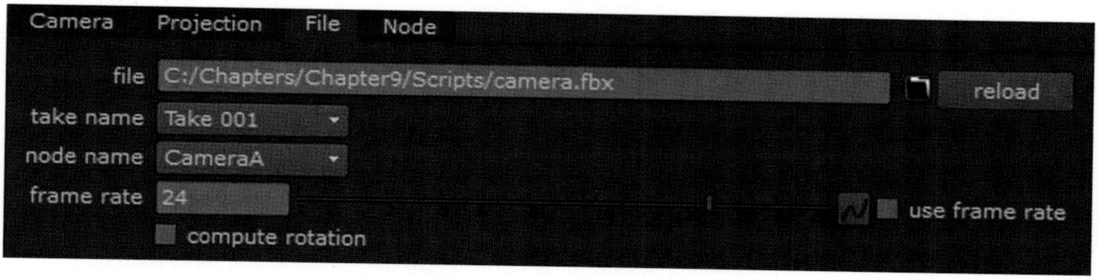

FIGURE 9.19 The Camera node's File tab with an imported camera listed.

3. Connect the Camera node to the Cam input pipe of the ScanlineRender node of an active 3D environment. Switch the Viewer's View Selection menu to 3D. With the Camera Or Light To Look Through menu set to Default, move the default camera so that the imported camera icon is visible. Play back the timeline. The imported camera remains static. If the camera was animated prior to FBX exportation, return to the File tab and change the Take Name menu to the appropriate animation take. The FBX format supports multiple animation takes, whereby unique sets of animation curves are stored in "take" nodes. With the camera.fbx file, the animation is stored in Take 001 (which is the default take name if only one take is present). Play back the timeline. The imported camera icon moves.

You can examine the animation curves of an imported camera by returning to the Camera tab and clicking an Animation Menu button beside a transform parameter and choosing Curve Editor. The curve keyframes are spaced one frame apart. You can edit the curves as you would any other animated parameter.

To import a light, follow these steps:

1. Choose 3D > Lights > Light. Open the new Light node's properties panel. Select the Read From File checkbox. Switch to the File tab. Click the File browse button and retrieve the FBX file that contains one or more lights. A sample file is included as `lights.fbx` in the `Chapters/Chapter9/scripts/` directory on the DVD; this file features two lights created in Maya.

2. In the File tab, change the Node Name menu to the light you wish to import. With the `lights.fbx` file, you have the choice of directionalLight or spotLight. If the lights were animated prior to exportation, set the Take Name and Frame Rate menus to appropriate values. To alter the imported light's intensity, adjust the Intensity Scale parameter.

3. Connect the Light node to the Scene node of the active 3D environment. The imported light is drawn with the equivalent Nuke light icon. For example, a Maya spot light is drawn as a Nuke spot light.

Importing and Applying Transforms

With Nuke, you can import transformation information and apply it to a TransformGeo node through an Axis node. To import transformations, follow these steps:

1. Choose 3D > Axis. Open the new Axis node's properties panel. Select the Read From File checkbox. Switch to the File tab. Click the File browse button and retrieve the FBX file that contains one or more nodes that carry animation curves. The nodes may represent geometry, lights, or cameras. A sample file is included as `transform.fbx` in the `Chapters/Chapter9/scripts/` directory on the DVD; this file features an animated polygon sphere.

2. In the File tab, change the Node Name menu to the node from which you wish to take transform information. With the `transform.fbx` file, the pSphere node carries the animation. Set the Take Name and Frame Rate menus to appropriate values. If you are using the `transform.fbx` file, set Take Name to Take 001 and Frame Rate to 24.

3. Select the geometry node you wish to transform and choose 3D > Modify > TransformGeo. Connect the Axis node to the Axis input of the TransformGeo node. Play back the timeline. The Axis node, which is represented in the 3D view as a six-armed icon, inherits the animation through the FBX file. In turn, the geometry follows the axis. For example, in Figure 9.20, the FBX animation is applied to a spiked ball imported through a ReadGeo node.

If the Axis properties panel is open, a motion path is drawn when there is a change in translation value over time. Note that Axis nodes are not rendered by the ScanlineRender node and are thus "null objects." Additionally, the TransformGeo node carries a Look input pipe. If the Look pipe is connected to another node, such as a geometry or light node, the TransformGeo node forces the geometry it affects to rotate so that it always "looks at" that other node.

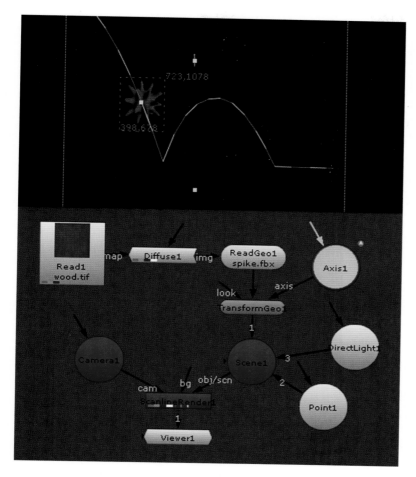

FIGURE 9.20 A spiked ball, imported through a ReadGeo node, follows an Axis node that receives its animation from imported transforms. A sample Nuke script is included as `importtransform.nk` in the `Chapters/Chapter9/Scripts/` directory on the DVD.

Exporting Geometry and Animation

You can export geometry as an FBX or OBJ file by using a WriteGeo node (3D > Geometry > WriteGeo). To do so, connect the output of a geometry node (or a downstream TransformGeo or other geometry modification node) to a WriteGeo node. In the WriteGeo node's properties panel, choose OBJ or FBX through the File Type menu and choose a file name and location through the File cell. By default, the output reflects any transformations and deformations that affect the geometry for a particular frame of the timeline. In fact, you can output a series of geometry files that represent an animation (Figure 9.21). In this case, you can set a specific frame range through the namesake parameter. As such, you must include the appropriate number of # signs in the file output name (e.g., `test.#.obj`). Note that you must click the Execute button to activate the WriteGeo node.

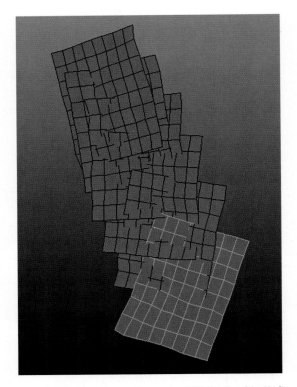

FIGURE 9.21 An animated, deformed card is exported as a series of OBJ files. Five of the OBJ files are imported into Autodesk Maya and are shown in this figure. A sample Nuke script is included as `writegeo.nk` in the `Chapters/Chapter9/Scripts/` directory on the DVD. Sample OBJ files are included as `plane.##.obj` in the `Chapters/Chapter9/Scripts/` directory on the DVD.

You can export Nuke transform animation by using the Chan file format. This may be useful for passing animation between different Nuke nodes or different Nuke scripts. To export or import a Chan file, click the File Menu button (Figure 9.22) carried by an Axis, Camera, or light node, and choose Export Chan or Import Chan from the dropdown menu. Chan files have the `.chan` extension. Chan files feature a list of frame numbers and transform values in a text format.

FIGURE 9.22 The File Menu button.

Fine-Tuning the ScanlineRender

By default, the ScanlineRender node produces a low-quality render. In particular, the geometry edge quality is poor. You can improve this by changing the Antialiasing menu, in the ScanlineRender tab, from None to Low, Medium, or High. Alternatively, you can switch to the Multisample tab and adjust the Samples slider, which drives subpixel sampling. The higher the Sampling value, the higher the quality and the slower the render. Although you can use Samples in conjunction with the Antialiasing menu, it's generally best to leave Antialiasing set to None if the Samples value is high.

By default, the ScanlineRender uses the project resolution to render. However, you can force it to render a different resolution by using the node's Bg pipe. For example, create a Constant node, set the Constant node's Format menu to the desired resolution, and connect the Constant node to the Bg pipe of the ScanlineRender node.

Blurring in 3D

To add motion blur to geometry moving in Nuke's 3D environment, apply MotionBlur3D and VectorBlur nodes. You can follow these steps:

1. Choose Filter > MotionBlur3D. Connect the output of the Camera node to the Cam input of the MotionBlur3D node. Connect the output of the network's ScanlineRender node to the unlabeled input of the MotionBlur3D node.
2. With the MoitonBlur3D node selected, choose Filter > VectorBlur. Connect the output of the VectorBlur node to the Viewer. Open the VectorBlur node's properties panel. Change the UV Channels menu to Motion.
3. Open the ScanlineRender node's properties panel. Switch to the Multisample tab. Change the Samples parameter to a high value, such as 24. Motion blur will not appear if Samples is set to 1. The motion blur will appear poor if Samples is set to a low value, such as 4. Switch the Viewer's View Selection menu to 2D to see the blur (Figure 9.23).

For more information on the VectorBlur node, see Chapter 6.

HDRI in Nuke

Nuke supports high dynamic ranges imaging (HDRI). HDRI takes advantage of 16- and 32-bit floating-point formats through the OpenEXR, TIFF, and Radiance (.hdr) image formats. Thus, Nuke is able to read and manipulate value ranges far beyond the capacity of nonfloat, lower bit depth formats. (See Chapter 3 for more information on bit depths.) HDRI is often employed

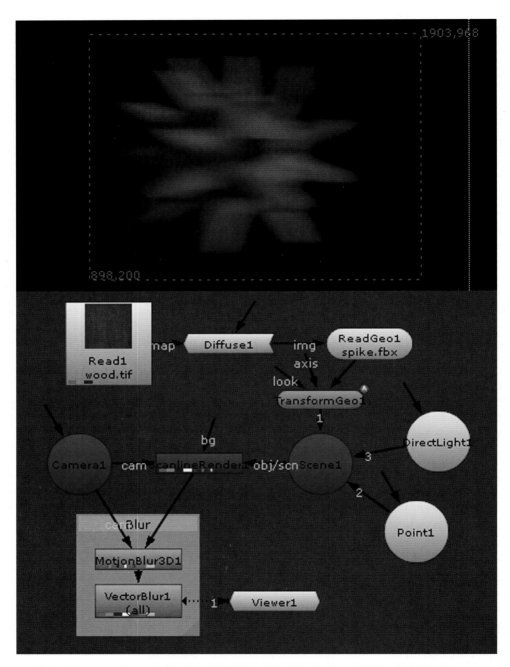

FIGURE 9.23 Animated geometry receives motion blur from MotionBlur3D and VectorBlur nodes. A sample Nuke script is included as `motionblur3d.nk` in the `Chapters/Chapter9/Scripts/` directory on the DVD.

in digital photography, 3D texturing, and 3D lighting, but has also found its way into visual effects compositing.

Nuke provides the Environment light node, which is designed to accept the input of a spherically mapped HDRI bitmap. When an HDRI bitmap is prepared, a specialized mapping is applied to fit the full view of a surrounding location into a rectangular space. Spherical maps (also known as latitude/longitude or lat/long) appear as horizontal images with the horizon generally at the vertical centerline (Figure 9.24). Other common mappings include light probe (angular) and vertical and horizontal cubic cross.

FIGURE 9.24 A spherical (lat/long) HDRI bitmap. Despite the large value range supported by HDRI, only a small exposure range can be displayed in print. Hence, the exterior appears overexposed in print, whereas the original HDRI bitmap contains proper exposure information for that area. Nuke's 32-bit floating-point architecture is able to access the full exposure range. This file, shot by Benjamin Ziegler, and similar spherical HDRI bitmaps are available for free download at www.turbosquid.com.

If a spherically mapped HDRI is unavailable, you can convert an HDRI with a different style of mapping with Nuke's SphericalTransform node (in the Transform menu). For example, in Figure 9.25, a Read node loads an .hdr image that has a light probe (angular) mapping. Its output is connected to a SphericalTransform node. The SphericalTransform node's Input Type menu is set to Angular Map 360 and its Output Type menu is set to Lat Long Map. The output of the SphericalTransform node is connected to the Map input of an Environment light node.

Note that the Output Type menu carries all the common HDRI mapping styles. For an additional demonstration of the Environment light, see the "Connecting Shaders" section earlier in this chapter.

FIGURE 9.25 A light probe HDRI bitmap is converted to a spherical (lat/long) HDRI output with a Spherical-Transfrom node. The HDRI bitmap, created by Paul Debevec, and similar light probe bitmaps are available for free download at *www.pauldebeved.com.*

Motion Tracking in a 3D Environment

NukeX includes the CameraTracker node, which creates a 3D camera based on tracking information gathered from an image sequence or movie with the goal of matching original real-world cameras. (In contrast, the Tracker creates motion paths based on the 2D movement of tracked features.) The basic workflow for the node follows:

- Connect an image sequence to the Source pipe of a CameraTracker node. Click the CameraTracker node's Track Features button (Figure 9.26). Features are automatically identified and tracked through the duration of the timeline. You can alter the number of features tracked and the sensitivity of the tracking through the Tracking tab. You can apply the Track Features button multiple times to create more accurate features tracks.
- To create a more accurate camera match, you can enter lens information into the Solver tab. For example, if you know the real-world camera used a 50-mm lens with an aperture size specific to a particular make of camera, you can set Focal Length Type to Known, Focal Length to 50, and Film Back Size XY to the correct aperture millimeter measurements.

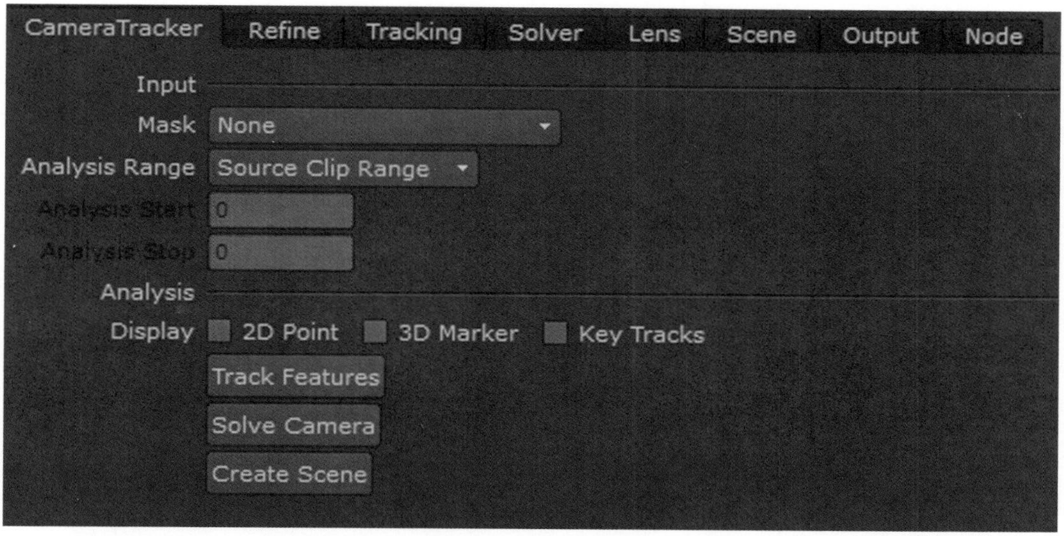

FIGURE 9.26 The CameraTracker properties panel.

- Determine the relative position and rotation of the real-world camera by clicking the Solve Camera button in the CameraTracker tab. Apply the data to a new Camera node and a new Scene node by clicking the Create Scene button. (For more detailed information on the CameraTracker node, see the Nuke User Guide.)

Two additional nodes, PointsTo3D and Reconcile3D, track points in 3D space. They both require a 3D camera and are found in the Transform menu. The PointsTo3D node determines the position of a feature in 3D space by examining the parallax between two or three motion-tracked 2D points. The basic workflow for the node follows:

- Create a 3D camera by applying the CameraTracker node to an image sequence.
- Connect the new camera node to the Cam input of the PointsTo3D node. Connect the original image sequence to the Img input of the PointsTo3D node.
- In the PointsTo3D node's properties panel, identify the XY positions of Point A, Point B, and Point C. Each Point represents a 2D location of a specific feature over time. For example, Point A may represent a tape mark on a wall at frame 1, Point B may represent the same tape mark on the wall at frame 15, and so on. To identity the XY position of a point, enter the values into the XY cells while the timeline is on a specific frame and click the corresponding Set Frame button (Figure 9.27). You can identify the location of any given pixel by dragging the mouse over

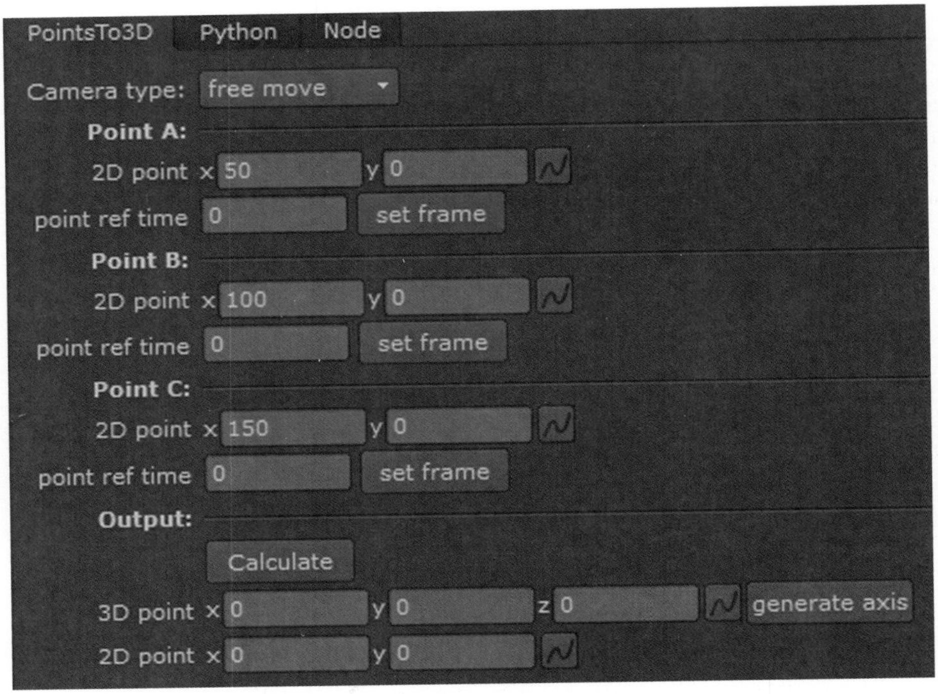

FIGURE 9.27 The PointsTo3D properties panel.

the Viewer and noting the XY readout at the bottom center of the Viewer panel.

- After the 2D Point positions are identified, click the Calculate button. An XYZ position in 3D space is determined and is stored by the 3DPoint parameter. You can feed the values into a new Axis node by clicking the Generate Axis node button. In turn, you can connect the new Axis node to a TransformGeo node and thus impart the position to geometry.

Reconcile3D converts an XYZ position in 3D space into an XY screen space position. This is useful for locking a 2D input, such as a bitmap, to a particular feature or object seen by a moving 3D camera. The basic workflow for the node is as follows:

- Create an animated 3D camera by applying the CameraTracker node to an image sequence. Alternatively, import a new camera through a Camera node's Read From File option or simply apply keyframe animation to an existing camera. Connect the Camera node to the Cam input of the Reconcile3D node.
- Define 3D position you wish to convert to 2D screen space by entering values into the Reconcile3D node's 3D Point parameter's XYZ cells. You

can also define the location by connecting an Axis node to the Axis input of the Reconcile3D node. The position/Axis must be within the Camera node's view.

· Click the Create Keyframes button. The 3D position is tracked. The resulting XY screen space position is stored by the XY Output parameter. Connect the 2D input you wish to track to the Reconcile3D node's Img input. The Img input inherits the motion. If the Img input has a smaller

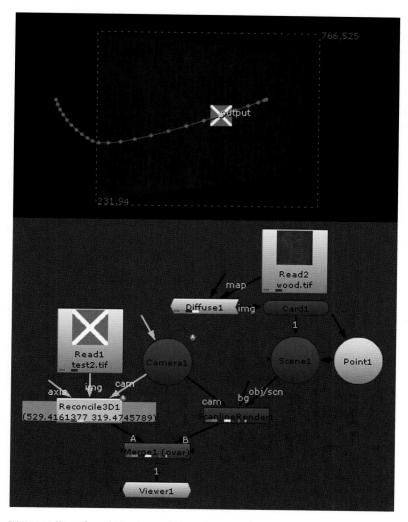

FIGURE 9.28 Using a Reconcile3D node, a small bitmap, featuring a white X, is tracked to a point in space that aligns with the center of a Card node. A sample Nuke script is included as `reconcile3D.nk` in the `Chapters/Chapter9/Scripts/` directory on the DVD.

resolution than the project resolution, you may need to alter the Reconcile3D node's Offset X and Y values to center the Img input over the new motion path.

- The output resolution of the Reconcile3D node is the same as its Img input. Therefore, to use the output in combination with the project-resolution ScanlineRender or PrmanRender node output, send both outputs through a Merge node (Figure 9.28).

Stereoscopic 3D

Stereoscopy creates the illusion of depth by presenting left- and right-eye views of the same subject. Stereoscopic motion pictures are commonly displayed as an anaglyphic image (where each view is hidden from the opposite eye with colored filters, such as cyan and red) or as a polarized image (where each view is hidden from the opposite eye with polarized filters). In either situation, either specialized glasses must be worn or a stereoscopic television set or monitor must be employed.

Nuke includes specialized nodes that can read, write, and display left- and right-eye stereoscopic bitmaps and image sequences. In addition, Nuke provides controls for setting the horizontal disparity—the disparity between object position in left and right views. Horizontal disparity is a natural by-product of binocular vision, where two eyes are a distinct distance apart (known as interocular distance). Ultimately, the adjustment of horizontal disparity alters the convergence point—the point at which there is no horizontal disparity. Objects behind the convergence point appear to be behind the screen, while objects in front of the convergence point appear to float in front of the screen.

Reading and Viewing Stereo Files

Before you can work with stereoscopic files, you must set up a stereo script. To do so, choose Edit > Project Settings from the menu bar. In the Views tab of the Project Settings panel, click the Set Up Views For Stereo button. Left and Right views are indicated in the view field (Figure 9.29). The Left view is color-coded red and the Right view is color-coded green.

There are two ways to read stereoscopic files: import each view through a separate Read node or import both views in a single OpenEXR file through a single Read node. If you use two separate Read nodes, you must combine the views with a JoinViews node (Views > JoinViews). Once the JoinViews node is connected to a Viewer, you can toggle between the Left and Right view by clicking the namesake buttons at the top of the Viewer panel (Figure 9.30).

Because the JoinViews node can only display one view at a time in the Viewer, you must connect a node from the Views > Stereo menu to create a stereo or stereoscopic effect. The following are descriptions of the nodes:

FIGURE 9.29 Stereo views are created through the Views tab of the Project Settings panel.

FIGURE 9.30 Stereo Left and Right view buttons at the top of the Viewer panel.

Anaglyph tints the Left view red, tints the Right view cyan, and overlaps the views (Figure 9.31). Thus, the node requires red/cyan glasses to be effective. You can change the horizontal disparity by entering a nonzero value into the Horizontal Offset parameter. Values above 0 bring the two views closer together and cause the convergence point to move farther way from the camera. Values below 0 push the views farther apart and cause the convergence point to move closer to the camera (causing objects to float in front of the screen). You can swap the red/cyan tinting by selecting the Right=Red checkbox. You can alter the saturation of the views by adjusting the Amtcolor slider.

SideBySide places the views next to each other. You can force a stereoscopic effect by clicking the Swap button and softly crossing your eyes until a third image appears in the center of the Viewer.

MixViews simply overlaps the views with partial opacity. To see each view equally, set the Mix slider to 0.5. The MixViews node offers a means to examine both views simultaneously, but does not create a stereoscopic result.

To pull a single view out of a stereo output, connect a OneView node and set the View menu to Left or Right. You can also use the Split And Join gizmo to pull each view out through a separate OneView node before recombining the views with a JoinViews node. Splitting out the views allows you to connect different filter nodes to each view. To swap the left and right views, connect a ShuffleViews node, click the Add button twice, and arrange the buttons to get the left view from the right and vice versa. You can find OneView, ShuffleViews, and the Split And Join gizmo in the Views menu.

FIGURE 9.31 Left- and right-eye views of a kitchen counter are turned into a stereoscopic output with JoinViews and Anaglyph nodes. A sample Nuke script is included as `anaglyph.nk` in the `Chapters/Chapter9/Scripts/` directory on the DVD.

OpenEXR Stereo Files and Split Parameters

To write stereo views into a single OpenEXR file, connect a Write node to a JoinViews node. The Write node automatically recognizes the stereo input, as is indicated by the Views parameter in the Write node's properties panel. Change the File Type to Exr. If you read an OpenEXR file that carries stereo views, the Read node displays a small "V" symbol at the top left of the node icon. (A sample stereo OpenEXR file is included as `stereo.exr` in the `Chapters/Chapter9/Bitmaps/` directory on the DVD.)

FIGURE 9.32 A Blur node's Size parameter is split into left and right subparameters with the View Menu button.

Any filter node that carries a stereo input features an additional menu beside every Animation button—the View Menu button. By default, the filter node affects both views equally. However, you can "split off" a view so that it can be affected separately. To make the split, click a View Menu button and choose Split Off Left/Right (v6.2) or Split Off Main (v6.3) from the dropdown menu. The View Menu changes to feature a small eye icon. Click the small arrow beside the associated parameter name to reveal the L (left) and R (right) subparameters (Figure 9.32). You can adjust each sub-parameter separately. To unsplit the split, click on the View Menu buttons and choose Unsplit Left/Right (v6.2) or Unsplit Main (v6.3).

Tutorial 9: Building a 3D Scene in Nuke
Tutorial 9 creates a 3D environment in Nuke with imported and texture bitmaps. We'll light the geometry with Nuke lights.

1. In the Node Graph, RMB-click and choose 3D > Scene. With no nodes selected, choose 3D > Camera. With no nodes selected, choose 3D > ScanlineRender. Connect the Camera1 node to the ScanlineRender1 node's Cam input pipe. Connect the Scene1 node to the Obj/Scn input pipe. Connect a Viewer to the output of ScanlineRender1. See Figure 9.33 for the final node network for this tutorial.

2. Change the View Selection menu from 2D to 3D. The menu is to the right of the Zoom menu at the top of the Viewer panel. Initially, the view of the 3D environment is empty. Alt-MMB-drag or MMB-scroll to dolly backward. A wireframe camera icon appears. This is the Camera1 icon. The view is presented through a default working camera.

3. With no nodes selected, choose 3D > Geometry > ReadGeo. Connect the output of ReadGeo1 to the Scene1 node. Open the ReadGeo1 node's properties panel. Click the File browse button and retrieve the `snowman.fbx` file from the `Tutorials/Tutorial9/Scripts/` directory. Create a new ReadGeo node. Connect the output of ReadGeo2 to the Scene1 node. Open the ReadGeo2 node's properties panel. Click the File browse button and retrieve the `ground.fbx` file from the `Tutorials/Tutorial9/Scripts/` directory. The imported geometry appears in the 3D view. However, the surfaces appear solid gray because there are no lights and no shaders in the scene.

Occula is a plug-in set designed specifically for stereoscopic work. Occula works with disparity fields, which are special channels that encode the location differences between pixels in left- and right-eye views. Occula can generate disparity fields from imported footage with the Solver and Disparity Generator nodes. Additional nodes support critical stereo adjustments, such as setting interocular distances. Occula also provides a means to carry out common nonstereo tasks, such as color grading and rotoscoping, in a stereo environment. Last, Occula offers the advantage of providing interlaced and checkerboard stereoscopic output, which the standard Nuke stereo nodes cannot provide.

Note that the ReConverge node, available in the Views > Stereo menu, requires a disparity field channel, which Occula can produce. With the ReConverge node, you can set the convergence point of a stereo input.

For more information, see the "User Guide for Occula" PDF available at The Foundry's website (*www.thefoundry.co.uk*).

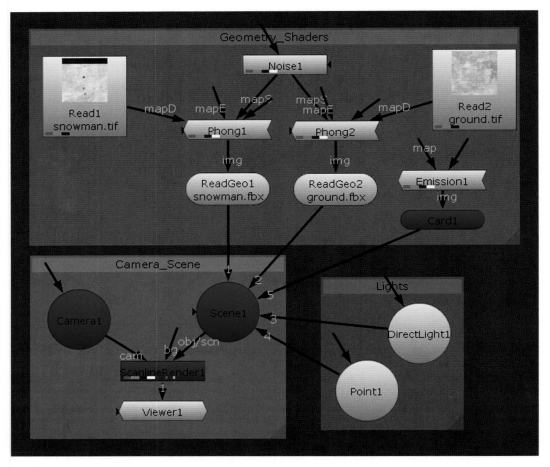

FIGURE 9.33 The final node network for Tutorial 9.

4. With no nodes selected, choose 3D > Shader > Phong. Connect the output of the Phong1 node to the input of ReadGeo1. The snowman geometry temporarily disappears. Create a new Read node. Import the `snowman.tif` bitmap from the `Tutorials/Tutorial9/Bitmaps/` directory on the DVD. Connect the output of the Read1 node to the mapD input of the Phong1 node. The mapD input maps the Diffuse parameter. The snowman reappears with a custom texture.

5. With no nodes selected, choose 3D > Shader > Phong. Connect the output of the Phong2 node to the input of ReadGeo2. Create a new Read node. Import the `ground.tif` bitmap from the `Tutorials/Tutorial9/Bitmaps/` directory on the DVD.

Connect the output of the Read2 node to the mapD input of the Phong2 node. The ground appears with a custom texture (Figure 9.34).

FIGURE 9.34 3D view of the snowman and ground geometry assigned to Phong shaders with custom bitmap textures. At this point, there is no shading as there are no lights in the scene.

6. Select the Camera1 icon and position and rotate the camera to frame the snowman. To interactively position the camera while looking through its lens, change the Camera Or Light To Look Through menu to Camera1 and Cmd/Ctrl+click the 3D View Mode button so that it turns green. Use the Opt/Alt and mouse key combination to scroll, dolly, and orbit. After the camera is positioned, click the 3D View Mode button so that it turns white again.

7. With no nodes selected, choose 3D > Lights > Direct and 3D > Lights > Point. Connect the DirectLight1 node and the Point1 node to the Scene1 node. Position the lights to aesthetically light the geometry. For example, position the Point1 light so that it sits to the screen left of the snowman. Change the DirectLight1 light's rotational values to −45,70,0 in XYZ; this aims the light downward as if it were the sun. Open the DirectLight1 node's properties panel and change the Intensity to 3. Open the Point1 node's properties panel and change the Intensity to 0.3. With this Intensity balance, the Direct light becomes the key light and the Point light becomes the weaker fill light. Change the View Selection menu to 2D and the Camera Or Light To Look Through menu to Camera1. The ScanelineRender1 node renders the camera view (Figure 9.35).

FIGURE 9.35 2D view, as rendered by the ScanlineRender1 node. A strong Direct light and a weaker Point light illuminate the scene.

8. Open the Phong1 and Phong2 nodes' properties panels and adjust the Diffuse, Specular, Min Shininess, and Max Shininess parameters. For example, to reduce the intense specular highlights, set Phong1's Specular to 0.3 and Phong2's Specular to 4. To give the specularity additional variation, choose Draw > Noise and connect the output of Noise1 to the mapS input pipes of Phong1 and Phong2. The mapS pipe sets the specular intensity based on values within the input. Open the Noise1 node's properties panel and set X/Y Size to 30; this shrinks the size of the noise pattern. To brighten the otherwise dingy snow, set Phong1 and Phong2's Diffuse parameters to 0.4 (Figure 9.36).

9. With no nodes selected, choose 3D > Geometry > Card. Connect Card1 to the Scene1 node. Open the Card1 node's properties panel. Change Translate XYZ to 0,15,−20 and Uniform Scale to 50. This moves the Card behind the snowman and ground (Figure 9.37). With no nodes selected, choose 3D > Shader > Emission. Connect the output of Emission1 to the Card1 node. The Card becomes gray. Open the Emission1 node's properties panel and change the Emission parameter to a sky-blue color by using the Color Sliders button. Because the Emission shader only provides the emission component, the shader is unaffected by lights in the scene. Hence, by assigning a blue Emission shader to a Card, a background sky is created.

FIGURE 9.36 The surface brightness and specular intensity are adjusted by changing the Specular and Diffuse values of the Phong nodes.

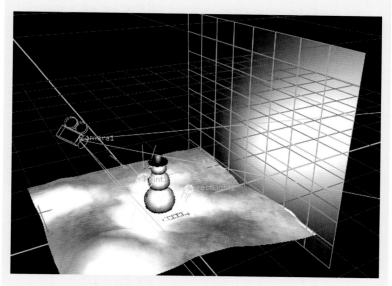

FIGURE 9.37 A Card is scaled and translated to sit behind the ground. Assigning the Card to an Emission shader allows it act like a self-illuminated sky.

10. Open the ScanlineRender1 node's properties panel and set the Antialiasing menu to High (Figure 9.38). Alternately, switch to the MultiSample tab and raise the Samples value. If you are using Nuke v6.2 or later, you can add shadows. Open the DirectLight1

FIGURE 9.38 The final render (without cast shadows).

node's properties panel, switch to the Shadows tab, and select the Cast Shadows checkbox. The ScanlineRender node creates depth map shadows. As such, the Depthmap Resolution parameter sets the size of the depth map and the Samples parameter sets the edge quality of the shadow. To avoid stairstepped shadow edges, raise the Depthmap Resolution and Samples above their default values. Raytraced shadows are available if the scene is rendered with the PrmanRender node (3D > RenderMan > PrmanRender). With raytraced shadows, the shadow softness is controlled by the Sample Width parameter.

This concludes Tutorial 9. As a bonus step, arrange and organize the node graph so that the scene is easy to understand. A sample Nuke script is included as Tutorial9.final.nk in the Tutorials/Tutorial9/Scripts/ directory on the DVD.

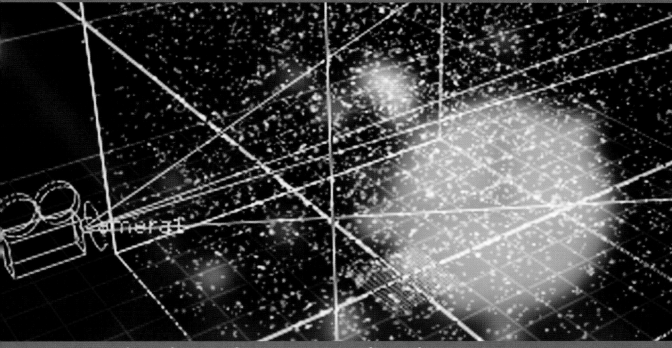

CHAPTER 10

Optimization, Scripting, and New Techniques

It's important to organize and optimize every Nuke script, whether it's simple or complex. The program provides various ways to group nodes, reduce calculation and rendering times, and automate common functions. The creation of links, expressions, and scripts can take the organization and automation even further by allowing you to create nodes, node connections, math-driven parameters, and custom interface elements through programming commands and saved script files.

This chapter includes the following critical information:

- Script optimization
- Gizmos and Group nodes
- Basics of TCL and Python scripting
- Links and expressions
- Deep compositing and particles

Organizing and Optimizing a Script

If you construct a large node network, the Node Graph can become difficult to navigate and interpret. In addition, if you work with large-resolution image formats or apply various processor-intensive filter nodes, Nuke may slow significantly as it calculates each frame. Thus, it is often necessary to organize and optimize the script. Nuke provides means to set program preferences, work with proxy resolutions, precomp outputs, create Group nodes and exportable gizmos, and annotate the network with notes.

System Preferences

Nuke provides a long list of user-defined preferences. These are accessible by choosing Edit > Preferences from the menu bar. The Preferences window includes the following tabbed sections:

- **Preferences** includes autosave, disk cache, and memory usage settings.
- **Windows** controls the functionality of GUI elements such as tooltips and snapping.
- **Control Panels** determines the behavior of the Properties panel.
- **Appearance** sets the program font and component colors.
- **Node Colors** sets its namesake. Note that the colors are divided into various categories, such as Drawing, Merge, or Keyer, and specific node names are typed in each category cell.
- **Node Graph** establishes the graphic qualities of pipes, arrows, and node boxes.
- **Viewer** sets the interactive qualities of the Viewer tabs. If you are working in Nuke's 3D environment and wish to mimic the camera controls of another program (e.g., Maya), change the 3D Control Type menu.
- **Script Editor** controls the font and colors used in the script field.

Customizing the Interface

You can customize the pane, panel, and tab layout of Nuke in several ways:

- You can close any tab (Node Graph, Curve Editor, Properties Bin, Script Editor, Group Node Graph, and so on) by RMB-clicking over the tab name and choosing Close Tab. Conversely, you can open any tab in any pane by LMB-clicking over the pane's Content Menu button (at the top left of the pane, as seen in Figure 10.1) and choosing the name of the tab from the dropdown menu (e.g., choose Node Graph).
- You can subdivide a pane into two panes by LMB-clicking the pane's Content Menu button and choosing Split Vertical or Split Horizontal. You can close a pane by choosing Close Pane for the Content Menu. You can

FIGURE 10.1 The Content Menu button, as seen to the left of a Node Graph tab.

break a pane or tab away from the main window and "float" it by choosing Float Pane or Float Tab from the Content Menu.

- You can save a current pane layout by choosing Layout > Save Layout *n* from the menu bar. You can restore a saved pane layout by choosing Layout > Restore Layout *n*.

Proxy Formats, Downrez, and Viewer Refresh

By default, Nuke processes the node network at full resolution, as determined by the Full Size Format parameter of the Project Settings properties panel. However, you can use a proxy resolution to temporarily speed up the node network processing. To do so, choose Edit > Project Settings, select the Proxy Mode checkbox, and set the Proxy Mode menu to Scale or Format (Figure 10.2).

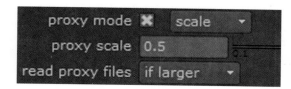

FIGURE 10.2 The Proxy section of the Project Settings properties panel.

Scale forces the composition to be scaled to a percentage set by the Proxy Scale slider. For example, if Proxy Scale is set to 0.5, the composition becomes 50% of the resolution size. The resulting pixel size is indicted by the output bounding box in the Viewer. The Format option scales the composition to a standard resolution, as is indicated by the Proxy Format menu. The Read Proxy Files menu determines how imported bitmaps, image sequence, and movies are interpreted by a Read node when the Proxy mode is activated. Regardless of the Read Proxy Files menu setting, the final output of the node network remains the proxy resolution. To return the composition to the full project resolution, deselect the Proxy Mode checkbox. You can remotely toggle on and off the Proxy Mode checkbox by pressing Cmd/Ctrl+P or clicking the Toggle Proxy Mode button at the top right of the Viewer tab (Figure 10.3).

FIGURE 10.3 Left to right: Toggle Proxy Mode button, Downrez menu, Region-of-Interest button, Recalculate button, and Pause button.

In addition to choosing a proxy format, you can downrez (downscale) the current Viewer input by choosing a non-one value from the Downrez menu

295

(see Figure 10.3). For example, if you set Downrez to 4, the input is scaled to one-fourth its original resolution.

You can prevent the Viewer from updating the entire bounding box by clicking the Region-of-Interest button (see Figure 10.3) so that it turns red. A region-of-interest handle appears in the Viewer. You can interactively LMB-drag the handle center to transform it or LMB-drag the handle corners to rescale it. If the node network is altered, only the area within the region-of-interest is updated. Additionally, you can force the Viewer to update by clicking the Recalculate button or pause a slow update by clicking the Pause button (see Figure 10.3).

Precomping and Caching

The Nuke Precomp node (Other > Precomp) acts as a subroutine, whereby a portion of a node network is exported as a separate Nuke script. The Nuke script is then re-read by the Precomp node and presented to the master script as a single output. This allows multiple artists to work on separate portions of a master script. To apply the Precomp node, follow these steps:

1. Select a node that has an upstream network you'd like to capture. RMB-click over the node and choose Other > Precomp. The Precomp Nodes dialog box opens (Figure 10.4). The Precomp script name and path are listed as well as the precomp render name, path, and file format (indicated by the file extension). You can change names and paths or leave them intact. Press the OK button. A new Precomp node is created. The Precomp node's output is connected to the network downstream of the node originally selected (Figures 10.5 and 10.6). By default, the original nodes are assigned to a new Background.

FIGURE 10.4 The Precomp Nodes dialog box.

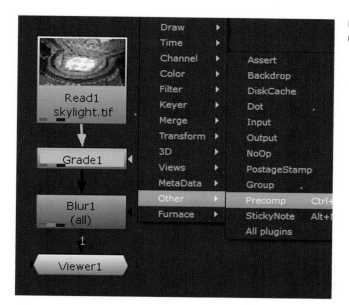

FIGURE 10.5 A Grade node is selected and Other > Precomp chosen.

FIGURE 10.6 The resulting Precomp node's output is connected to the Blur node, while the Grade and Read nodes are separated and indicated by a new Background.

2. Open the Precomp node's properties panel. The precomp script is listed. You can force the node to render an image sequence and thus save calculation time by clicking the Render button. When the Render is complete, the Read File For Output checkbox is automatically selected and the rendered files are used for the node's output. The node icon turns green to indicate this. You can force the node to use the saved script instead of the renders by deselecting the Read File For Output checkbox.

In contrast, the DiskCache node, in the Other menu, writes the scanline data produced by the upstream node network to a temporary disk cache. (*Scanlines* are rows of pixels sent to the Viewer.) This allows downstream nodes to use the disk cache data and thus skip the necessity of calculating the upstream scanlines until the upstream network is changed. The cache location is set by the Preferences window (Edit > Preferences from the menu bar).

Splitting the Viewer

A Viewer node can accept 10 inputs. Each input is consecutively numbered. You can quickly connect an input to a Viewer by selecting the input node and pressing a number key, such as 2, 3, or 4. If two or more inputs exist, you can toggle between them by pressing the 1 through 9 keys on the keyboard (pressing 0 switches to input 10). Once two or more inputs exist, you can create a split screen with one input on the left and another input on the right. To activate the split, change the Composite menu, at the top center of the Viewer panel, to Wipe (Figure 10.7). Change the Read A menu to one input. Change the Read B menu to a second input.

FIGURE 10.7 Left to right: Read A input menu, Composite menu, and Read B input menu.

A wipe handle is placed at the center of the bounding box (Figure 10.8). You can LMB-drag the handle left or right to change the split line. You can reduce the opacity of the Read B input by LMB-dragging the diagonal line at the top right of the handle. For example, in Figure 10.8, Viewer1 carries two inputs. The first input is provided by a Read node and the second input is provided by a Blur node that blurs the Read node's bitmap.

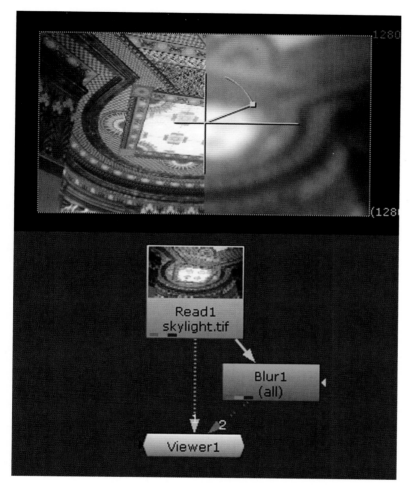

FIGURE 10.8 A wipe handle, provided by the Wipe setting of the Composite menu, combines two inputs. In this case, input A is set to the Viewer input 1, which is the unaltered Read1 node. Input B is set to the Viewer input 2, which is the Blur1 node.

Using Metadata

You can loosely define *metadata* as data about data. In the realm of digital photography and cinematography, metadata is hidden information carried by a file. For example, a bitmap created by a digital still camera can carry metadata in an EXIF (exchangeable image file format) where the photo's date of creation, the camera's f-stop, file bit depth, file size, and similar information is stored. In Nuke, you can view or modify existing metadata. You can also create custom metadata to fit the specific project you are working on. Nuke provides the following metadata nodes through the MetaData menu.

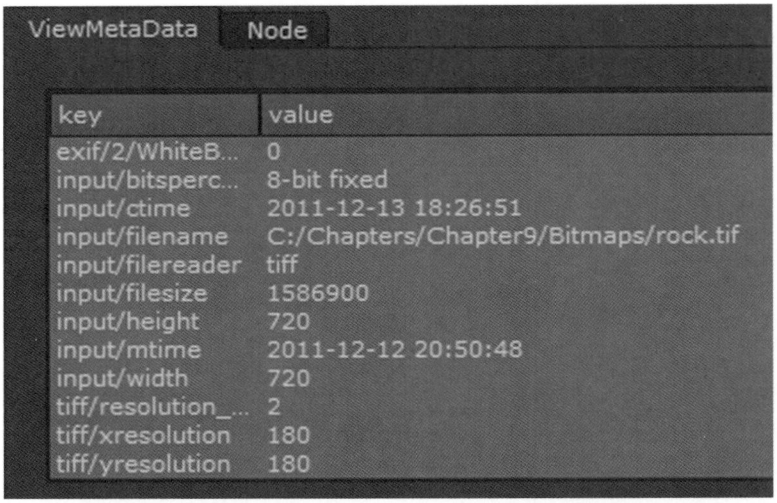

FIGURE 10.9 A small portion of the metadata carried by a bitmap. A ViewMetaData node is connected to the output of a Read node.

ViewMetaData displays metadata flowing into its input pipe (Figure 10.9). **ModifyMetaData** allows you to overwrite existing metadata. You can modify the data one key at a time. A *key* is a variable with a specific name and value. For example, a key name may be Exif/FocalLength and the key value may be 35. To modify a key, click the + button, double-click the orange cell below the Key column, select a key name in the Pick Metadata Key dialog box, double-click the orange cell below the Value column, and type the new value into the cell. You can add a custom key by typing a key name into the Pick Metadata Key dialog box text cell.

AddTimeCode adds time code (HH:MM:SS) to the metadata stream as a new key. The key is listed as Input/timecode.

CopyMetaData allows you to copy metadata from a node connected to the Meta input pipe. You can copy all the keys and values or choose a specific key name.

CompareMetaData compares metadata between its input A and input B pipes. Differences with key names and key values are listed in the node's properties panel.

Sticky Notes and Postage Stamps

Nuke provides the StickyNote node, which you can use to annotate a node network. The StickyNote text appears in the Node Graph, but is not connectable to other nodes. The PostageStamp node, on the other hand, creates a node-sized thumbnail of its input. The PostageStamp node allows you to check a portion of a network without having to reconnect or create a Viewer node. Both nodes are available through the Other menu.

Creating Groups

Nuke node networks often become complex and difficult to interpret. Thus, Nuke provides a means to group nodes together. When nodes are grouped, they are replaced by a Group node and are otherwise hidden in the Node Graph. However, the nodes are accessible through their own Group tab. To create and utilize a Group node, follow these steps:

1. Shift+select the nodes that you would like to convert to a group. Choose Other > Group. A new Group node replaces the selected nodes in the Node Graph. In addition, the original nodes appear in a new Group tab named Group*n* Node Graph (Figure 10.10).
2. You can manipulate the original nodes within the Group tab. This

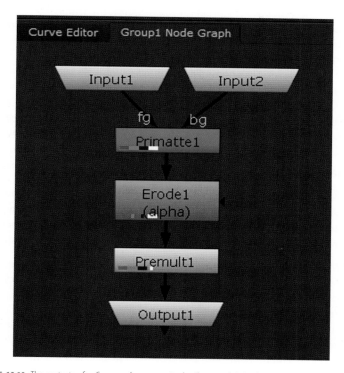

FIGURE 10.10 The contents of a Group node, as seen in the Group node's Node Graph tab.

includes changing parameter values, animating parameters, deleting nodes, adding nodes, and connecting or disconnecting pipes. That said, do not change the new Input or Output nodes as they represent incoming and outgoing connections to the Group node.

3. To close the Group tab, RMB-click over the tab name and choose Close Tab from the dropdown menu. To open the Group tab of a Group node, select the Group node and choose Edit > Node > Group > Open Group Node Graph from the menu bar or press Cmd/Ctrl+Enter.
4. To delete a Group node and restore the original nodes to the Node Graph, select the Group node and choose Edit > Node > Group > Expand Group from the menu bar.

Writing and Reading Gizmos

In Nuke, a *gizmo* is a set of nodes or a node network that is saved as a unique script. Gizmos are useful sharing sections of larger scripts among multiple compositors or savings routines that are used in multiple scripts over the duration of a lengthy production. To create and read a gizmo, follow these steps:

1. Select a Group node. (To create a Group node, see the prior section.) Open the Group node's properties panel. Click the Export To Gizmo button. In the file browser, choose a name and location to write the gizmo file to. Gizmo files are special text files that carry the `.gizmo` extension.
2. To read a gizmo file, choose File > Import Script from the menu bar. A new, unconnected Gizmo node is placed in the Node Graph. Although a Gizmo node represents a set of nodes with specific connections and parameters settings, the nodes are not visible. To access the original nodes, choose Edit > Node > Group > Expand Group from the menu bar.

Managing Knobs

In Nuke, a *knob* is a specific parameter of a specific node. In general, a knob is represented by a slider, numeric cell, or checkbox. You can add a custom knob to a node at any time. This may be useful for creating custom parameters when scripting with Python or TCL. To add a knob, follow these steps:

1. RMB-click over an empty area of a node's properties panel and choose Manage User Knobs from the dropdown menu. An unlabeled knob dialog box opens. Click the Add button and choose a parameter style from the dropdown menu. For example, select Integer Knob to create a numeric cell.
2. A new knob dialog box opens (Figure 10.11). Enter a parameter name into the Name field (this is the variable name used by expressions and similar scripting). Enter a name into the Label field (a *label* is the name that appears to the left of the parameter slider, cell, or checkbox). Optionally, enter text into the Tooltip field (a *tooltip* is the descriptive text that appears when the mouse hovers over the parameter). Click the OK button. The box closes and the new knob is added to the user knob list. Click the Done button of the unlabeled dialog window. The new knob is added to the User tab of the node's properties panel.

FIGURE 10.11 Knob dialog boxes. The top box sets the name, label, and tooltip for the added knob.

3. Additionally, you can add a standard Nuke knob by clicking the Pick button instead of the Add button and selecting the knob name from the Pick Knobs To Add dialog box. To delete a user knob, RMB-click over an empty area of a node's properties panel, choose Manage User Knobs, highlight the knob name in the unlabeled knob dialog box, and click the Delete button.

For more information on Python and TCL scripting, see the following "Scripting and Expressions" section.

Updating Help Boxes

When you click the question mark at the top right of a node's properties panel, a default help message appears in a yellow dialog box. You can change the help message by RMB-clicking over an empty area of the properties panel and choosing Edit Help from the dropdown menu. A Edit [?] Help Message dialog box opens, which you can type into. Note that any change affects the current node but no other node (old or new) is affected.

Scripting and Expressions

Scripting is a form of programming that provides greater control over a program such as Nuke. Nuke supports TCL and Python scripting through the Nuke interface. In addition, Nuke provides a means to create expressions. *Expressions* are small mathematical formulas with which you can automatically update parameter values.

Introduction to TCL

Nuke is built on the Tool Command Language (TCL), which is an open-source programming language. You can use TCL commands to manipulate the timeline, customize the Nuke interface, expand the functionality of nodes, retrieve node information, and read or write to or from Nuke scripts and other databases.

To enter a TCL command, choose File > Script Command from the menu bar or press the X key in the Node Graph to open the Script Command dialog box (Figure 10.12). Select the TCL radio button and enter the command in the Command field. Click the OK button to execute the command.

FIGURE 10.12 Script Command dialog box.

A few TCL commands are included here. Note that the term *knob* is often used by Nuke to refer to a specific node parameter.

- `version` returns the current version of Nuke in a dialog box.
- `memory info` prints a detailed memory report, including node memory demands, convolution filter sizes, and resolutions passed between nodes to Viewers.
- `frame` *n* moves you to frame *n* on the timeline.
- `setkey` *knob n value* sets a keyframe for the named knob on frame *n* with a stated value. The proper knob name must be used and should include the node name, parameter name, and channel name separated by periods. For example, a proper knob name is `Blur1.size.w`. Thus, a command might be `setkey Blur1.size.w 10 2`.
- `knobs -a` *node* lists all the knobs carried by a node in a dialog box. Commonly used knobs represented by cells, sliders, and checkboxes appear first in the list.
- `script_save_as` *name* saves the script. For example, enter `script_save_as C:/comp/test.nk`.
- `menu` "*menu_name*" "*hotkey*" "*icon_name*" "*tooltip*" {*command*} adds a custom menu to the menu bar. When the menu is selected, a TCL command is executed. For example, to create a custom undo menu that uses the F1 hotkey, enter `menu "Undo" "F1" "" "" {undo}`. Empty quotes

signify that a particular option is not used, such as an icon bitmap name and tooltip text. Note that the custom menu is not permanent and disappears if Nuke is restarted.

You can also execute a TCL command in the Script Editor. However, you must precede the command with a Python command `nuke.tcl` and place the TCL command within parenthesis and quotes. For example, enter `nuke.tcl ("memory info")`. For information on the Script Editor and the Python scripting language, see the next section. For a detailed list of TCL commands, choose Help > Documentation and click on the TCL Scripting link in the browser that opens.

Introduction to Python

Python is an open-source, dynamic scripting language used widely in the realm of 3D animation and digital compositing. Nuke supports the use of Python scripting through its Script Editor. You can open the Script Editor by clicking a Content Menu button at the top-left corner of a pane and choosing Script Editor from the menu. The Script Editor appears in a new tab, which you can close at any time by RMB-clicking the tab name and choosing Close Tab.

The Script Editor is divided into two sections: a top Output window and a bottom Input window. You can type a Python script in the Input window and execute the script by pressing Cmd/Ctrl+Enter. For example, type `print "Nuke Rocks"` and press Cmd/Ctrl+Enter. The Input window is cleared and the result of the script is displayed in the Output window (Figure 10.13).

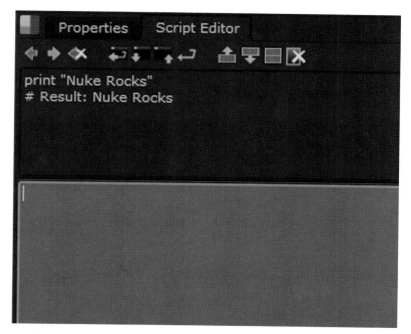

FIGURE 10.13 Top-left corner of the Script Editor tab. The Input window is light gray and the Output window is dark gray.

Python Object.Method Examples

Python is an object-oriented language. An *object* is a unique data set. Similar objects are considered instances of a *class*. Classes are grouped together into *modules*. Objects within a class provide various means to manipulate the contained data, each of which is known as a *method*. Within Nuke, a Python command is composed of an object and a method separated by a period. As such, the syntax follows `object.method(value)`, where `value` is a variable passed to the method to alter its behavior. For example, the command `nuke.message("Nuke Rocks")` creates a dialog box with the text "Nuke Rocks"; in this case, `nuke` is the object and `message` is the method.

Nuke provides a long list of modules, classes, objects, and methods. For a detailed description of these components, choose Help > Documentation and click on the Python Scripting link in the browser that opens. A few example object.method commands follow (note that Python is sensitive to capitalization):

- `nuke.undo()` undoes the previous step.
- `nuke.frame(n)` moves to frame *n* on the timeline.
- `nuke.selectAll()` selects all the nodes in the Node Graph.
- `nuke.createNode("node_name")` creates a new node. A standard node name, such as Blur, must be entered within the parentheses.
- `nuke.addFormat("width height pixel-aspect-ratio format_name")` adds a new format to the Project Settings panel Full Size Format menu. For example, enter `nuke.addFormat("1280 720 1 720HD")` to create an HDTV format.
- `nuke.value("knob")` returns the value of a knob. The knob name must include the node name, parameter name, and channel name. For example, enter `nuke.value("Blur1.size.w")` to retrieve the current value of the Size parameter of the Blur1 node.
- `nuke.extractSelected()` breaks connections between selected nodes and the rest of the network and moves the selected nodes to the right.
- `nukescripts.autoBackdrop()` adds a backdrop to a selected node.
- `nukescripts.infoviewer()` prints the state of a selected node in a dialog box, including the current value of every knob.

Note that you can enter Python commands into the Script Command dialog box. Press X in the Node Graph and select the Python radio button.

Python Variables and Operators

Python scripting supports the use of variables. A *variable* is a value that may change within the scope of a program or script. You can create a variable by choosing a variable name and declaring what it's equal to. For example, Cmd/Ctrl+Entering `val=10` creates the variable `val` and declares that it is equal to 10. You can retrieve the variable value at a later time. For example, Cmd/Ctrl+Entering `print val` displays `10` in the Output window. There are three common variable types, each of which you must declare differently:

`val=10`	integer
`val=10.3725`	float
`val='Hello'`	string

In addition, you can assign nodes to variables. This allows you to retrieve or update the node's parameter values at a later time. The following are example commands:

- `bn=nuke.createNode("Blur")` creates a new Blur node and assigns it to the `bn` variable.
- `bn["size"].getValue()` displays the Blur node's Size parameter value.
- `newvar=bn["size"].getValue()` assigns the parameter value to a new variable, `newvar`.
- `bn["size"].setValue(10)` updates the Size parameter value to 10.

You can update a variable value at any time. In addition, you can apply mathematical operators. For example, you can Cmd/Ctrl+Enter the following:

```
val=0
val=val+100
print val
```

To enter a multiline script, press the Enter key at the end of each line and press Cmd/Ctrl+Enter to execute the script. Python uses the following mathematical symbols: + (plus), − (minus), * (multiply), and / (divide). In fact, you can use the `print` command as a calculator; for example, `print 2048*.13` displays `266.24` in the Output window.

Python supports complex programming structures such as `if` statements and `for` loops. For example, the following script locates every Blur node in the script and tests whether its input is connected to a Read node. If the Read node is present, the Size value is changed to 5.

```
for nodename in nuke.allNodes():
    if nodename.Class() == "Blur":
        if nodename.input(0).Class() == "Read":
            nodename["size"].setValue(5)
```

In this case, the double equals sign (==) is required when comparing variables with an `if` statement. The `for` statement cycles through all the Nuke nodes found within the Node Graph; with each step, the variable `nodename` is set to one node. The first `if` statement tests whether or not the `nodename` variable is a Blur node. If the first `if` statement is true, the second `if` statement tests whether the Blur node's input pipe is connected to a Read node. If the second `if` statement is true, the Blur node's Size parameter is set to 5. If either of the `if` statements are false, the script jumps back to the first line. Note that Nuke is sensitive to indentation when `for` and `if` statements are involved. For more information on Python syntax and programming structures, visit *www.python.org*.

Managing Hotkeys

Nuke provides an extensive list of hotkeys for various nodes and operations. To examine the list, choose Help > Key Assignments from the menu bar. To edit the hotkey assignments, you must update the `menu.py` Python file. By default, the file is placed in the Nuke plug-ins directory. For example, on a Windows 7 64-bit operating system, the file is located at the `C:\Program Files\Nuke[version_number]\plugins` directory. If you are running a non-Windows system, you can use the Python command `nuke.pluginPath()` to find the directory. Within `menu.py`, each Nuke menu item and associated hotkey is declared. For example, the following two lines create the File menu and Save submenu in the menu bar:

```
m = menubar.addMenu("&File")
m.addCommand("&Save", "nuke.scriptSave(\"\")", "^s")
```

In this case `nuke.scriptSave` is the object.method Python command associated with the Save menu and `^s` represents the Cmd/Ctrl+S hotkey. You can alter the hotkeys by using such symbols as ^ for Cmd/Ctrl, ^# for Cmd/Ctrl+Opt/Alt, and + for Shift. Once you save the `menu.py` file in a text format and restart Nuke, the hotkey updates take effect. You can also edit the `menu.py` script to add or remove your own custom menus. For example, to add your own menu named "Quit" to the menu bar with a submenu that closes the Nuke script with a Cmd/Ctrl+Q hotkey, add the following lines:

```
m = menubar.addMenu("&Quit")
m.addCommand("&Quit Script", "nuke.scriptClose()", "^q")
```

Script Editor Buttons

The Script Editor includes a row of buttons that allow you to open and save Python scripts, cycle through script history, and control the Input and Output windows. These are illustrated by Figure 10.14 and are described here.

Previous Script/Next Script loads previously executed scripts. The scripts appear in the Input field.

Clear History clears the script history used by Previous Script/Next Script.

Source A Script loads a script into the program and executes it immediately. The result of the script is displayed by the Output window.

Load A Script loads the script into the Input window but does not execute it.

Save A Script saves the Input window script as a text file with the `.py` extension. You can edit a `.py` file with an external text editor, such as Windows Wordpad.

FIGURE 10.14 Script Editor Buttons: (1) Previous Script, (2) Next Script, (3) Clear History, (4) Source A Script, (5) Load A Script, (6) Save A Script, (7) Run The Current Script, (8) Show Input Only, (9) Show Output Only, (10) Show Both Input And Output, and (11) Clear Output Window.

Run The Current Script runs the Input window script. It has the same functionality as Cmd/Ctrl+Enter.

Show Input Only/Show Output Only determine if Input and/or Output windows are visible.

Clear Output Window fulfills its namesake.

Working with Links and Expressions

In Nuke, you can link two parameters together, forcing the second parameter to adopt the values of the first parameter. After a link is created, the relationship between the parameters is automatically maintained until the link is removed. To create a link, follow these steps:

1. Open the properties panels for the two nodes you wish to connect with a link. Determine which node will be the "parent" and which will be the "child" (the parent supplies values to the child). Determine which parameters are to be linked.
2. Cmd/Ctrl+LMB-drag from the parent parameter Animation Menu button to the child parameter Animation Menu button. For example, Cmd/Ctrl+LMB-drag from the Rotate Animation Menu button of one node to the Rotate Animation Menu button of a second node. A green link line is drawn between the nodes in the Node Graph. An arrow indicates the flow of information (Figure 10.15).

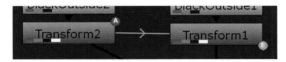

FIGURE 10.15 A link drawn between two nodes.

3. Test the link by updating the parameter value of the parent node. The child node parameter value changes automatically. The link will remain until you LMB-click the child node's Animation Menu button and choose No Animation.

A link represents a simple expression. Initially, the expression carries a 1-to-1 relationship, where the child value is exactly equal to the parent value. You can modify the expression, however, by LMB-clicking the child Animation Menu button and choosing Edit Expression. The Edit Expression dialog box opens and displays the initial expression (Figure 10.16).

FIGURE 10.16 Expression dialog box.

The expression uses the syntax `node.parameter.channel` where `node` is the node name, `parameter` is the parameter name, and `channel` is the optional channel name, such as `x`, `y`, `z`, `w`, `h`, and so on. (Nuke may add the word `parent` to the start of the expression; the expression will function with or without it.) You can update the expression by adding a mathematical formula. For example, to reduce the rotation of the child parameter to half of the parent parameter, add `/2` to the end of the expression line. To update the expression click the OK button. For example, in Figure 10.17 the Rotate

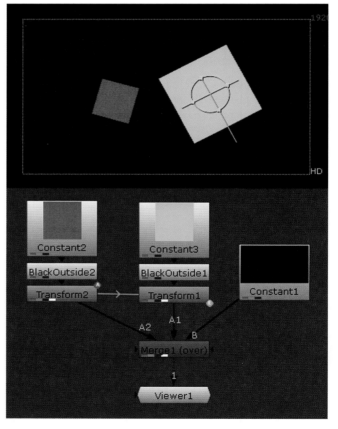

FIGURE 10.17 A link causes a yellow Constant to rotate four times faster than the red Constant. The red Constant's Transform node is animated, while the yellow Constant carries no animation. A sample script is included as `linking.nk` in the `Chapters/Chapter10/Scripts/` directory on the DVD.

parameters of two Transform nodes are linked. The child parameter, which affects a yellow Constant square, rotates four times faster than the parent parameter, which affects a smaller red Constant square. The expression is written as `Transform2.rotate*4`.

As an alternative to Cmd/Ctrl+LMB-dragging between Animation Menu buttons, you can LMB-click a child Animation Menu button and choose Add Expression. The Expression dialog box opens. If the parameter carries more than one channel, each channel receives its own expression field. In this situation, there is no initial expression and you must type one from scratch. Note that you can "mix and match" parameters when creating expressions. For example, you can link Rotate to Translate X. In such a case, you can Cmd/Ctrl+LMB-drag between the Rotate Animation Menu button and the Translate X numeric cell.

Using Expression and Math Nodes

The Expression node, available through the Color > Math menu, allows you to affect color, alpha, depth, and motion channels with complex expressions. The node's properties panel offers four Channels menus, which you can set to the channel or channels of your choice (Figure 10.18). Below each channels menu is an = field, into which you can type an expression. For example, to set the input alpha channel to 1, set the first Channels menu to Alpha and enter 1 into the first = field.

To make the expressions more complex, you can add mathematical operators or functions. Functions signify a complex value or math operation with

FIGURE 10.18 The Expression node properties panel. The first Channels menu selects the alpha channel, which in turn is set to a value of 1 by the first = field.

Much like the CornerPin2D node (see Chapter 8) the Stabilize2D node requires expressions to work. The general work flow for the Stabilize2D node follows:

1. Create motion paths for an input using a Tracker node (see Chapter 8). Two tracks are often necessary, so activate Tracker1 and Tracker2.

2. With the Tracker node selected, choose Transform > Stabilize. Change the new Stabilize2D node's Type menu to 2 Point.

3. Enter 1—into the Stabilze2D node's Track1 X and Y and Track2 X and Y cells. This inverts the incoming motion path data.

4. Create links or expressions between the Tracker node's Tracker1 and the Stabilize2D node's Track1 parameters. (The Tracker node is the parent and the Stabilize2D node is the child.) Do the same for Tracker2 and Track2. For example, the final expression for Track1 X should look like 1—Tracker1. tracker1.x.

5. Adjust the Stabilize2D node's Offset X and Y parameters to slide the output back into the output bounding box area.

a simple name. For example, to assign each pixel of the green channel with a random value plus 0.2, set one of the Channels menus to RGB, select the matching Green checkbox, and enter `random + 0.2` into the matching = field (Figures 10.19 and 10.20).

To see a full list of functions supported by Nuke, choose Help > Documentation and click the Knob Math Expressions link in the browser that

FIGURE 10.19 Each pixel of the green channel is brightened by adding 0.2 and a random value assigned by the `random` function.

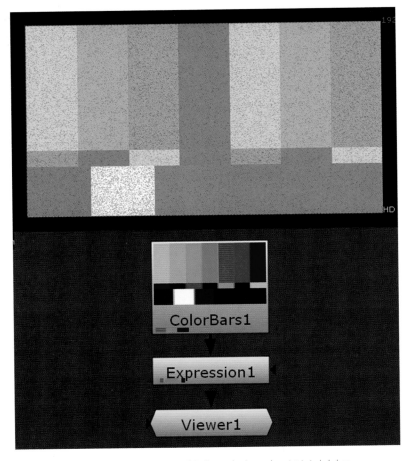

FIGURE 10.20 The result of the expression on a ColorBars node. A sample script is included as `expression.nk` in the `Chapters/Chapter10/Scripts/` directory on the DVD.

opens. Other useful functions include `pi` (value of pi, rounded off to 3.141592654), `sqrt(x)` (square root of *x*), `log(x)` (natural logarithm of *x*), and `pow(x, y)` (*x* raised to the power of *y*). If a function requires a variable, like `x` or `y`, you can use a fixed value or a channel name. For example `pow(red, 2)` is equal to the red channel pixel value to the power of 2. Note that the Expression dialog box, described in the previous section, supports the use of functions.

At the top of the Expression node's properties panel, four slots are provided for creating temporary variables. For example, if you enter `t = pow(r, g)`, then the variable `t` is equal to the red channel pixel value to the power of the green channel pixel value. Once a variable is established, you can use it in any of the = fields below the Channels menu.

The remaining nodes in the Color > Math menu apply mathematical operations to their input. The Add node adds a value set by the Value parameter to every pixel within the channels defined by the Channels menu. The Multiply node multiplies the value. Gamma applies a power function. The ClipTest node adds a zebra-stripe pattern to any part of the input that exceeds the values set by the Lower and Upper parameters. ColorMatrix multiplies the input by a 3×3 matrix, which is useful for converting one color space to another.

New Techniques

Nuke v6.3 adds several new techniques: deep compositing, image-based modeling, and in-program particle generation. These techniques are explored in this section.

Introduction to Deep Compositing

With deep compositing, each pixel of a deep image stores camera-relative depth and opacity information in addition to standard RGBA channel information. When compositing deep images, you have the flexibility to determine the relative *depth* of a rendered element without relying on a separate depth map render pass or forcing the 3D animator to reanimate and re-render the scene. Deep compositing also produces superior results when compositing 3D objects that have been rendered with partial transparency or motion blur.

NukeX v6.3 supports the DTEX deep-image format, which is generated by the RenderMan rendering engine. To read a DTEX file, choose Deep > DeepRead. If you don't have access to RenderMan, you can convert the depth channel of a Maya IFF or OpenEXR file to the deep format. For example, in Figure 10.21, a Maya IFF file is loaded into a Read node. The Read node is connected to a DeepFromImage node, which converts the Depth channel information into the deep-image pixel data.

FIGURE 10.21 The Depth channel of a Maya IFF bitmap is converted to the deep-image data format with a DeepFromImage node.

You can examine the "deepness" of any given pixel within a deep image by displaying the Deep Graph (expand the small forward-slash button above the timeline and to the left of the Viewer pane). When you move the mouse across the Viewer, a white line moves across Deep Graph to indicate the pixel depth (distance from camera) (Figure 10.22).

The Deep menu provides a series of nodes designed to work with deep images. Many of the nodes are similar to nondeep Nuke nodes. For example, DeepColorCorrect offers the same Saturation, Contrast, Gamma, Gain, and Offset sliders as the ColorCorrect node. However, several nodes have unique functionality. For example, the DeepTransform node is able to transform a deep image in the X, Y, and Z directions. This allows the 3D object in the image to intersect or move between the 3D objects of another deep image. Such transformations are not available to nondeep images. DeepTransform carries X, Y, Z, and Z-scale parameters. Changing the Z parameter to a negative value pushes the 3D objects of the input further from the camera; positive values bring the objects closer to the camera (Figures 10.23, 10.24, and 10.25). (Note that there is no change in the object scale.) The Z-scale parameter serves as a divisor for the depth value of a pixel; this is useful when converting Depth channels created by different 3D programs. For example, Maya creates a default Depth channel where values change from small negative numbers (close to camera) to 0

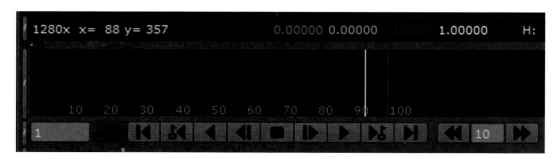

FIGURE 10.22 The Deep Graph. The white line signifies the pixel depth.

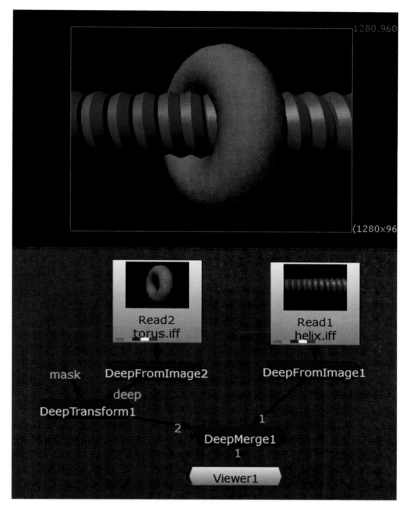

FIGURE 10.23 A DeepTransform node positions a render of a red helix. When the Z parameter is set to 2750, the helix lines up with the center of a torus from a separate deep image. (A DeepMerge node combines the helix and torus render.) A sample script is included as deep.nk in the Chapters/Chapter10/Scripts/ directory on the DVD.

(far-clipping plane); hence, changing the Z-scale parameter to −1 makes the Maya Depth channel positive and easier to work with once it's converted to deep data.

Other useful deep nodes include DeepExpression (allows you to write expressions for deep channels), DeepCrop (crops depth data in front of and behind defined planes), and DeepMerge (merges together deep inputs). For more information on deep compositing theory, visit *www.deepimg.com.*

315

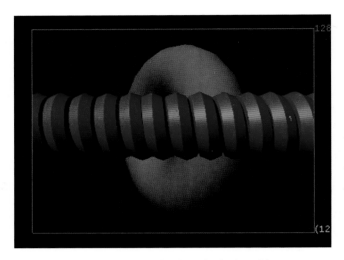

FIGURE 10.24 When the Z parameter is set to 0, the helix is placed in front of the torus.

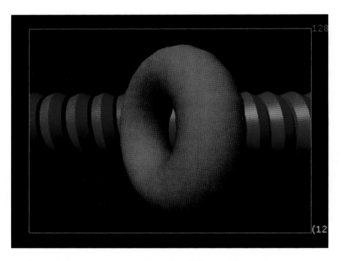

FIGURE 10.25 When the Z parameter is set to 4000, the helix is placed behind the torus.

Introduction to Particles

Nuke v6.3 introduces a set of particle tools. The tools are divided into two menus: Particles and Toolsets > Particles. An easy way to create a particle system is to choose one of the preexisting particle tool sets. For example, to create a snow simulation, follow these steps:

1. Choose Toolsets > Particles > SnowBox. Choose 3D > Scene, 3D > Camera, and 3D > ScanlineRender. Connect the Camera1 node to

the Cam input of the ScanlineRender1 node. Connect the Scene node to the Obj/Scn input of the ScanlineRender1 node. Connect a Viewer to the ScanlineRender1 node. In Nuke, the particles simulations occur in a 3D environment.

2. Connect the P_SnowBox1 node to the Scene1 node. The Progress dialog box opens as the particle positions are calculated for the current frame. Change the View Selection menu to 3D. Use the Opt/Alt-mouse button keys to move the default camera back. The P_SnowBox1 node creates a system box that emits numerous snowlike particles (Figure 10.26). Play back the timeline. The particles drift downward. Select the Camera1 icon and interactively move it so that it has a good view of the particles. Change the View Selection menu back to 2D.

3. Open the P_SnowBox1 node's properties panel. You can adjust the system scale, particle speed, particle scale, particle opacity, and the quality of the turbulence that causes the particles to move in a semi-random fashion.

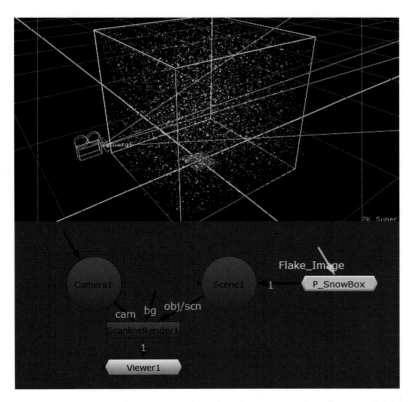

FIGURE 10.26 The SnowBox tool set creates a particle simulation that mimics snow. A sample script is included as snow.nk in the Chapters/Chapter10/Scripts/ directory on the DVD.

317

To create a particle simulation from scratch, you can follow these basic steps:

1. Choose Particles > ParticleEmitter. Connect the ParticleEmitter node to a Viewer.
2. Connect a geometry node to the ParticleEmitter node's Emit input pipe. The node emits particles from the surface of the geometry. If the Emit pipe is not connected, particles are emitted along the Y axis. To hide the geometry, change the geometry node's Display menu to Off.
3. To specify a unique look for the particles, connect a geometry node or Read node with a bitmap to the ParticleEmitter node's Particle input pipe.
4. Adjust the particles' emission rate, lifetime, velocity, size, and mass through the ParticleEmitter node's properties panel.
5. To render the particles from a 2D view, construct a 3D environment with ScanlineRender, Camera, and Scene nodes. Connect the ParticleEmitter node to the Scene node's input pipe. You can connect shader nodes to the geometry as you would any other 3D scene. To light the particles, add one or more light nodes to the scene.
6. To combine multiple particle simulation, connect the output of one ParticleEmitter node to the Merge input pipe of a second ParticleEmitter node.
7. To alter the speed, direction, and randomness of the particle movement, add one or more force nodes to the scene. For example, connect a ParticleDrag node between the ParticleEmitter node and the Scene node and raise the ParticleDrag node's Drag value to slow the particles. You can chain several force nodes together.
8. To create the illusion that the particles are bouncing off a surface in the scene, add a ParticleBounce node between the ParticleEmitter node and the Scene node. The ParticleBounce node creates a planar, spherical, or cylindrical boundary, as determined by the node's Object menu. You must position the boundary to correspond with the surface the particles should "bounce off." The boundary does not render.
9. To motion blur the particles, raise the Samples parameter in the MultiSample tab of the ScanlineRender node above 1.

For a step-by-step guide to creating an article simulation from scratch, see Tutorial 10 at the end of this chapter.

Image-Based Modeling

Nuke v6.3 includes the Modeler node (3D > Geometry > Modeler), which gives you the ability to create image-based geometry inside the program. Image-based modeling uses photographs or motion picture/video footage to triangulate reference points and thus generate geometry that accurately recreates real-world objects. To apply the Modeler node, you can follow these basic steps:

- Using the CameraTracker node, create a 3D camera to match an image sequence or movie with a moving camera.
- Connect a Modeler node's Camera pipe to the Camera node and Source pipe to the Read node that carries the image sequence or movie. Switch the View Selection menu to 2D.
- Open the Modeler node's properties panel. A Modeler toolbar is added to the left side of the Viewer panel. Select the Add Faces tool. Interactively click in the Viewer to add three or more vertices to create a polygon face. Follow the contours of the feature you wish to recreate as geometry. For example, click four times at the corners of a window pane. To close the face, press the Enter key or click the first vertex in the Viewer.
- Move to a different frame on the timeline (preferably one where there's a significant shift in the camera position). Select the Select/Edit tool. In the Viewer, LMB-drag the vertices to match the current position of the feature you are recreating. For example, move the vertices back to the corners of the window pane. As soon as the node has the positions of vertices for two frames, a 2D polygon face is generated and is visible in the 3D view.
- You can build upon the polygon face by moving, splitting, or extruding it. To split a face, choose the Select/Edit tool, select a polygon edge by LMB-clicking the edge in the Viewer, RMB-click, and choose Split Edge. To extrude a face, choose the Select/Edit tool, press Cmd/Ctrl while selecting the face in the Viewer, and Cmd/Ctrl+LMB-drag the face along the handle. To move a selected face, LMB-drag the face by the handle center. You can continue to adjust vertex positions of all the faces as you move to different frames on the timeline.

For more information on the CameraTracker node, see Chapter 9 or the "CameraTracker User Guide" PDF available at The Foundry website (*www. thefoundry.co.uk*).

Tutorial 10: Creating a Particle Simulation from Scratch
This tutorial creates a simple particle simulation that includes particle forces and collisions.

1. Create a new script. Choose 3D > Scene, 3D > Camera, and 3D > ScanlineRender. Connect the Camera1 node to the Cam input of the ScanlineRender1 node. Connect the Scene node to the Obj/Scn input of the ScanlineRender1 node. Refer to Figure 10.27 for the final node network. Connect a Viewer node to the ScanlineRender1 node. In Nuke, the particles simulations occur in a 3D environment. Change the View Selection menu to 3D. Interactively move the default camera back.

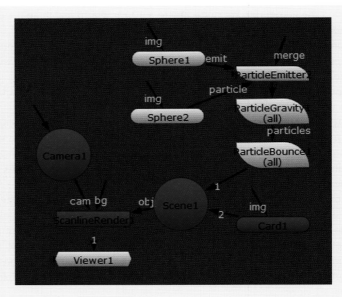

FIGURE 10.27 The final node network for Tutorial 10.

2. Choose Particles > ParticleEmitter. Connect the ParticleEmitter1 node to the Scene1 node. Play back the timeline. Particles are generated along the Y axis and form a straight line. Choose 3D > Geometry > Sphere. Connect the Sphere1 node to the Emit input pipe of the ParticleEmitter1 node. Return to frame 1 and play back the timeline. Particles are generated from the surface of the sphere (Figure 10.28). Open the Sphere1 node's properties panel. Change Translate Y to 5. Simplify the sphere by changing Rows/Columns to 6,6. Hide the sphere in the 3D view by changing the Display menu to Off.

3. By default, the particles are white squares. To change the shape, create a second Sphere node and connect it to the ParticleEmitter1 node's Particle input pipe. Open the Sphere2 node's properties panel and set Rows/Columns to 3,3. Open the ParticleEmitter1 node's properties panel. Adjust the Size parameter to scale the particles.

4. At this point, the particles are moving in all directions from the surface of the Emit sphere and are unaffected by any forces. To add gravity to the simulation, choose Particles > ParticleGravity and drop the new node on top of the pipe connecting the ParticleEmitter1 and Scene1 nodes (see Figure 10.27). To increase the gravity's strength, change the ParticleGravity1 node's To Y parameter to a larger negative number (e.g., −0.5). When you play back the timeline, the particles arch from the Emit sphere and fall downward (Figure 10.29).

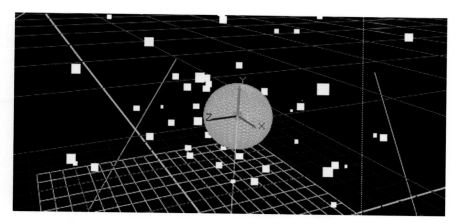

FIGURE 10.28 Particles are emitted from the surface of a sphere.

FIGURE 10.29 Particles are pulled downward by the ParticleGravity1 node.

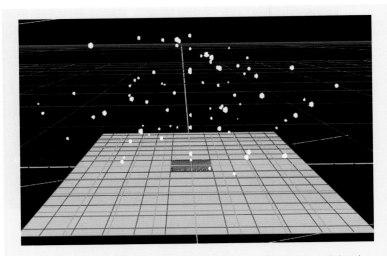

FIGURE 10.30 Particles "bounce" off a card through the assistance of a ParticleBounce node boundary.

5. Choose 3D > Geometry > Card. Connect the Card1 node to the Scene1 node. Scale and rotate the card so that it lies on the "ground" below the particles. Play back the timeline. Note that the particles pass through the card. To create the illusion that the particles are bouncing off the card, choose Particles > ParticleBounce and insert the new node between the Scene1 node and the ParticleGravity1 node. The ParticleBounce1 node creates a planar collision boundary. Through the ParticleBounce1 node's properties panel, scale the boundary so it matches the scale of a card. Play back the timeline. The particles "bounce" off the card before succumbing to gravity once again (Figure 10.30).

6. Experiment by changing the ParticleBounce node's Bounce and Friction values, as well as the Lifetime, Velocity, Size Range, and Mass parameters of the ParticleEmitter1 node.

    This concludes Tutorial 10. As a bonus step, add lights to the 3D scene, add shaders to the Sphere1 and Card1 nodes, and create a test flipbook render through the 2D view. A sample Nuke script is included as Tutorial10.final.nk in the Tutorials/ Tutorial10/Scripts/ directory on the DVD.

Appendix A

Shake/After Effects to Nuke Conversion Chart

Important Shake nodes and After Effects (AE) effects/operations are listed in the following tables along with the equivalent Nuke nodes.

Reading/Writing Files

Shake Node	AE Effect/Operation	Nuke Node
FileIn	File > Import > File	Read
FileOut	Composition > Add To Render Queue	Write

Merging/Combining Layers

Shake Node	AE Effect/Operation	Nuke Node
IAdd	Add blending mode	Merge (Operator = Plus)
IMult	Multiply blending mode	Merge (Operator = Multiply)
ISub	Subtract blending mode	Merge (Operator = Minus)
Max	Lighter Color blending mode	Merge (Operator = Max)

Creating Shapes/Text and Rotoscoping

Shake Node	AE Effect/Operation	Nuke Node
Color	Layer > New > Solid	Constant
AddText	Horizontal text tool	Text
QuickShape	Pen tool	Roto
QuickPaint, RotoShape	Brush tool	RotoPaint

Color and Channel Manipulation

Shake Node	AE Effect/Operation	Nuke Node
ColorCorrect	Color Balance, Curves	ColorCorrect
HueCurves	Hue/Saturation, Curves	HueCorrect
Clamp	Levels	Clamp
LogLin	Color Management tab of the Interpret Footage window	Log2Lin
Reorder	Shift Channels	Shuffle
MDiv	Imported files are interpreted as premultiplied or unpremultiplied through the Alpha section of the Interpret Footage window	Unpremult
MMult	Imported files are interpreted as premultiplied or unpremultiplied through the Alpha section of the Interpret Footage window	Premult

Filters and Keying

Shake Node	AE Effect/Operation	Nuke Node
Blur	Gaussian Blur	Blur
Convolve	(unavailable)	Convolve
DilateErode	Matte Choker	Erode
ChromaKey	Color Key, Color Range	HueKeyer
LumaKey	Luma Key, Color Range	Keyer
Keylight	Keylight	Keylight

Appendix B

Working with Interlacing, Pulldown, and Rolling Shutters

Interlacing and Deinterlacing

Nuke is designed to work with progressive frames. When an image sequence or movie is loaded into a Read node, the frames are imported at the frame rate determined by the Fps parameter of the Project Settings panel. In contrast, interlaced video breaks each frame into two interlaced fields. For example, HDTV supports 1080i at 30 frames per second, where each frame is broken into two fields; thus, 1080i runs at 60 *fields* per second. Interlacing was developed for predigital standard-definition television but continues to be supported by digital television and video. Note that HDTV also supports 1080p with progressive frames and no fields.

You can import an interlaced QuickTime or AVI movie through a Read node (assuming that the FFmpeg library is installed). You can deinterlace the footage, and thereby remove the interlacing, by using Nuke's hidden DeInterlace node. To do so, follow these steps:

1. In the Node Graph, press the X key to bring up the Command dialog box. With the box set to TCL, enter **DeInterlace** into the Command field (note the capitalization of the D and the I). A new DeInterlace node appears. The DeInterlace node is actually a gizmo composed of two FieldSelect nodes, two Reformat nodes, and a Dissolve node. To access the hidden nodes, select the DeInterlace node and choose Edit > Node > Group > Expand Group from the menu bar.
2. Open each of the Reformat nodes and set the Output Format parameters to a resolution that matches the resolution of the QuickTime or AVI file. By default, Output Format is set to 720 × 486 NTSC video with a nonsquare pixel aspect ratio, which may not be desirable. The DeInterlace network extracts the top and bottom field from each frame, rescales the frames with the Reformat nodes, and recombines them through a Dissolve node.

Alternatively, you can install the FieldsKit plug-in, which is available at *www. creativecrash.com*. FieldsKit offers a set of parameters for deinterlacing and interlacing footage.

Note that you can use the FieldSelect node without the DeInterlace gizmo to extract a single field from each interlaced frame. To create the node, press the X key to bring up the Command dialog box, select the TCL checkbox, and enter **FieldSelect** into the Command field (note the capitalization).

Removing and Adding 3:2 Pulldown

3:2 pulldown is a product of the telecine process, whereby motion picture film is transferred to video. Because motion picture film runs at 24 fps and standard-definition NTSC video runs at 30 fps (or more accurately, 29.97 interlaced fps), the telecine process must repeat 6 fps. Nuke provides a Remove32p node for removing the repeated frames. To use the Remove32p node, follow these basic steps:

1. Import an interlaced, 29.97 fps QuickTime or AVI movie trough a Read node (see Chapter 1 for information on QuickTime and AVI file format support).
2. Connect a Remove32p node (Time > Remove 3:2 Pulldown) to the output of the Read node. The output of the Remove32p node is deinterlaced and is designed to run at 24 fps. To review the output at 24 fps, set the timeline's Desired Playback Rate cell to 24.

To readd interlacing and the 3:2 pulldown so that the output runs at 29.97 fps, add an Add32p node (Time > Add 3:2 Pulldown).

Removing a Rolling Shutter Artifact

The RollingShutter plug-in, made available by The Foundry, removes its namesake from video footage. A rolling shutter artifact is created by the Complementary metal-oxide-semiconductor (CMOS) sensor of a video camera. CMOS sensors expose one scanline at a time. Hence, if the camera and/or subject is in motion, the background or subject is distorted in a skewed, trapezoidal fashion. This is due to the lag time between the exposure of the first and last scanline of a frame. The RollingShutter plug-in removes the skew through motion estimation techniques. For best results, enter an accurate value for the node's Correction parameter. Correction represents the time, in frames, between the exposure of the first scanline and the last scanline. If your camera scans from the bottom to the top of the frame, enter a negative Correction value. For more information, see the "RollingShutter User Guide" available at The Foundry's website (*www. thefoundry.co.uk*). Note that CCD sensors do not create rolling shutter artifacts.

Index

Page numbers with "f" denote figures; "t" tables; "b" boxes.